Driscoll & Knight's Map

of

EDMONTON

and

Environs

(1907)

Historic Edmonton

Historic Edmonton

AN ARCHITECTURAL AND PICTORIAL GUIDE

Jac MacDonald

With a foreword by Diana Thomas Kordan

The Edmonton
Journal

LONE
PINE

The Publishers:
Lone Pine Publishing
414, 10357 - 109 Street
Edmonton, Alberta
T5J 1N3

Typesetting by Pièce de Résistance Typographers, Edmonton.
Printing by Commercial Colour Press Ltd., Edmonton, Alberta.

Canadian Cataloguing in Publication Data

MacDonald, Jac Charles, 1954-
    Historic Edmonton

    Includes index.
    ISBN 0-919433-33-2

    1. Historic buildings - Alberta - Edmonton.
2. Edmonton (Alta.) - Buildings, structures, etc.
3. Edmonton (Alta.) - Description - Tours.
I. Title.
FC3696.7.M23 1987   971.23'3   C87-091446-4
F1079.5.E3M23 1987

Design and layout: Yuet C. Chan
                   Ewa Pluciennik

Alberta Culture

This book has been made possible through a significant contribution in time, commitment and expertise from Alberta Culture and Multiculturalism, Historic Sites Service.

Photo Credits

Contemporary Photography:
    The Edmonton Journal, principal photographer, Ken Orr, and contributing photographers, Michael Dean, Petr Honcu, Colin Shaw.

Archival Photography:
    City of Edmonton Archives
        98
    Glenbow Archives
        187
    Provincial Archives of Alberta
        31, 34, 38, 39, 47, 50, 62, 63, 66, 71, 86, 87, 91, 94, 103, 105, 110, 126, 143, 146, 158, 175, 195.

Map Credits

    City of Edmonton Archives
        148
    Provincial Archives of Alberta
        68, 93
    The University of Alberta, Map Collection
        Endsheets, 10.

The publisher gratefully acknowledges the assistance of the Federal Department of Communication, Alberta Culture, the Canada Council and the Alberta Foundation for the Literary Arts in the production of this book.

"Historic Edmonton"

Newspapers are the first stewards of history, of those elements that connect us to our past and shape the directions of our future.

What can be more tangible evidence of our origins than the historic buildings in which the past was once the present? Their embellishments and design offer us important hints of the lives spent in them; lives that laid the foundations for the future that is our life today.

This book first appeared as a series of articles in *The Journal*. In the service of our public obligation to history, we considered the documenting of historic architecture important enough to develop a more permanent record. So, with both pleasure and a sense of fulfilled purpose, *The Edmonton Journal*, with the kind assistance of Alberta Culture, and SPARE (Society for the Protection of Architectural Resources in Edmonton), brings you this record of the buildings that nurtured the spirit from which Edmontonians moulded the cultural essence of a great city.

William Newbigging,
Publisher,
The Edmonton Journal

Acknowledgements

Lone Pine Publishing and the author join in thanking the many people whose kind support and valuable contributions made this book possible. They are William Newbigging, publisher of *The Edmonton Journal*, general manager Steve Hume, editor Linda Hughes, managing editor George Oake, promotions manager Dennis Skulsky, assistant promotions manager Dave Reidie and assistant advertising director Fred Castle.

Special thanks to graphics editor Steve Makris who contributed expertise and valuable advice; Ken Orr for his outstanding photography; and, *The Edmonton Journal* photographic staff and darkroom technicians.

We gratefully acknowledge the involvement of Alberta Culture and Multiculturalism, Historic Sites Service. Special thanks to architectural historian Diana Thomas Kordan who prepared the foreword, provided editorial advice and support materials; historic site designation officer Aart Looye, architectural historian Dorothy Fields and media consultant Judy Berghofer.

Senior archivist Dave Leonard skillfully provided chapter introductions, guided tours information, editorial advice and archival materials. Thanks also to city archivist Helen La Rose and her staff June Honey, Bruce Ibsen and Jeanne Kormysh. A note of thanks to archivist Mike Kostek and staff of the Edmonton Public School Board archives.

We wish to acknowledge and thank The Board of Directors of the Society for the Protection of Architectural Resources in Edmonton (SPARE). In particular, Elly de Jongh, Tom Ward, Abdule Rampuri and, Diana Thomas Kordan and Dave Leonard, both mentioned earlier in this acknowledgement, who assisted SPARE in its initiatives.

Finally, a special note acknowledging the participation of Cathie Bartlett who wrote the articles on Norwood School, McDougall United Church, St. Albert Church and Holy Trinity Anglican Church; Lesley Francis who wrote on Grandin School and the Ross Block; and Gail Gravelines who provided Emily Murphy House and LeMarchand Mansion. ■

Contents

The Buildings

The following buildings are listed by
name, original function and style.

A
Alberta Hospital
Institutional
Jacobethan Revival Style

Arlington Apartments
Residential Apartments
Classical Revival Style

Arts Building
Educational Building
Beaux-Arts Classicism

Ash Residence
Residence
Georgian Revival Style

Assiniboia Hall
Institutional/Educational
Jacobethan Revival Style

Athabasca Hall
Institutional/Educational
Jacobethan Revival Style

B
Birks Building
Commercial
Commercial Style

The Boardwalk
Commercial
Renaissance Revival Style

Bowker Building
Governmental Building
Beaux-Arts Classicism

Buena Vista Apartments
Commercial/Residential
Commercial Style

C
Canada Permanent Building
Commercial
Renaissance Revival Style

Canadian Bank of Commerce
Commercial
Commercial Style

Christ Church
Church
Tudor Revival

Church of St. Jean Baptiste
Church
French-Canadian Church Style

Civic Block
Governmental Building
Commercial Style

Bank of Commerce
Commercial
Commercial Style

Corbett Hall
Institutional/Educational
Jacobethan Revival Style

D
Dental Pharmacy Building
Institutional/Educational
Renaissance Revival Style

Duggan House
Residence
Queen Anne Style

E
Eastwood School
Educational Building
Collegiate Gothic Style

Edmonton Brewing and Malting
Industrial
Scottish Baronial

F
Fire Hall No. 6
Institutional/Fire Hall
Classical Revival Styling

G
Gainer Block
Commercial
Romanesque Revival/Boomtown
Front Architecture

Gariepy House
Residence
Second Empire Style

Gibbard Block
Commercial/Residential
Classical Revival Style

Gibbons House
Residence
Georgian Revival Style

Gibson Block
Commercial/Residential Apartments
Commercial Style

Grandin School
Educational Building
Renaissance Revival Style

H. Allen Gray School
Educational Building
Collegiate Gothic Style

Government House
Governmental Residence
Jacobethan Revival Style

H
Hecla Block
Residential
Classical Revival Style

Highlands Junior High School
Educational Building
Collegiate Gothic Style

Holgate Mansion
Residence
Tudor Revival Style

Holy Trinity Anglican Church
Church
Gothic Revival Style

Holy Trinity Ukrainian Catholic Ch.
Church
Ukrainian-Canadian Church Style

Hub Cigar Store
Commercial
Boomtown Front Architecture

K
King Edward School
Educational Building
Collegiate Gothic Style

Knox Church
Church
Gothic Revival

L
Father Lacombe Chapel
Church
Mission Style

Lambton Block
Commercial/Residential
Classical Revival Style

Legislature Building
House of Parliament
Beaux-Arts Style

LeMarchand Mansion
Residential Apartments
Beaux-Arts Classicism

M
Hotel MacDonald
Hotel
Chateauesque Style

MacLean Block
Commercial
Renaissance Revival Style

Magrath Mansion
Residential
Georgian Revival Style

Malone Block
Commercial/Residential
Classical Revival Style

Masonic Temple
Social Hall
Late Gothic Revival Style

McCauley School
Educational Building
Collegiate Gothic Style

John A. McDougall School
Educational Building
Collegiate Gothic Style

McDougall United Church
Church
Romanesque Revival Style

McIntosh House
Residence
Queen Anne Style

McKay Avenue School
Educational Building
Renaissance Revival Style

McLeod Building
Commercial
Commercial Style

Morehouse House
Residential
Georgian Revival Style

N
Norwood School
Educational Building
Renaissance Revival Style

Notre Dame Convent
Religious
Second Empire Style

O
Old RCMP Barracks
Institutional
Gothic Revival Style

Old St. Stephen's College
Theological School/Dormitory
Collegiate Gothic Style

Oliver Elementary School
Educational Building
Jacobethan Revival Style

Orange Hall
Social Hall
Mission Style

P
Parkdale Elementary School
Educational Building
Collegiate Gothic Style

Pembina Hall
Institutional/Educational
Jacobethan Revival Style

First Presbyterian Church
Church
Late Gothic Revival Style

R
Revillon Building
Commercial
Commercial Style

Donald Ross School
Educational Building
Georgian Revival Style

Ross Block
Commercial
Romanesque Revival/Boomtown
Front Architecture

Rutherford House
Residence
Jacobethan Revival Style

S
Sacred Heart Catholic Church
Church
Gothic Revival Style

St. Albert Roman Catholic Church
Church
Romanesque Revival

St. Joachim's Roman Catholic
Church
Church
French-Canadian Classical Revival

St. Josaphat's Cathedral
Church
Ukrainian-Canadian Church Style

St. Joseph's Basilica
Church
Gothic Revival

St. Joseph's College
Religious/Educational
Jacobethan Revival

St. Vital Church
Church
French-Canadian Classical Revival
Style

Schwermann Hall
Institutional/Educational
Collegiate Gothic Style

Old Scona High School
Educational Building
Renaissance Revival Style

Sheppard House
Residential
Georgian Revival Style

Smeltzer House
Residence
Canadian Four-Square Style

Strathcona Post Office
Institutional/Government
Romanesque Revival Style

Strathcona Public Library
Institutional/Library
Renaissance Revival Style

CP Rail Strathcona Public Library
Commercial/Transportation
Queen Anne Style

T
Alex Taylor School
Educational Building
Georgian Revival Style

Tipton Block
Commercial
Boomtown Front Architecture

U
Union Bank Building
Commercial
Renaissance Revival Style

V
The Villa
Residence
Tudor Revival Style

W
Prince of Wales Armoury
Institutional/Military
Gothic Revival Styling

Wesley Sunday School
Religious Institution
Gothic Revival Style

Robertson Wesley United Church
Church
High Victorian Gothic Revival Style

Westmount Junior High School
Educational Building
Collegiate Gothic Style

The White House
Residence
Georgian Revival Style

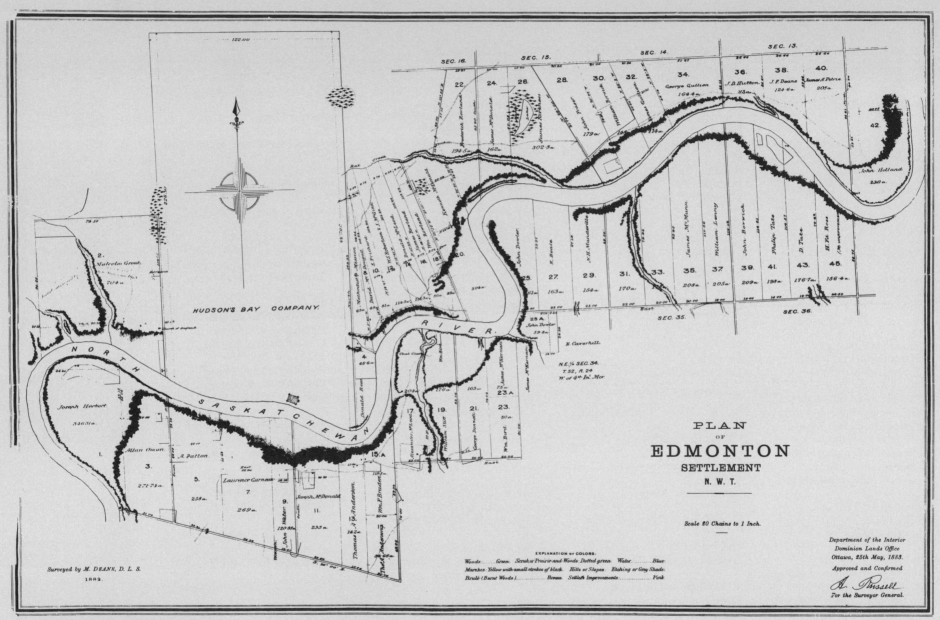

Surveyors plan of Edmonton, 1882.

Foreword

We all feel a sense of familiarity with the historic buildings of Edmonton, and because of this we seldom give them the consideration they deserve. Our attitude toward our architectural environment has in fact changed little over the years. As early as 1914, the author of the publication *Edmonton: Alberta's Capital City* remarked that Edmonton "has been spoken of as a city with no past, some present and an illimitable future." It is a view still expressed today, and one which does little to validate the importance of our historical traditions. It is also an attitude that has colored the general perception of Edmonton's historic buildings. In comparison to other major Canadian metropolises, Edmonton is relatively young. Consequently, many consider it void of a 'past' and its architecture of moderate value or little interest. Yet this sentiment has been challenged as of late, by bringing into focus the specific character of Edmonton's architectural heritage and its relevance within a Canadian context.

Usually the idea of historic architecture evokes images of 19th century homes in Ontario or the walled city of old Quebec. Rarely do local architectural examples come to mind. This is largely due to our perception of Alberta's historical development. The period between settlement and extensive urban development was much shorter and more recent than it has been in the formation of the cityscapes of eastern Canada. We have, therefore, become accustomed to looking elsewhere for standards by which to gauge the value of our built heritage. Moreover, we hesitate to compare Alberta's architectural tradition to other regional developments in Canada because we consider our buildings to be, in most cases, not as old or stylistically ornate. Yet in recent years we have come to realize that these criteria must be altered to reflect more accurately the significance of our regional history.

Most of the pre-Second World War heritage buildings which remain in Edmonton today were constructed between the years 1903-1916. During these years, migration to the city was constant as new arrivals from other parts of Canada, the United States and Europe continued to settle in Edmonton. Edmonton came to represent a human collage with disparate ideas about what buildings should look like. By the time extensive urban development occurred in Edmonton, a broad range of historic revival styles had been popularized by architects for more than twenty years across Canada. Thus, when architects and builders began practicing their trade here, numerous variations on the Gothic Revival, Queen Anne Style and classical revival styles for example, had already appeared in other parts of North America. Architects were confronted with the challenge of adapting these architectural forms to the local scene, which included considerations of landscape features, building types, and the availability of both construction materials and capital. It is not surprising that when adequate funds were available to hire a trained architect or to obtain quality architectural detailing, the buildings of Edmonton appear as though they could have been designed for most any other larger urban community in Canada. The grander building projects in the city, such as the Bowker Building, the Legislative Building, the Hotel MacDonald and numerous other structures are easily identifiable as styles, and readily linked to the national scene. All the architectural clues have been provided for us.

We have seen them elsewhere. It is when we are confronted by smaller scale projects, such as private residences, individually owned commercial blocks, apartments and community churches, that we lose sight of the tradition or traditions from which they were derived, and the degree of interest we should have in them. But it is only natural to expect that these architectural ideas would evolve over several years, or decades, of interpretation and re-interpretation before being applied in the city, and that the need for architectural purity—loosely defined—would no longer be required. It is exactly this blending of architectural sources or variations of a given theme that characterize the majority of our built heritage.

In Alberta, the influence of English architectural models have been by far the most visible and widespread. This is particularly evident in architectural designs for residences and institutional buildings. Domestic architecture in Edmonton's earliest subdivisions such as Old Strathcona, the Groat Estate, and the Highlands usually drew upon the late 19th century historical revival styles based on both classical and picturesque English antecedents. The Georgian Revival and Queen Anne styles appear in various forms throughout these historic neighborhoods as the two most common residential types. The Magrath Mansion located in the Highlands, for instance, is a unique and exemplary adaptation of the Georgian Revival Style in its most palatial form. More typical representations of the style can be seen in the design for the Gibbons Residence situated in the Groat Estate. Like many homes modeled after this style, the Gibbons residence may not look like other domestic Georgian Revival designs built in North America twenty years earlier, but the basic features of the style are discernable. Its symmetrical appearance, central hall plan and ornamental detailing distinguish the house as a decendent of the Georgian Revival tradition.

Architectural designs for education structures in Edmonton further illustrate the impact of English-inspired styles. Throughout the city, English Renaissance Revival Style schools were built to combine the new concerns for incorporating modern conveniences (such as proper ventilation and lighting) with the traditional styling that recalls the institutions of higher learning in England. Norwood School, Alex Taylor School and McKay Avenue School each exhibit classical detailing of a similar kind. Pedimented central pavilions are flanked by wings that house classrooms well lit by natural lighting from the numerous square—and round—arched windows which punctuate the walls. Tall, proud chimney stacks enliven the hipped roof line. Columns, quoins, keystones, pilaster strips, Palladian windows and ornamental cornices further distinguish these structures as fine adaptations of English classicism in Edmonton.

Collegiate Gothic architecture was the second most popular style for educational buildings in the city. It was imitated with great regularity throughout North America, recalling again the prestigious institutions of learning that had flourished for centuries in England. The John A. McDougall School, King Edward School and Westmount Jr. High School are representative of this trend. Each of the structures is

dominated by a central, crenellated tower and the facade is boldly brought to life through the contrasting of horizontal ribbing and polychromatic ornamental accents capping piers, delineating entryways, and defining tracery.

In spite of the dominance of English-inspired sources in Edmonton architecture, other architectural influences had a significant impact on the development of the urban landscape. Although many motifs were of English origin, it is not always clear whether these designs were brought to Alberta directly by English trained architects, or by Canadian and American architects and builders who were influenced by English traditions. Inevitably, it was all three. To illustrate this point, one need only look to the history of the Legislature Building. It was designed in the Beaux-Arts Style by the then provincial architect, Allan Merrick Jeffers, an American citizen later to become a naturalized British subject. The theoretical premises on which Beaux-Arts Classicism was based emanated from the 19th century teachings of the Ecole des Beaux-Arts, in Paris. When theory was transformed into an identifiable style, it soon began to appear throughout Europe and North America. Jeffers' design has, in fact, been linked specifically to American sources, namely the Rhode Island and Minnesota State Capitol Buildings. Although Jeffers' sources have been specifically associated to American origins, Beaux-Arts Classicism had already become the accepted style for provincial capital buildings across Canada.

American influence was also imported as building types which were largely products of the American cityscape. This was particularly true in the development of commercial architecture, including the early 20th century skyscraper and the luxury middle-class apartment block. The McLeod Building is perhaps the premier example of an American-style skyscraper in Edmonton with its early multi-storey features and the exterior of a functionally modern structure. The unique flatiron shape of the Gibson Block was also based upon an American precedent. Due to increased New York land values, the firm of Burnham and Company shaped the 1902 Fuller Block (now the Flatiron Building) to fit a wedge-shaped lot. It was a novelty, a practical one, which was quickly replicated across North America.

The proliferation of the luxury apartment block in the United States as an alternative to the expensive, urban single-family dwelling provided models for architects and builders throughout Canada. The Arlington Apartment constructed in 1909, was representative of many of the smaller scale modern residential blocks. Because these apartments were nestled in lots provided by the patterned urban streetscape, plans were symmetrical, and usually rectangular, to maximize the use of land and increase profitability. Sympathetic to the formal and regularized plan shapes, classical ornament was characteristically applied to the cornice and concentrated around window and door openings.

An exception to the classically-derived ornament of the city's apartment blocks is the French-inspired design of the LeMarchand Mansion. The LeMarchand, like numerous other historic buildings in the province, is a reminder of the ethnocultural nature of early Edmonton. When René LeMarchand arrived from Paris, he commissioned the design of the exclusive 1911 apartment block, complete with interior touches of Art Nouveau styling. Most French influence in Edmonton, however, is attributed to French-Canadian sources and not those linked directly to Europe. For example, Rosary Hall—formerly the Joseph Gariépy House—was designed in the French Second Empire Style, which was a common feature in French Canada. Gariépy came to Edmonton in 1892 and had his house built ten years later. Historic photographs of the home capture its original splendour, complete with the painted wood-carved detailing on its wrap-around verandah.

Nowhere is the ethnocultural flavour of Edmonton and its surrounding communities more apparent than in the architectural designs of French-Canadian and Ukrainian-Canadian churches. St. Joachim's in Edmonton and St. Jean-Baptiste, which dominates the centre of Morinville, were designed to resemble late 19th century Quebec parish churches. St. Joachim's triple-tower facade became a prototype for many Catholic churches throughout the province, including the church at Morinville built in 1907, eight years after St. Joachim's. Ukrainian-Canadian churches also became a visible form of ethnic identity with the distinct styling of both St. Josaphat's in Edmonton and the church of the Holy Trinity in the neighbouring community of Leduc. Although both these churches differ from others of Ukrainian origin in that an architect trained in Europe designed them, Father Philip Ruh was sensitive to Ukrainian sources in both instances when he drew upon the 17th century wooden and masonry traditions of western Ukraine.

A convergence of a great variety of architectural sources over an approximate twenty-five year span contributed to the rich architectural vocabulary which characterize many of Edmonton's historic buildings. A collection of these buildings presented in this publication examined from both an historical and architectural point of view will serve to encourage a better understanding of the nature of Edmonton's architectural heritage. In doing so, our misgivings about comparing Edmonton's heritage to the broader Canadian scene will be laid to rest and its contribution to the historical and architectural development of Canada acknowledged.

Diana Thomas Kordan
Architectural Historian, Inventory Program
Alberta Culture and Multiculturalism

Indians encamped on Rossdale Flats at foot of McKay Avenue School.

Introduction

*T*hey intrude onto the landscape. Some get in the way and others are forgotten. Some are swept away in the course of time, while still others are elevated and revered.

They are of course our historic buildings, those vestiges of another time that many say Edmonton is lacking. It is true of course that many of this city's more salient architectural jewels are no longer with us. But here and there, scattered throughout this sprawling prairie-parkland metropolis, bits and pieces remain. Some are plainly ugly while others are spectacular in their elegance. Most are somewhere in between, combining form with function in a way that is often lacking in much of our modern architecture.

These older buildings are not readily apparent to the eye of the casual visitor. Some long-time residents are unaware of this city's remaining architectural heritage. But this collection of aging bricks and boards ties contemporary communities to the founders of this, North America's northernmost major metropolis. If we allow, these edifices can reach out and grab us, connecting us to the flitting ghosts of our rudimentary beginnings. It is worth savoring before we join them.

The lasting contribution of our predecessors represents a saga of human triumphs, real tragedies, achievements and growth, made all the more amazing by the relatively primitive conditions of their era. We all know it began in the quest for the coats of the beaver and the muskrat. Sating the demand of European high fashion was a tough job, and with the exception of the Cree, it was not easy to convince most Plains Indians to abandon their traditional way of life in favor of a mercantile economy.

As a result, trading posts were moved farther and farther inland. Fort Augustus was established near present-day Fort Saskatchewan by the North West Company in 1795, and Edmonton House was built beside it in 1796. Due to rampant over-trapping in the immediate area, they both subsequently moved upstream in 1802 to the present-day Rossdale Flats, and again shared common ground. After moving downstream in 1810, the forts came back to stay in 1813.

The Hudson's Bay Company called its first post Edmonton House, which later became Fort Edmonton. That name honors the town in Middlesex, England, whence hailed Sir John Lake, HBC deputy governor. In 1821 the two companies merged.

The Company of Adventurers Trading into Hudson's Bay, commonly known as the Hudson's Bay Company, became the dominant economic force in the area. After disastrous floods in 1825 and 1830 (such as the North Saskatchewan River is known to throw at the flats every so often) the fort was moved to its last location. Higher ground on the north bank, near where the Centennial Flame flickers on the Legislature Building's south lawn, was the trader's last repose.

Fort Edmonton became a major post, serving tributary posts at Jasper and Rocky Mountain House. Rumors of gold in the river brought more white men and their wares and their whiskey.

The trade attracted Indians, and the white traders and gold miners married Indian

Fort Edmonton below Legislature Building, circa 1920.

women. It attracted Metis from Saskatchewan and Manitoba, and the presence of rough and rowdy white men, religious Metis and heathen Indians, attracted the missionaries.

It is there that this book really begins, for the presence of those courageous and sometime open-minded men of the cloth presaged all that which followed. For while the forts are all long gone, the beginnings of life outside the fort which started with the church, are still with us.

Edmonton's pioneers achievements occurred for the most part within the 82 years spanning the building of the Lacombe Chapel in St. Albert in 1861, and the

completion of St. Josaphat's Cathedral in 1943.

Edmonton now ranks among the most recent of the world's great cities. But the forces and people that brought it and us here are worth deliberating upon, not only for the lessons they teach us, but in simple appreciation.

Take Father Albert Lacombe. The Reverend Father for all his incredible energy, accomplishment and compassion, is said to be too earthy for sainthood. God bless him.

But to spend some time in his presence would be more than an honor. Born in St. Sulpice, Quebec, in 1827, ordained a priest in 1849, he was one of the first Roman Catholic missionaries sent to bring the word of God to the frontier in 1852.

As well as founding the City of St. Albert on Edmonton's northwest doorstep, he oversaw the erection of a chapel—Alberta's oldest building. His love of the wild and of the Native people caused him to abandon St. Albert a few years after the building of the chapel, saying it had become too civilized.

Father Lacombe prevented bloodshed between Indian tribes and between Indians and the white man. As well as learning to speak English, he created a dictionary and grammar of the Cree Indian language. He died in 1916, in a home he established for the aged in Midnapore, now part of Calgary.

For all of his contributions, Father Lacombe was but one. Others preceded and more followed. There were other missionaries, including the Methodist Reverend George McDougall who established the first building—his first church here—well outside the protective walls of the fort in 1873. That church has since been moved to Fort Edmonton Park, and was succeeded by a much grander structure in 1910.

There were the men of the Hudson's Bay Company who saw promise and opportunity and left the safety of company employ to lay the foundations of a city, hopefully pocketing a living if not a small profit on the way. They included John Walter, who built his first home on the Walterdale Flats about 1874, and Malcolm Groat who parlayed his west-end farmlands into a small fortune in real estate during the residential development of Glenora.

Then there's ex-HBC man Donald Ross, whose genial and rotund appearance and fondness for the liquor trade drove earnest preachers into a froth. Ross established the first hotel with bar and poolroom of course, and proved that fat and healthy crops could be grown in abundance in this northern Eden.

Our buildings were either built by, or for, or to honor those who were over-achievers—

men like Matthew McCauley, businessman, school board founder, vigilante, mayor, MLA, father of 16 children, farmer and prison warden. He arrived here in 1879 and he couldn't stop if he tried. McCauley died breaking new ground as a homesteader in the Peace River Country in 1930.

As the missionaries and ex-HBC men laid the groundwork, merchants like John A. McDougall and Frank Oliver followed, setting up humble businesses and successfully competing with the monopolistic Hudson's Bay Company. Their efforts in turn brought the trappings of civilization which brought another wave of early settlers. Men like Alex Taylor and Robert McKernan who brought in the telegraph from Battleford to the Hay Lakes and then to John Walter's first

Alberta coat of arms above Speaker's chair.

humble home on the south bank next to the boarding docks of the Belle of Edmonton.

The growing presence of settlers here was still outranked by the settlement at St. Albert, so much so that Alex Taylor built the first telephone line from his telegraph office to the Bishop's Palace (now known as Vital Grandin Centre) on the north bank of the Sturgeon River. Taylor also entered into partnership with Frank Oliver, and together they began Alberta's first newspaper, *The Edmonton Bulletin*, on December 6, 1880. Oliver of course, took over and dominated the media business and politics here until his defeat at the polls in 1917.

Walter Scott Robertson arrived in 1883 and became the district's first sheriff. He also brought in Edmonton's first piano about 1885. In 1874 the law arrived in the form of 20 Mounties under the command of Inspector W.D. Jarvis. But the Mounties camped downstream at Fort Saskatchewan until 1909 before drifting into Edmonton.

The railway arrived in 1891, though it wouldn't cross the river until 1905 as the Edmonton, Yukon and Pacific Railway that never made it much past 118th Avenue. The completion of the Calgary and Edmonton Railway in 1891 brought a land boom, especially in Strathcona, then called South Edmonton.

That year early south side settler Thomas Anderson and others sold their holdings to Nanton and Munson, Winnipeg real estate brokers for the CPR. They turned around and flipped them at a small profit to south side settlers and merchants. Strathcona began under the cold gaze of miffed north siders.

But Matt McCauley helped to assure the north side's supremacy when he took the law into his own hands during the Land Office Rebellion of 1892. McCauley held the Mounties and the federal government at bay until they recognized Edmonton as the rightful spot for the land office.

When the Grand Trunk Railway and the

Canadian Northern Railway arrived in 1910, the web was fully spun. Civilization had truly arrived in these parts. Now it had to be filled in, with schools, homes, businesses and institutions.

The first 13 years of this century were exciting ones. The economic spin veered up exponentially, egged on by the declaration of Edmonton as the capital of one of Canada's newest provinces in 1905.

Thousands flocked here prior to the First World War, as the world economy hummed in an ever-ascending economic boom and the west offered cheap land and boundless opportunity. Governments added to the economic din in quest of quarters and facilities.

The city scrambled to find ways and means of accommodating and serving the influx, a daunting task considering the complete lack of services. But pioneers didn't stop to deliberate and complain. They went on with the business of doing.

Consider the year 1912. The Legislature Building, the jewel in our crown, was completed and Edmonton's first city hall was built. Edmonton swallowed its cross-river rival Strathcona that year, its population jumped to 50,000, and Alberta's first university was in the construction stages. Numerous luxury homes were being built from the Highlands through to Glenora and south of the river. Building permits were worth $3.6 million in 1911, and they peaked in 1913 at $9.2 million.

From 1904 to 1914 the public school board went through an unprecedented construction spree, which wouldn't be repeated until many years later when the city was much more developed. EPSB Archives show 16 schools were built at a cost of $1.9 million. Only two brick schools—Queen's Avenue School (1903) and College Avenue School (1895) existed previously, and they are long gone.

Governments, businesses and the common people would suffer the effects of economic hangover when the boom went bust after the declaration of war August 4, 1914. The city's population peaked at 72,516 in 1914 and like the more recent collapse of the 1980s, out-migration coupled with war diminished the ranks of Edmonton residents. In 1917, the population shrank to 51,000.

That fact is reflected in this book. Of the 113 buildings mentioned, 59 were built in the period from 1905 to 1913. Thirty-seven were constructed between 1914 and 1943. From 1874 to 1904, 17 buildings were erected. These figures, simple as they are, show the growth of the city during the pre-war period.

But let's return to those times before the Great War, when resource-based, cyclical economy, boom and bust, were unknown concepts. Instead, embrace the era, when electricity, telephones, and running water were making their first appearances. The crank phonograph was just taking the city by storm—a Victor Gramophone was selling for $31, and radio was still in the future.

Turn back the pages to 1910. The latest popular songs, according to the Eaton's catalogue, were "Daisies Won't Tell" and "I Wish I had a Girl." Robert Lee was city mayor, while across the river, J.J. Duggan occupied that chair in Strathcona.

The Union Bank and the Canada Permanent Loan Company were expressing confidence in our economic future with the completion of their lofty Edmonton headquarters. At the top of McDougall Hill, the congregation of McDougall Church were proudly celebrating the opening of their new church, just next to the coal-fired Edmonton Incline Railway Company, which was cranking horses and buggies, the odd motorcar and foot passengers up and down the hillside.

The seven-year-old upstart *Edmonton Journal* was competing with Frank Oliver's *Bulletin*, and working out of quarters at 657 First Street, part of the now-demolished Tegler Building. The first building at the University of Alberta, Old St. Stephen's College, was being completed at land's end in a farmer's field. Certainly it wouldn't be there if it weren't for the crass political machinations of Premier Alexander Rutherford.

But he won't be around long. Rutherford was in the throes of a scandal that would push him out of office. Sir Wilfrid Laurier was still Prime Minister.

Out in more rolling fields on the east bank of Mill Creek Ravine, the Oblates of Mary Immaculate were setting to work on what is now called Faculté St. Jean.

As the sun rose in the early morning, the chef at the Dominion Hotel laid on the bacon from Gainer's piggery while the smoke from coal-fired stoves and backyard incinerators wafted through the city.

It wasn't so long ago...

Downtown West

In 1891 the area of downtown Edmonton west of 101st Street was subdivided by the Hudson's Bay Company and sold to enterprising local residents for modest amounts. With the Klondike gold rush and the boom economy that followed, this district effectively replaced Jasper East as the commercial centre of the city.

With the announcement in 1907 that a new provincial "parliament building" would soon be erected on 109th Street, even greater encouragement was given to the westward development of the city, and commercial buildings like the MacLean Block began to appear.

Vestiges of the pre-World War I economic high can still be seen in the restored Boardwalk and Revillon buildings on 102nd Avenue. In later years these would be complemented by the Birks building and others.

The heart of the city served other purposes as well, and in the First Presbyterian Church and McKay Avenue School are seen two of the finest religious and scholastic buildings in Edmonton. The Gariépy house was the home of one of Edmonton's early entrepreneurs, while Arlington Apartments reflected the transition from boarding house to apartment dwelling as an answer to the city center's growth. In later years, the diversity of activity and architectural style in the city's downtown core would be seen in such landmarks as the Old Citadel and the Masonic Temple.

Downtown West

1. *Legislature Building*
2. *Bowker Building*
3. *McKay Avenue School*
4. *Land Titles Building*
5. *Arlington Apartment*
6. *First Presbyterian Church*
7. *Gariépy House*
8. *Masonic Temple*
9. *Old Citadel*
10. *The Boardwalk*
11. *Revillon Building*
12. *Birks Building*
13. *McLean Block*

LEGISLATURE BUILDING • 1912

The Jewel in Edmonton's Crown
9718-107 Street

THE YEAR was 1912 and quaint trams of the Edmonton Radial Railway rumbled up and down 97th Avenue beside the crumbling clay embankment that supported Alberta's new Legislature Building.

"Versailles of the North," or versions thereof, were nothing but far-flung visions of hopeful politicians and forward-thinking landscape architects. Palatial reflecting pools and an underpass lined with owls in flight were yet to unfold.

On what is now the south lawn, near today's Centennial Flame, the last historic Fort Edmonton was collapsing. It had already become a favorite haunt of many a young lad with time on his hands.

In 1912 a real estate and economic boom was still in full force. Clapboard homes were being erected north across the avenue in the tract between 107th and 109th Streets. About 70 years later, that space would house a $66-million landscaping effort that some unforgiving wag dubbed "Versailles of the North."

The Legislature Building was the biggest and latest jewel in Edmonton's crown when it was formally opened in 1912 by the Duke of Connaught, then Governor General of Canada. Despite the downpour of rain which plagued his visit and prevented inspections of the university and the mission at St. Albert, the Duke was complimentary. "You gentlemen have shown your sentiment of the dignity of the duties which have to be performed here," he told assembled dignitaries.

Costing taxpayers about $4-million, the T-shaped building was an achievement for its time and place that present day architect Brian Woolfenden still marvels over. Woolfenden, the consulting architect on the $877,000 worth of renovations to the

The splendour of the Legislature Building and surrounding landscape.

legislature chamber and the rotunda undertaken in 1987, says ''it was a mammoth undertaking for those days—a credit to the government of the day and the architect who designed it.''

It seems like a safe bet now, but then both the city and the province were less than 10 years old. Their approximate populations at the time were a modest 54,000 and 375,000.

The five-storey Beaux-Arts architecture was described by some as pretentious and by others as simple. The building had little overall sculpture compared to its contemporaries, and a lack of sculpture in the round. But simple is a relative term, especially for such a young prairie city.

Its adornments include Ionic pilasters, six grand Corinthian columns at the main portico, the Alberta coat of arms above, elaborate capitals—some derived from an Egyptian motif—scrolls, dentils, gables, carved balustrades, light wells, and a dome within a dome capped with a cupola.

With the exception of the granite base and the six entrance colonnades, a yellowish-brown sandstone mined from the Glenbow Quarry near Calgary provides its finish. Now under water and known as the Glenbow Reservoir, the quarry could not provide stone in large enough chunks for the front columns, so these were imported from Bedford, Indiana.

The building was designed by the provincial architect Allan Merrick Jeffers, an American citizen who later became a naturalized British subject. Jeffers left provincial employ for that of the city prior to the building's completion, and the interior design was finished by Richard Palin Blakey.

Then-Premier Alexander Rutherford's good friend Percy Nobbs, professor of architecture at McGill University in Montreal, reviewed and approved the plans. Nobbs' influence was heavily felt in the early buildings of the University of Alberta.

Jeffers' design is believed to have been influenced by the Rhode Island and

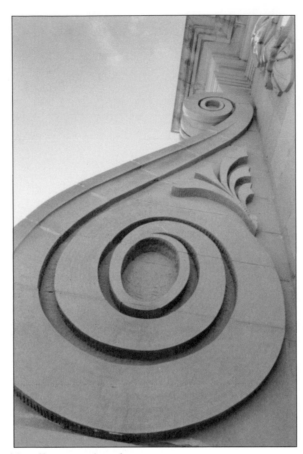

Scroll supporting dome.

Minnesota State Capitol Buildings. Its capitol building in Providence was designed in 1895 by the firm of McKim, Mead, and White.

The Minnesota building completed in 1905, was designed by Cass Gilbert, a noted and widely-published architect of his day. One of Gilbert's famous works was the 66-storey Manhattan skyscraper—The Woolworth Building of 1913 vintage—still considered one of New York City's major landmarks today.

Then-Public Works Minister W.H. Cushing, and later Rutherford, visited St. Paul, Minnesota, to inspect Gilbert's design, which has marked similarities to our capital building.

Beaux-Arts Classicism was championed in the late 19th century by one of the most famous of architectural schools in Europe— the Ecole des Beaux-Arts in Paris. The pictorial Beaux-Arts design of the Legislature Building is characterized by the symmetrical T-shaped plan and massing of building parts such that the climatic central entryway and grand, lantern-capped dome dominate the composition, Alberta Culture has noted.

Other typical features include the portico, supported by six large, fluted Corinthian columns. ''The appearance of coupled half columns and the combination of round and flat arched windows in the same elevation are additional features that are common to the style, a style which could turn classical restraint into a lively profusion for detail,'' says Alberta Culture.

In her 1979 thesis for a Master of Arts degree at the University of British Columbia, entitled ''The Prairie Legislative Buildings of Canada'', Diana Bodnar says that part of the *raison d'être* for such a building was that ''geographically isolated communities attempted to link their prairie environment, architecturally at least, with American and European centres for cultural, economic, and political activity. They wanted to prove that they were respectable, that they were progressive and equal.''

For statistics buffs: the dome was built with 200 tons of reinforced steel. The front Corinthian columns are 12 metres high and 1.2 metres in diameter, the administrative wing is 104 metres long and the legislative wing is 77 metres long.

To decorate the interior there is 22,000 square feet of marble weighing 1,950 tons, quarried in Quebec and Pennsylvania. The legislature chamber measures 17 by 16 metres, and the top of the dome is almost 57 metres off the ground.

A beacon in the cupola on top of the dome is meant to signal the populace when the assembly conducts an evening session. But building superintendent, Bill Kreibom, mused that it may have had more to do with quelling the anxiety of members' wives about the reality of all that night work.

To help MLAs keep their eyes on their work are 600 light bulbs on the vaulted ceiling of the chamber. All of these must be changed with a cherry-picker. Initially that took a week, but in 1943 workers finished it in two days.

There are eight arched windows in the drum of the dome, topped with portholes believed copied from the design of the Brazilian pavilion at the St. Louis World's Fair.

The fountain and flower bed was installed in the main floor light-well in honor of the 1959 visit of Queen Elizabeth to this province. It was the second fountain and longest-lasting, the first being built in honor of the 1939 visit of her father, King George VI.

Recent renovations to the chamber and rotunda to help mark the building's 75th anniversary included restoring the rotunda to its original color. In the chamber, new green carpeting, sound and video systems, desk consoles, mahogany panelling, and in the galleries, new chairs and wheelchair facilities were added.

While further renovations were planned, fiscal restraints have thus far prevented their fruition. They included painting the chamber ceiling and making it more accessible for changing light bulbs, installation of acoustical enhancements for the hearing impaired, digital speech timers for the members, and a state of the art television system.

In a 1987 interview, the Speaker of the Legislature, David Carter, called it "the number one building in the province in its combined importance—its political, architectural, and historical focus. It's a great old building and a very fine building for its day, but nobody at that time envisioned all of the electronic requirements that would be needed in the future."

As a result, the building is overloaded

Window trim on dome.

electronically and there isn't enough air circulation. Carter and Kreibom detailed other problems: the soft sandstone, lack of flashing, and too many flat surfaces all contribute to weather-induced decay, especially of the stone embellishments. Excessive interior moisture from the fountain has caused freeze and thaw problems in the dome, which is now being monitored and hopefully rectified.

Edmonton was designated the provisional capital of Alberta by the federal government in 1905, but it took a 16-to-8 vote by the first Legislative Assembly before the choice was ratified a year later.

The assembly first met in the Thistle Rink and then in the assembly hall of the McKay Avenue School. Upon the completion of the first Terrace Building on the Legislature grounds, the assembly met there until its first sitting in proper quarters in 1911.

The government purchased the 21-acre site of the old fort from the Hudson's Bay Company in 1906 for $84,000. The fort was torn down in 1915 in the belief that it spoiled the view of the Legislature Building.

Excavation for the building began in 1907. A building permit was taken out a year later for the modest sum of $1.25 million. Governor General Earl Grey laid the cornerstone in October 1909.

The last stone was laid on the dome in May 1912, and by December the incomplete costs had risen to $2.1 million. By the time of completion, Rutherford was no longer in office—a victim of the Alberta and Great Waterways Railway scandal. Then-Premier A.L. Sifton occupied his official new quarters in the east wing on January 20, 1913.

No story of the legislature is complete without at least one anecdote. One story has it that when legislature business dragged in the spring, Premier Ernest Manning (1943 to 1969) had a habit of opening the doors to the balcony overlooking the south lawn after it was freshly spread with ripe manure. With the hot spring sun beating down, the odiferous scent would waft into the chamber, reminding farmer members that it was seeding time, thus expediting business. ∎

Above: Elegant entranceway to the Legislature.
Left: Mahogany entrance doors to chamber.
Opposite page: The Legislature Building, which opened in 1912, cost taxpayers $4 million to build.

BOWKER BUILDING • 1931

Example of Beaux-Arts Style
9835-109 Street

CECIL BURGESS and Brian Woolfenden have something in common—a love of traditional architecture. Their mutual interest joined—albeit half a century apart—at the provincially-owned edifice now called the Bowker Building.

Burgess, a professor of architecture at the University of Alberta, was the original consulting architect when the Bowker was erected for the princely sum of $940,000 in 1931. Woolfenden was the consulting architect when the Bowker's interior was overhauled for $7 million in 1980. Woolfenden judges the only other building of this calibre in Edmonton is the Legislature.

Formerly known as the Administration Building, and also the Natural Resources Building, it is one of the few remaining examples in Edmonton of the Beaux-Arts architectural style, and one of the last to be built here.

Beaux-Arts Style was derived from the academic teachings of one of the most influential of 19th century architectural institutions, the Ecole des Beaux-Arts in Paris. Features of the building include its U-shaped symmetrical plan, and the focus of design on the central pavilion. Rectangular and round-arched windows, coupled columns supporting the pediment and the ornate roof balustrade all contribute to this classical style.

The Bowker is more than a last hurrah marking the end of an architectural era. Its erection symbolized the transfer of Alberta's natural resource wealth from federal to provincial jurisdiction in 1931. Much of its original price tag was applied to the exterior finish of limestone. Fifty years after it was erected, the province was able to give it an improved interior.

Woolfenden was asked to renovate to

Corinthian columns above Bowker Building entrance.

modern standards, and to preserve those parts which warranted it. Only the front vestibule with its oak doors, stained glass windows, marble flooring and the washrooms remain the same. The remainder was gutted and re-built in the style of another era.

Renovation highlights include a 900-square-foot east portico addition with circular staircase and centre decorative column with a fountain-burst effect achieved with jute covered with pre-cast plaster. The portico connects the building to the Legislature's underground pedestrian mall.

The redesigned front foyer or rotunda incorporates a groin vault ceiling. The fifth floor features the mahogany-finished conference room with elaborate Corinthian and Ionic columns and pilasters. Dentil and frieze work grace the ceiling.

Woodwork throughout is mahogany. Three copies were made of the original stained glass coat of arms in the front foyer—two of which were also installed there, and the third in the fifth floor conference room.

Woolfenden's appreciation of the original craftsmanship was incorporated in a myriad of interior details. All of the bronze door plates incorporate a 75 per cent reduction of the original coat of arms found on the front door escutcheons. ■

McKay Avenue School • 1904

Red Brick School of Renaissance Style
10424-99 Avenue

MODERN HIGHRISE apartment buildings and office towers surround two buildings that played a prominent role in early Edmonton.

McKay Avenue School, a four-storey red brick building served as Alberta's first Legislative Assembly in 1906 and 1907.

On the grounds beside it is a grey wood frame building—Edmonton and Alberta's first public school fully restored to 1881 conditions, right down to the desks and slates used by the city's first pupils. It was built on four lots donated to the fledgling school board by the Hudson's Bay Company.

Both buildings were named after the avenue, which had taken its name from Dr. William MacKay, a pioneer Hudson's Bay Company doctor. The name was originally misspelled on the brick school's front and has remained unchanged ever since.

The wood frame school is architecturally significant as the first building constructed of dressed lumber in Edmonton—all others at the time were of logs. It was built for $968. The money was raised by public subscription, as the legal school district was not established until 1885. During its first 20 years of public service, it served as a courtroom and social centre, as well as providing the city with its first centre of learning.

The old school house has been restored and is used as a living museum where present-day students can experience the lessons and the discipline of century-old academia.

The brick school, built in 1904, was described by *The Edmonton Bulletin* as of the "Renaissance style of architecture constructed of pressed brick and stone trimmings."

The brick school was designed by H.D. Johnstone, and built at a cost of $51,450 by a Mr. Manson. Its cornerstone was laid by

1912 classroom in McKay Avenue School.

Lord Minto, Canada's governor general at the time.

During its construction, the school board sold the 1881 school house to the contractor for use as a construction shack. The old school then made its way to the river valley, where it was used as a private residence on the Rossdale Flats until 1980. During the 1915 flood of the North Saskatchewan River, it almost floated away but was secured with a hook and cables by its owner, David Mawhinney.

The Legislative Assembly which used the third floor assembly hall for two years paid $400 in rent. Many momentous issues were decided at this time, including establishing Alberta's first speed limits for automobiles at 20 miles per hour and formalizing Edmonton as the capital of Alberta.

McKay Avenue School was designated a Provincial Historical Resource in 1976. The brick school is now used to house the board's museum and archives. One of the classrooms has been restored to 1912 era conditions. In the process, seven coats of paint were removed from the wainscotting by students at W.P. Wagner High School. The third floor has been restored to look as it did when it housed the Legislative Assembly. ■

The Bowker Building is one of the few remaining examples of Beaux-Arts architecture in Edmonton.

Above: Stained glass coat of arms, Bowker Building.
Right: Mahogany-panelled conference room, Bowker Building.

LAND TITLES BUILDING • 1893

Building Subject of Rivalry

10523-100 Avenue

THE HUMBLE Land Titles Building stands as a monument to the success and growth of Edmonton, and as a tombstone marking the demise of Strathcona.

In an 1893 article, *The Edmonton Bulletin* commented that the building's construction "is the first tangible acknowledgement from the government that the town of Edmonton had any right to exist."

Plans were drawn by the federal public works architect Thomas Fuller. The design is similar in style to English rural houses and barns, which have large, jerkinhead roofs and comparable proportions. The building was designated a Provincial Historical Resource by Alberta Culture in 1977.

Its erection was the culmination of a tumultuous tug-of-war that could easily have resulted in bloodshed. The tussle between Edmonton and Strathcona residents marked the beginning of the end for Strathcona's aspirations to become the major city.

The success of loyal Edmontonians who rallied around the defence of the land office may have bordered on treason, but it assured the pre-eminence of this city in the early struggle to become a leading provincial centre.

"Strong antipathy arose between the two settlements on the north and south banks of the river," *The Bulletin* said in a 1909 article. "South Edmonton was puffed with pride at the acquiring of railway facilities, and Old Edmonton, perched on its regal throne on the high bank to the north, viewed with wrath the attempt to rob it of its glory."

Stories are mixed as to just how Edmontonians discovered the affair. One dark night in June 1892, the land office was being loaded onto wagons for a furtive trip across the river. It seems boosters of that impetuous overnight clapboard sensation—otherwise known as Strathcona—had convinced Interior Minister Edgar Dewdney or "Dirty Dewdney" as *The Bulletin* called him, that the office would be better located close to the end of the recently-completed Calgary and Edmonton Railway.

One account had it that a Reverend Fauquier, a Roman Catholic priest, alerted the populace, while *The Bulletin* claimed it found out when the land office placed a late classified advertisement that night to advise the public of its new location. In any event, "the trumpet of Mars was sounded on Jasper Avenue" and "'blue was the ozone with the deprecations which were called on the head of the offenders," *The Bulletin* said.

Mayor Matt McCauley, who had already garnered a reputation for expedition, led a troop of indignant residents to the offending wagons, quickly removed the "whiffletrees" and the nuts on the axles, and placed a guard around the wagons.

On orders from Dewdney, Captain Arthur Griesbach of the Northwest Mounted Police led 20 Mounties from Fort Saskatchewan with orders to ensure the land office's removal. But they were met by McCauley and the "home guard."

McCauley told Griesbach that the "building will not be moved without bloodshed. I am prepared to take my chances, if you care to do the same." Griesbach backed off and, four days later, the land office was back in business in its old location.

"The excitement had barely time to subside, when on July 11, 1892, tenders were called for a new land office to be built in Edmonton," *The Bulletin* said.

The land office had occupied a number of locations up to that point. The first was opened in 1884 by Pierre Gauvereau in a log house formerly occupied by *The Bulletin*. This original Dominion Land office was moved to Fort Edmonton Park in the 1970s.

In 1887, registrar George Roy built the first house on 100th Street and moved his office into his home. In 1893, the combined land, timber, and registry office moved to 106th Street and 100th Avenue and became known as the Land Titles Building. It featured a galvanized iron roof with a steep pitch, and B.C. fir for interior woodwork.

It served as the land office until 1909, when the office moved to the Jasper Block at 105th Street and Jasper Avenue, where it stayed until new offices were built in 1912.

During the First World War, the Old Land Titles Building was occupied by the 19th Alberta Dragoons, and subsequently it became known as Victoria Armories. The Dragoons used it until the late 1930s when the Edmonton Fusiliers moved in, remaining there for the duration of the Second World War. The 19th Armored Car Regiment then occupied the building until it was acquired by the province in 1949. It was then used by the provincial department of health and social development for offices and laboratories.

The province vacated the building in 1978, and rented it to the Red Cross Society. In 1986, the Alberta Publishers Association, the Writers Guild of Alberta and numerous other organizations established WordWorks in the building. ■

ARLINGTON APARTMENTS • 1909

Block's Features Are of a Bygone Era

10524-100 Avenue

THE ARLINGTON APARTMENTS, one of Edmonton's first tenement houses when constructed in 1909, continues to express the grace and craftsmanship of another age.

Its creaky maple floors, high ceilings, and quaint interior design betray the whimsies and social habits of another era—when servants were common, and entertaining at home was a city event.

Many prominent people took up residence here over the years due to its luxury status and proximity to the Legislature Building. They included Richard Hardisty, son of a former factor at Fort Edmonton, and noted historian John Blue, Alberta's first provincial librarian.

There are 49 apartments on five floors. A partial sixth floor, now used for storage, was once a tea room. Oak woodwork runs along the ceilings and room entryways. Large oak pocket doors divide the parlors from the dining rooms.

Each of the suites featured a built-in reversible Murphy bed and oak buffet, inset with a mirror and flanked with oak spindles. Oak closet doors are faced with a small china cabinet, built-in writing desk and shelving.

The Edmonton Historical Board described The Arlington as a red brick building "of relatively austere architecture. It depends for its success on careful brick detailing, expressed in the corbelled cornice, the brick corner piers, and the well-proportioned arched and recessed entry with its brick piers and corbelled shelf above."

The Arlington "provides color, texture and human scale to 100th Avenue in contrast to the glass or concrete office towers which have been built nearby."

The block cost $130,000 and was built to take advantage of Edmonton's first real estate boom. Contractor Robert Grant of Winnipeg

Builders of the Arlington Apartments, 1910.

managed to complete it in just a few weeks—a storey a week—using 25 brick layers and 50 carpenters.

Original owners included G. Swaisland, manager of Molsons Bank, D.R. Fraser of Fraser Lumber Mills, and P.O. Dwyer, who built the Transit Hotel. In 1943 it was sold to Mickey and Garret Ryan of Northern Transportation. In 1947, Garret Ryan became the sole owner and held the title until the present owner, Phyllis Barham, purchased the building. ■

31

Old Land Titles Building as it appears today.

FIRST PRESBYTERIAN CH. • 1912

Late Gothic Style Church
10025-105 Street

THIS RED BRICK edifice with its six-storey bell tower, once had a commanding view of the Edmonton area, reputedly as far away as Stony Plain.

Built in the Late Gothic Revival Style, the structure traces its roots to 1881 when Reverend Andrew Browning Baird established the faith's first city church. Those first services were held in Reverend George McDougall's Methodist church. The congregation then moved to a room above a grain warehouse at 98th Street and Jasper Avenue, where the Convention Centre now stands.

In 1882, the Hudson's Bay Company granted the church four lots at 104th Street and 99th Avenue, across from McKay Avenue School. Two were for a manse, and two for a wooden church, which opened that fall.

The congregation met there until 1902, when a new 500-seat brick church was built at 103rd Street and Jasper Avenue. That old church is gone and its site occupied by the office tower that was once the flagship of Don Cormie's Principal Group of Companies.

But in the early years of this century, Edmonton was booming, and capitalists cast envious eyes upon the congregation's prime Jasper Avenue location. So the present structure was built to seat 1,250 people. Speculators paid $195,000 for the old church, and the astute congregation paid $172,000 for its new one plus another $14,000 for its three lots.

The Reverend Baird was succeeded as pastor in 1887 by the highly respected Reverend David George McQueen, who served the church for 41 years.

The church was designated a Provincial Historical Resource in 1978 by Alberta Culture. Its design is considered a good

First Presbyterian Church built in Late Gothic Revival Style.

example of Late Gothic Revival Style with transept and a 114-foot corner bell tower.

The church was designed by the south side architectural firm of Arthur Wilson and D.E. Herrald, who designed many early Strathcona structures, including the Strathcona Public Library and the university home of Alberta's first premier, Alexander Rutherford.

First Presbyterian was built of Redcliffe pressed brick with Bedford stone trim, and erected with a concrete basement on a stone foundation. Predominately English-inspired, the style also incorporates some French Gothic elements, such as the triple-arch motif of the main porch. As well, the large pointed arched windows on the sides and front facade, are filled with French Gothic flamboyant tracery, characterized by its flowing and flame-like motif.

Building features include a sanctuary with a U-shaped gallery, a semi-dome housing the organ, a double vestibule, a fir-panelled arched ceiling, and oak and fir woodwork. The pulpit from the 1902 church is still being used. The tower features 20 tubular chimes, a gift in 1913 from John A. McDougall, a pioneer city businessman.

The organ with oak case and mahogany console was built in 1909 by Casavant Frères of St. Hyacinthe, Quebec. It has 1,572 pipes ranging from three-eighths of an inch to 16 feet in length.

Historical mementoes abound. Above the pulpit are the colors of the 63rd Battalion of the Canadian Army, presented to McQueen in 1916, the same year his son Alex was killed in France. A silver trowel, a mallet, and plumb line, all presented to McQueen at the cornerstone ceremony in 1911, are encased in the church's social room, as is a 100-year-old desk, once used by Baird. The first pulpit used in the 1882 church is found in a hall at the rear of the church.

Much of the church's history is tied to that of McQueen. Although he was later beloved

Laying cornerstone. First Presbyterian Church, July 1911.

by his congregation, he first received an icy welcome. Members were miffed at not having had any say in his appointment, and did not officially induct him as minister until 1893.

McQueen served as inspector of schools until that time. He married Catherine Robertson in 1890, and they had three sons and four daughters. Two of them, Jean Learmonth and Helen Siemens were church members in the 1980s.

McQueen became the first moderator of the Alberta Synod of the Presbyterian Church, and a moderator of the Presbyterian Church of Canada. He died in 1930. ■

GARIEPY HOUSE • 1902

A Tenuous Lease on Life
9947-104 Street

THE FORMER home of leading pioneer Edmonton merchant Joseph Gariépy was almost destroyed in the early 1980s.

When a building evaluation showed the building to be sound and worth renovating, the mansion and its eastern annex underwent substantial renovations in 1983. The original mansion with additions, is owned by the Sisters of Providence of St. Vincent de Paul.

But while the building could easily qualify for historic resource designation on architectural and historic grounds, and gain protection from redevelopment, it has never been requested by any group.

When built, its location was known as the corner of Victoria Avenue and Fourth Street, our city's first bourgeois neighborhood. Today it is near the heart of downtown in the middle of a bustling commercial and residential high-rise area.

Gariépy, who made his fortune in real estate as well as retailing, purchased the land for $620 from carriage builder John Walter in1898, and built Gariépy House in 1902.

It was constructed by P. Anderson and Company, a prominent local brick firm for an unknown sum, however it is known that Gariépy took out a $25,000 mortgage with John McDougall.

Joseph Hormisdas Gariépy came to Edmonton in 1892 when our fair city's population was less than 200 souls. He had previously owned a grocery store in Montreal.

Shortly after his arrival, he astounded Edmontonians by paying the then unheard-of price of $1,200 for the northwest lot at Jasper Avenue and McDougall Street (100th Street) as the site for a general store.

His business was successful due to the influx of fortune-seekers en route to the Klondike. In 1908 he added a second store in Morinville.

He went on to become a town councillor in 1897/98, held numerous directorships in various early Edmonton companies, and was a founding member and president of the Board of Trade, forerunner of the Chamber of Commerce. Gariépy's son, Wilfrid, became a provincial cabinet minister, and later a member of parliament.

The Edmonton Historical Board called the mansion one of few remaining pre-incorporation Edmonton buildings and one of the few early grand mansions which remain in the city's earliest upper middle-class neighborhood.

The square, two-storey brick structure was built in the French-inspired Second Empire architectural style, and is considered the best example in the city. Features include a corner tower and Mansard-type roof. The second storey has segmentally-arched windows projecting through the cornice onto the Mansard roof-like dormers. These are topped with decoratively carved wood ornaments.

The turret roof is accented with small round French-inspired windows, and both the turret and Mansard roofs are covered with green painted wood shingles.

In 1923 it was sold to capitalist John A. McDougall for $25,000 in full settlement of his mortgage. McDougall in turn sold it for $12,500 to the religious order in 1924. The sisters added an eastern wing in 1925 of similar architecture, which was designed by McLean Engineering Company.

Today the home is a residence for female outpatients and nuns, a role it assumed in 1962 after serving as a temporary residence for single women coming to the city to work. ∎

MASONIC TEMPLE • 1931

Gothic Hall Home to Masons
10318-100 Avenue

THE GRAND GOTHIC style hall that Edmonton's Masonic Order built in 1931 remains in pristine condition over half a century later.

The Masonic Temple, a centre of social life in Edmonton prior to the Second World War, continues to serve the various rites and orders of about 8,000 Masons.

The lodge, which replaced another building on 102nd Street, is city headquarters for the order which is dedicated to the moral improvements of good men. Among its first members was Dr. Edward Ainslie Braithwaite, a veteran of the 1885 Rebellion and Edmonton's first medical officer. He was first grand master of the lodge prior to Alberta becoming a province.

Funds for the building, which is owned by Central Masonic Temple Company, were raised by share subscription as early as 1910. Its total cost reached $170,000.

The building was designed by architect William Blakey, who also prepared the plans for Christ Church and the Stony Plain Multicultural Centre, a former regional high school. The four-storey lodge is of steel and concrete construction, with red brick and artificial stone on the exterior. The medieval lines of the facade include the Masonic emblems of the compass and square. Six canopied niches were included to hold statues.

Alberta Culture speculated that Blakey chose the Late Gothic Revival Style for the design of the temple in an effort to link buildings to the origins of Freemasonry. Freemasons were members of medieval craft guilds, which were often involved in large crown building projects.

The building was designed to have two entrances—the right for public access to cloakrooms and the main floor auditorium,

and the left for the "special prerogative of the craft," according to a 1931 article in *The Journal*.

The double oak doors at both ends featured bronze lock plates, while inside special door plates and handles were struck with the Masonic emblems. The main floor included an auditorium that could seat 500 people. It retained the original light fixtures, described in the article as "12 delicately-wrought brass electroliers of refined and tasteful pattern." A library, replete with turn of the century books, and a foyer, with terrazzo flooring inlaid with copper masonic emblems, is also on the main floor. Offices occupy the second floor. A large and small lodge room are located on the third floor. Both feature stained glass windows and ornate woodwork.

Braithwaite's significance for the Masons is no less than his historic significance for the city and province. He joined the Masons in 1893. In 1929, he sold the majority of his property, save for his home, to the Central Masonic Temple Association Limited. He also turned the first sod for the building. He served as a medic for the North West Mounted Police in the 1885 Rebellion and witnessed the hanging of Louis Riel.

He was posted to Fort Saskatchewan in 1890 and, two years later, established a medical practice in Edmonton. In 1896, he became Edmonton's first coroner. He performed the first surgery at several city hospitals. He retained his affiliation with the RCMP until 1931, becoming one of its longest serving members. Braithwaite died at the age of 87 in 1949. ∎

Former home of Joseph Gariépy.

Above: Detail of fine workmanship above front door to Masonic Temple.
Left: Window detail, Masonic Temple.

OLD CITADEL • 1925

From Salvation to Beauty Salon
10030-102 Street

Exterior of Masonic Temple.

THE OLD CITADEL has gone from soup and salvation to the snipping and buzzing of nattily-coiffed hairstylists at work—and it's had a mid-life flirt with theatre to boot.

The fundamental exhortations of the Salvation Army—born in the social distress of the Victorian industrial revolution—have long since faded away from inside the prim and proper clinkered brick exterior of the Old Citadel. Originally the centre for the Salvation Army on a mission from God to save souls, the building now houses Marvel Hairstyling and Esthetics School.

With about 13,000 square feet, the Old Citadel was built in 1925 for $30,000 as a centre for administration and religious services. It was the sixth city home for the Sally Ann.

It was designed by Herbert A. Magoon and George Heath MacDonald—one of the city's more prolific early architectural firms, who also counted Old St. Stephen's College, Knox Church, and the now-demolished Tegler Building among other credits.

In 1965, the Salvation Army acquired larger premises in the former Central Pentacostal Tabernacle. So, Joe Shoctor and a group of enterprising businessmen and theatre buffs—including Sandy McTaggart, Ralph McMillan, John Soprovich and the late J.L. Martin—purchased the structure for $100,000.

The building was converted into the city's first professional live theatre since the Second World War. With 277 gold seats, chandeliers, and a balcony, the facility opened that November to a packed and critically-acclaimed run of Edward Albee's ''Who's Afraid of Virginia Woolf.'' The building continued as the city's professional theatre centre until 1976 when the new Citadel Theatre opened.

The Old Citadel then became a disco and,

Aerial view of city showing Legislature Building, 1956.

Vertical brick piers link towers of the Old Citadel.

two years later it was purchased by Frank Cairo for $560,000. More renovations were made to make the building suitable for use as a beauty school. Little remains of the original building except for the facade, double doors, and ornate open beam ceiling.

The Edmonton Historical Board noted the unusual architecture of the Old Citadel. While the building was designed to have a fortress-like appearance, the board pointed out that "the emphasized verticality of the centre portions suggests ecclesiastical qualities as well."

It called the brick detailing ornate and careful. The flat roof is bordered by gable parapets at each corner, and polychrome bricks and tiles accent the facade. The board said the central tower is the building's most significant feature with two slender towers linked with an intricate pattern of vertical brick piers, recessed panels, and a recessed and arched entrance.

There is an off-centre corbelled brick balcony halfway up the north tower, which makes the overall composition slightly asymmetrical. Except for the canopy and closure of two street-level windows, the facade remained unaltered. ■

THE BOARDWALK • 1910

Former Warehouse Transformed
10220-103 Street

THE ROSS BROTHERS warehouse has undergone many a transformation, including a few stabs at becoming a successful retail mall.

Now known as The Boardwalk, the structure was built in 1910 as the most modern hardware warehouse west of Winnipeg, for the thriving retail and wholesale firm of Ross Brothers Limited.

Its most recent owners, N.A. Properties Limited, a subsidiary of North West Trust Company, have made $17 million worth of changes to the 96,000-square-foot, four-storey building, along with its partner, The Revillon Building.

Its centrepiece is a four-storey glass-enclosed canopy between the two buildings. Inside, an atrium mall with restaurants caters to office workers. The changes were completed in 1986, and won an award from the Alberta Historical Resources Foundation.

The Renaissance Revival styling features a series of symmetrical arches with a centre bay window over the original entrance. Corbelling and a subdued cornice distinguish the brick finish. The building was originally 130 by 80 feet wide with only five arches. It was built of B.C. fir, with double-planked flooring, steel and plaster partitions, and fireproof vaults on the first and second floors. There were two electric freight elevators, a trolley, scales and indoor tracks.

Built in the city's warehouse district during Edmonton's pre-First World War economic boom, Ross Brothers Hardware was a thriving concern. The firm was started by James Ross who first arrived here in 1878. Besides a successful business career, he was in the home guard during the 1885 Rebellion, and served four terms as an alderman. ■

Above: The Revillon building is an example of commercial architecture.
Right: The Boardwalk and The Revillon are connected by a four-storey glass canopy.

REVILLON BUILDING • 1912

Fashionable Furs to Fashionable Offices
10221-104 Street

THE REVILLON building has gone through numerous transformations in an attempt to find a paying niche in the modern streetscape.

The building began its life as a fur trading and hardware warehouse. The six-storey structure with a two-storey annex was originally northern headquarters for the Revillon Frères Trading Company, a Paris-based rival of the Hudson's Bay Company.

Revillon Frères Trading which was established in 1723, arrived here in 1900 and owned two other buildings before this one was built in 1912 at a cost of $350,000. The arrival of the firm's new quarters resulted in a gush of civic pride by *The Edmonton Bulletin* and *The Edmonton Journal*. It was noted that $2 million of furs passed through the firm's warehouse annually en route to New York and Paris where they were made into fashionable outer wear.

Through the years the building has housed countless businesses and survived two major fires, in 1928 and 1949. An annex was added to the original six-storey structure in 1920 at a cost of $200,000.Architect and contractor for both was J. McDiarmid of Winnipeg.

In 1912 its modern conveniences were considered a technological marvel—an automatic telephone exchange system connecting 26 phones, three electric hoists, an electric passenger elevator, a pneumatic tube to deliver orders and memos between offices, and a spiral chute to send orders to the shipping room.

Architectural features of this six-storey poured concrete brick-clad structure include a flat roof bordered by a parapet with brick corbelling. The facade is divided into bays of paired rectangular windows, separated by full-height piers. The ground floor on 104th Street is sheathed in limestone which contrasts with the building's brick finish.

The Edmonton Historical Board notes that although "not as pure as that developed by the Chicago school, The Revillon is a fine example of that straightforward, clean, functional approach" of commercial architecture.

At last reckoning, The Revillon was attempting to find a profitable life reincarnated as one of Edmonton's first festival markets. ■

BIRKS BUILDING • 1929

Former Home of Famous Jewelry Firm
10123-104 Street

ELEGANCE NOTWITHSTANDING, it was considered a marvel of medical technology when the Birks Building was built in 1929 to house the famous Canadian jewelry firm of Henry Birks and Sons Limited. The building was the first in the city to incorporate custom-built medical features, including a compressed air system to power dental and other tools which still functioned at publishing time.

The Edmonton Historical Board has called its architecture an example of the transition from the older Commercial Style to the Moderne Style. It features classical details such as a modest cornice and the plain arcading of the first two floors. Decorative highlights include bronze panels, leaded windows above the canopy, mosaic tile incorporated with the beige brick, and the use of polished and unpolished marble.

It was constructed for $350,000, primarily to house Birks' Edmonton operation. The design was patterned after a Montreal building and drawn up by the Montreal architectural firm of Percy Nobbs and George Hyde, with Cecil S. Burgess as the resident architect. This arrangement had served the threesome well on a number of Edmonton projects. Their biggest contribution to Edmonton architecture was the design of numerous early buildings at the University of Alberta, including the Arts Building and the first Medical Building. Burgess was also the university's professor of architecture.

About 5,000 people attended the building's grand opening on November 15, 1929. It was hosted by none other than Henry G. Birks, grandson of the firm's founder.

The Edmonton Journal lauded the building as presenting "a distinct compliment to the structural and architectural dignity of this city."

The Birks store was first managed by D.A. Kirkland, who had plied the jewelry trade here since 1910, and was locally known as the "Diamond Prince."

In 1947 the building was sold to Edmonton Buildings Limited, a group of city businessmen headed by Francis Winspear—a former Dean of Commerce at the University of Alberta. Birks continued operations under a long-term lease. In 1971 Birks abandoned its first city foothold and moved to the Edmonton Centre downtown shopping mall.

One of the building's notable tenants was Radio Station CJCA, whose famous bespectacled tiger topped the building until the mid-1980s. CJCA occupied the fourth floor of the building from 1934 to 1973.

Other than customary office renovations for tenants, the building remains much as it was. An air conditioning system has been added and electrical and plumbing systems have been upgraded. ■

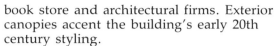

Corporation Revitalizes Building
107 Street & Jasper Avenue

THIS ATTRACTIVE turn of the century commercial block on Jasper Avenue has aged gracefully and usefully—thanks to new life breathed into it by former owners.

The three-storey MacLean Block could easily have met the wrecker's ball, except for the plans of Daon Development Corporation. In 1977, the firm purchased the block and completely gutted the interior. A modern building was then erected within the MacLean's exterior shell.

Inside, its years are belied by an elegant marble tile and oak panelled foyer. Only the original sandblasted brick walls in the modern open-plan offices tell the visitor that this is indeed an older building.

The 25,000-square-foot block has attracted a number of tenants, including restaurants, a

book store and architectural firms. Exterior canopies accent the building's early 20th century styling.

The Jasper Avenue landmark was an early product of the pre-First World War real estate boom. In the first ten years of this century, growing city businesses pushed development west along Jasper Avenue from the central core. A successful physician and surgeon come real estate developer, Dr. James D. MacLean, took advantage of his profits and the city's need for commercial and apartment space, and constructed the building in 1909. It was then the furthest west of any commercial building.

Dr. MacLean arrived in Edmonton in 1906, and married Lottie Belle Ross, daughter of Edmonton pioneer John Ross (no relation to Donald Ross).

The building was designed by James Wize, who also designed the now-demolished Corona Hotel. It was constructed by Pheasey and Batson for $35,000. Shortly after it opened, its major ground floor tenant was the Imperial Bank of Canada, which maintained a west branch here until 1959.

Dr. MacLean sold the building to his father-in-law in 1911 and moved to Strathcona. The structure was resold that year to the Belgian Investment Corporation of Canada. Belgian Investment and its successor held title until Daon's purchase in 1977.

The Edmonton Historical Board terms the MacLean Block "an excellent local example of the Victorian Italianate Renaissance Style."

The MacLean Block was renovated into modern offices in 1977.

Birks Building, former home of famous jewelry firm.

McCauley · Rossdale

The oldest settled area in Edmonton is the McCauley-Rossdale district. Indians trading at Fort Edmonton camped on Rossdale Flats, and when a white settlement emerged outside the Fort in the late 1870s, it was along High Street, later Jasper Avenue, east of 101st Street.

Rossdale was named after Donald Ross, the first man to build a farm outside the fort and on the flats in 1876. The McCauley district was named for Matt McCauley, Edmonton's first mayor whose livery stable stood just off Jasper Avenue.

After the turn of the century, McCauley emerged as a hotel district to the south, a finance and business district to the west, and a red light neighbourhood to the north-east, with a civic centre in the middle. Vestiges of all elements have survived, including the Civic Block, the McLeod, Canada Permanent and Union Bank buildings. Fronting the area was the Hotel MacDonald, Edmonton's finest for over half a century. On the other hand, Rossdale emerged as an industrial district. Although the Rossdale Brewery is the only industrial structure remaining, many of the small dwellings in the community reflect the life style of the working class people who lived there in the early part of the century. Likewise, the Donald Ross School and Diamond Park add to the sense of community that prevailed long after the small industries closed down.

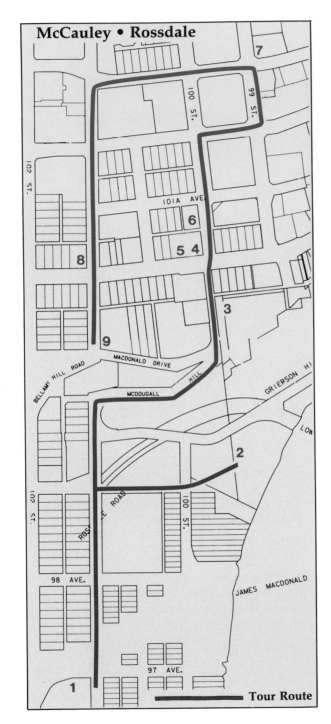

DONALD ROSS SCHOOL • 1917

If Only Initials Told Tales...

10125-97 Avenue

IF THE LOVERS whose initials are inscribed on the weathered brick walls of Donald Ross School are still as together as their Alma Mater, perhaps love and old architecture can endure in this world.

The school, in one of Edmonton's oldest neighborhoods, was named after a prominent Edmonton pioneer. Donald Ross was the third white man to build a house in Edmonton outside the fort. He was also the city's first gardener and hotelier, and probably first saloon-keeper and billiard hall manager.

Ross served as a member of the first public school board in 1883. He was the original owner of most of Rossdale, once known as River Lot Four.

Donald Ross School was built for $33,895 by the Dunlop, Johnson Construction Company, to help accommodate growing enrolments as the city's economy and population grew prior to the First World War.

The school, built near the end of Ross's life, has been twice threatened with demolition—first in the late 1960s to make way for traffic interchanges, and in the 1980s as a possible site for the space sciences centre which was later built in Coronation Park.

The school was closed in 1974 due to declining enrolment and has since been used as the headquarters for the Commonwealth Games, Universiade '83 and Summerfest. Interior renovations costing $80,000 transformed classrooms and hallways into offices and meeting rooms. By 1985 the school was primarily used as a natural and human history interpretive centre by the city's parks and recreation department.

The five-classroom structure trimmed with Bedford stone succeeded the Saskatchewan Avenue School—a two-storey wood structure built in 1907. The main floor had two classrooms, an assembly area, and an office for the principal. The second floor had three more classrooms, an infirmary, a staff room and a spacious hallway.

Mary McIvor, the school's first principal, served for 41 years. She was regarded as a strict disciplinarian and an excellent teacher.

Alberta Culture has described the building as a good example of utilitarian educational designs used at the turn of the century. ■

Aerial view of the McCauley neighbourhood

ROSSDALE BREWERY • 1905

Brewery Faces Uncertainty
9843-100 Street

THE CRUMBLING red brick brewery in Rossdale faces some uncertainty, despite or perhaps because of its status as a Registered Historical Resource.

In the mid-1980s, the city changed its long-standing policy of buying river valley properties to create a park. Having decided to retain existing river valley communities as residential areas, the Rossdale community plan was to be redrafted. This could allow a commercial use, currently not permitted.

The new community plan may mean changes in zoning, land use, and traffic patterns in Rossdale and other river valley communities. As part of those plans, the city would like to see the brewery restored and used again in some form.

The two-storey brewery, forerunner of Molson Alberta Brewery Limited, was built in 1905. It was the first owned by the Edmonton Brewing and Malting Company.

Alberta Culture calls it the oldest unaltered industrial structure of its type in Alberta. Two other breweries predate it, but Calgary's Cross Brewery built in 1892 has been greatly altered and the Lethbridge Brewery built in 1901 is only partly standing. Designation was granted by Alberta Culture in 1980.

After passing through many hands over the years, the Edmonton building became part of the estate of entrepreneur Allan Hardy. He died shortly after its purchase by his Saxon Group of Companies in 1980. In 1985, trustees of Hardy's estate said the brewery's Registered Historical Resource tag scares away prospective owners who might view the designation as limiting their ability to develop the site as they wish.

The original owner of the brewery was William Henry Sheppard, who became a councillor and mayor of Strathcona. He also owned several hotels, the Arctic Ice Company adjacent to the brewery, and an insurance brokerage.

Some accounts also say that Sheppard also became a shareholder of the Edmonton Incline Railway Company, which ran up and down McDougall Hill from 1908 to 1913 where the Chateau Lacombe stands today. The combination elevator and railway enabled him to get his wagons loaded with kegs of beer up the formidable grade of McDougall Hill. The demise of the incline railway came with the completion of the High Level Bridge in 1912.

When the brewery was built, the top floor was used as a malt room. A malting plant was on the ground floor, which was designed with a 21-foot high ceiling to allow for the installment of a drum system to sprout barley.

Output for the year ending in March 1908 was said to be 20,000 barrels, 10 times production in the first year. Business grew to the point that in 1913 the brewery moved to 121st Street and 104th Avenue, which is most recently known as the Molson's Brewery. ■

Above: Rossdale Brewery awaits its future.
Opposite page: South facade of Hotel MacDonald.

HOTEL MacDONALD • 1915

Grande Dame Seeking Suitor
Jasper Avenue & 100 Street

IN 1986 they finally unloaded the box the Mac came in, but for concerned Edmontonians and their city fathers, too much time and uncertainty has elapsed in the long-anticipated reconditioning of the grande dame of Edmonton hostelry.

The Hotel MacDonald was built in 1915, but by 1987 it was celebrating its fourth year with a 100 per cent vacancy rate. It was shut down in 1983 for a restoration job that at last count had been set back at least four times.

The only visible evidence that something was happening was the 1986 demolition of a 16-storey rectangular wing, which opened in 1953—the so-called box the Mac came in. At last word, the $24 million renovation was to be finished by the spring of 1990, while CN continued its search for a buyer.

The Mac was Edmonton's pre-eminent hotel for at least 50 years and it played host to royalty, politicians and show business personalities. Among them were King George VI and Queen Elizabeth, Prime Minister John Diefenbaker, Bob Hope, Jack Benny and Zsa Zsa Gabor.

The toned-down renovations are to see the Mac with 190 rooms, with classy modern amenities in a traditional setting. The Wedgewood Room and Empire Ballroom are to be restored to their former glory, and there will also be a bar, a restaurant and various meeting and banquet rooms.

The original 10-storey hotel had 175 rooms and was built for $2.2 million at the end of one of Edmonton's first economic booms. The hotel was built by the Grand Trunk Pacific Railway on land selected for its proximity to the business district and its prime southern view of the meandering North Saskatchewan River. The hotel's origins with the Grand Trunk Pacific Railway are retained—the original doorknobs are

Hotel MacDonald dining room, circa 1955.

emblazoned with the GTP logo.

The exterior of the building, which was designed by the Winnipeg and Montreal architecture firm of Ross and MacFarlane, was finished in Indiana limestone with a copper roof now blackened with age. Its interior featured steel frame construction, reinforced concrete flooring, gypsum rock walls, and terracotta interior partitions.

The Mac was formally opened on July 6, 1915. The *Edmonton Daily Capital* described the gala affair as the most important social

event in the city's history.

"Another mile-post in the social life of Edmonton was passed last night when the MacDonald Hotel made its formal debut as an operating hostelry," the paper boasted. "The splendid structure was the mecca of society and upwards of 420 Edmontonians can lay claim to having feasted in the magnificent dining room on the night that the portals of the MacDonald were thrown open to the public.

"It was perhaps the most brilliant social

event in the city's history, for never before has it been possible to carry out a similar function upon so colossal a scale."

Some of the hotel's features included the octagonal Palm Room which in later years became known as the Wedgewood Room because of its groin ceiling with Wedgewood design plaster sculptures. The rotunda and corridors were paved in Lepanto marble.

The Confederation Room, with its two-storey height and arched doorway to the south patio, included a massive 9-by-18-foot painting of the Fathers of Confederation. The 1915 painting by Frederick S. Challener remains where he supervised its hanging. Following the fire in Parliament in 1917 and the destruction of the original, this became the earliest surviving copy of this famous work.

The ballroom occupied the entire end of the east wing. Two-storeys high, and known as the Empire Ballroom, it featured plaster sculptures of hunting scenes in the ceiling. This prompted some to name it the Hearth and Hound Room.

The hotel has a long history of seeking tax concessions from city council. Tax concessions were wrested before it was built in 1910, including paying cost only on water and power for 20 years, and no taxation on property above $50,000.

The building of the 300-room addition many years later cost $4.5 million and concessions were again granted. With the city experiencing a boom after the Second World War and the discovery of oil at Leduc, more hotel rooms were badly required. So council bowed again, reducing the hotel's tax rate to $75 a room from $338.

CN Hotels was so happy with the addition that the company's then president, Donald Gordon, said the old wing of the Mac might be replaced by a modern addition to conform to the style of the new tower. But even before the new wing was built, a 1949 editorial in *The Journal* defended the gracious lines of the old Mac.

The final seconds – Tegler Building, 1982.

"The new wing, as the CNR hotel officials pointed out, will become the hotel and the present MacDonald will be the wing in reality," the paper said. "This is too bad. The MacDonald is a beautiful building and while it will still be beautiful when it becomes a mere "wing," it will be overshadowed by the far from beautiful 16-storey rectangular mass."

Finally, in 1983, council made some of its more recent concessions. For the pleasure of designating the Hotel MacDonald as the city's first and only municipal historic resource a year later, the city agreed to $3 million in concessions, including a freeze on tax assessments in the first five years of operation. ■

McLEOD BUILDING • 1915

Chicago Style Block Was City's Tallest
10136-100 Street

THE McLEOD BUILDING is no longer the premier office block it once was. Its "A" class standing is past, and so are the days when it towered over the downtown core. At one time, it and the now-demolished Tegler Building were Edmonton's largest and finest office buildings. But if it's been a few years since the nine-storey McLeod has been able to claim the title of tallest and most up-to-date building in the city, its timeless elegance will always be worthy of an appreciative look.

The edifice now serves as temporary office space for arts and social organizations. If it is no longer sought by the most prestigious business clients and its stature is shrinking on the city skyline, the McLeod will remain as a solid example of one of Alberta's first skyscrapers.

The building, a prime example of the Chicago Commercial Style of architecture, was saved from destruction by the city and subsequently purchased by the province for $4.8 million in 1980 when its then owner, Oxford Development Group, threatened to demolish it. The government's long-term plans call for a complete restoration of its interior, and eventual use as government offices.

The structure, finished in terracotta—a type of clay tile—represented the culmination of the rise to fortune of one of Edmonton's first settlers and real estate speculators—Kenneth McLeod. The Ontario-born McLeod came here in 1891 and at one time was an alderman. He was sole owner of the McLeod until 1929, when he began divesting his holdings. He died in Vancouver in 1940.

McLeod claimed it would be the largest in the city—25 feet taller than the Tegler, built in 1911 and demolished in 1983. Until 1951 and the rise of the addition to the Hotel MacDonald with its 16 storeys, the McLeod ranked as the city's tallest structure.

One of the building's tenants was A.C. Rutherford, Alberta's first premier, who had a law office in it. But because it was completed after the economic bust, it wasn't until 1924 that the McLeod was fully occupied.

The interior was made of the finest wood and marble. Corridor floors were set with marble, and the office floors were laid with terrazzo on concrete slabs, resembling mosaic.

Italian Pavanosse marble was used in the main entrance and the wainscotting of corridor walls. Doors, doorjambs, windows, and baseboards were made from oak. The building was heated with high pressure steam and was piped for gas lighting.

Because most office buildings were then populated largely by men, the building had only one washroom for women—on the fifth floor.

The Edmonton Historical Board described the McLeod as Alberta's best remaining example of the Chicago school of architecture, developed in the American metropolis at the turn of the century.

Chicago school features include massing, verticality, heavy overhanging cornices, the use of terracotta on exteriors, and the three-part division into ground storey, intermediate floors, and top floors with cornice. ■

Above: Wrought iron and marble in McLeod Building.
Right: McLeod Building, worthy of appreciation.

UNION BANK BUILDING • 1910

Recession Stopped Project Plans

10053 Jasper Avenue

THE DERELICT Union Bank Building, one of the few bank buildings in Edmonton predating the First World War, is probably better known as the former home of the North West Trust Company.

The classic structure was built for $60,000 in 1910 to house the Union Bank of Canada. It was also home to several other financial institutions until the early 1980s when it was abandoned by North West Trust for the modern confines of the IPL Building.

Little remains of the building's original elegant decor. Some of the ornate first floor ceiling with dentilled moldings could be glimpsed through gaps in a lower tiled ceiling. Only the third floor escaped the veneer office decor that replaced the original mahogany and oak. An old oak staircase leads to a number of rooms, former offices with oak doors and overhead transoms. One features a brick fireplace.

The building was destined for redevelopment in Alberta's energy-based economic boom. But the boom ended before its owners, Patrician Land Corporation, could get their plans for a 38-storey office building to first base. Patrician was owned by Peter Pocklington.

One of the architects commissioned for the office tower project was David Murray. He said in a 1985 interview that the project would have fully integrated the old Union Bank facade and offset the tower so that it didn't compete with the old building front. Murray called it ''one of the most perfect facades of its kind in the city.'' Alberta Culture has also expressed interest in designating the facade.

The North West Trust Building was designed for the Union Bank by architect Roland Lines, whose other credits included the Canada Permanent Building, the original

Facade of Northwest Trust Company (Union Bank Building).

Royal Alexandra Hospital, and Norwood and Alex Taylor schools.

The exterior design is derived from Renaissance Revival architecture, with Ionic pilasters, and a base of solid Bedford stone from Indiana, complemented with pressed red brick. An imposing entrance was mounted with the bank's coat of arms.

The Union Bank of Canada, with headquarters in Quebec City, had purchased the land for its future building for $50,000 from Frank M. Gray in June 1909. Gray had paid $1,000 for the property eight years before.

The building was purchased by The Canadian Realty Corporation for $121,554 in 1911. James Richardson and Sons Limited bought it for the devalued sum of $90,000 in 1928. That firm owned it until 1979, when it was purchased by North West Trust for $1.9 million.

North West Trust sold it to Patrician Land Corporation for $3.1 million in 1982. Patrician then took out a $3.8 million mortgage with North West Trust.

In addition, Morguard Trust Company has a second mortgage of $3.8 million on the building to protect its interest in the possible redevelopment of the site. In 1984, Morguard filed a $46 million writ of execution on the building because of Patrician's failure to pay mortgages on other unrelated properties.

Northwest Trust foreclosed upon the building in August 1985. It was then acquired by Hartford Properties. ∎

Detail on Canada Permanent Building.

CANADA PERMANENT BLDG. • 1910

City's First Fireproof Bank
10126-100 Street

THE CANADA Permanent Building site has turned full circle from restaurant to the classicly detailed headquarters of a prestigious loan company, to restaurant once again, housing the Japanese Village Restaurant since 1972.

The lot was originally home to the Criterion Restaurant. The building was levelled in 1908, and in 1909 its owner Kenneth McLeod—who built the McLeod Building next door—sold the lot to Canada Permanent Loan Company for $24,000.

In 1910 the firm erected a handsome three-storey structure for $65,000. This building, designed by local architect Roland Lines, was said to be the first fireproof bank in the city. Lines' other projects included the Union Bank Building, the old Royal Alexandra Hospital (now the Glenrose) and Alex Taylor School.

The building's design has earned accolades from Alberta Culture and the Edmonton Historical Board. Alberta Culture describes its design as the city's best example of the High Victorian Italianate Style used before the turn of the century for commercial structures in major eastern Canadian urban centres.

The city's historical board notes that despite the dissimilarity in both size and style to the neighboring McLeod, the two buildings complement each other.

The structure served as Canada Permanent's Alberta head office for 40 years and was then leased for office space before becoming a restaurant in 1972. About $750,000 was spent to renovate the building and bring in the Oriental decor.

In the early 1970s the Oxford Development Group planned to demolish both the Canada Permanent and the McLeod Buildings for redevelopment. However, because of public concern the plans were never carried out.

Both buildings were purchased by the province in 1980 for $4.8 million. Despite its age, the building is structurally sound. The only recent renovation was replacement of the roof in 1982.

The building is made of reinforced concrete with red stretcher bond brick and sandstone. The three-bay front facade has extensive classical detailing. According to the historical board, its architecture is one of imagery. The symmetrical lines were meant to convey the banking message of solidity, security, and a sense of historical continuity harking back to the classical world. For example, the front attached columns or pilasters were meant to impart security visually by being securely grounded on a base and sweeping upward through the pilasters, culminating in Ionic capitals and an overhanging cornice.

The third storey is capped with a stone balustrade with symmetrical Grecian urns. The year of its erection—1910—is carved in stone and surrounded by a gala of garlands.

■

CIVIC BLOCK • 1912

Former City Hall Sits Empty
4 Sir Winston Churchill Square

IT DOESN'T look like an old building—in fact some might say its post-war exterior is only surpassed by city hall for sheer lack of architectural appeal.

But beneath the 1960s veneer of brown and buff aluminum cladding lies our first city hall. The six-storey building saw its last use as a police station. Built in 1912, the Civic Block is the last remaining brick building on the square.

The vacant building is said to be in solid condition, but would likely require an overhaul of its electrical and mechanical systems to meet current building code requirements. Possible future uses include housing the city archives, or once more becoming Edmonton's city hall.

The Civic Block's Edwardian brick and stone facade was covered during a major 1961 renovation that saw it transformed into a police station. Inside, little remains of the traditional elegant office decor save for a wide iron, oak, and granite staircase connecting all six floors and the basement. The building was never intended to serve as city hall for as long as it did.

The Civic Block's architect was Allan Merrick Jeffers, who had just signed on as a city employee after working for the province. Among his provincial credits are the Legislature Building and Government House. Jeffers was instructed to design a utilitarian office building with little embellishment, until a more fitting building could be erected. Our city fathers waited 45 years for that more fitting building.

The residue of 20 years of police occupation litters the building. Nothing has been done to the building since the police department's departure. A shooting gallery, armory and boiler room are found in the basement. An adjoining garage with a

Above: Hotel MacDonald has commanding view of river valley.
Right: Facade of the Canadian Bank of Commerce

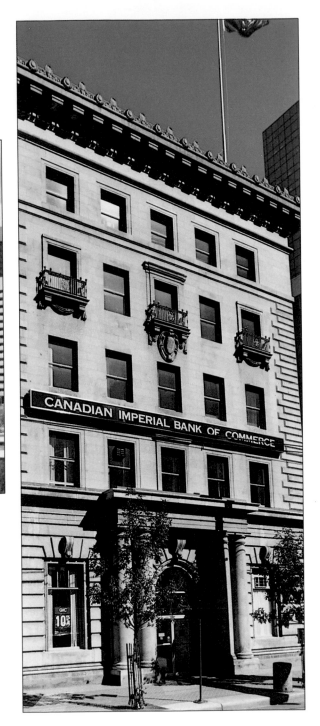

gymnasium above was added on the side when the building was converted to a police station.

The 52,000-square-foot building cost $225,000 to construct in 1912. It was large enough to accommodate all city offices with one floor left empty for future expansion. It was called modern commercial architecture in its day. Prior to that time, city offices were located in an annex to the first fire hall at 98th Street and 101A Avenue.

In 1912, Jeffers said in a report: "No attempt has been made in the design to elaborate the architectural lines, as it is a general belief that some day this site will demand a more pretentious structure and one in harmony with its surroundings. But until that day arrives, this structure should well satisfy the wants required..." ■

BANK OF COMMERCE • 1929

Edwardian Architecture Enhances Bank

10102 Jasper Avenue

THE REGAL BEARING of the Edwardian commercial style structure at Edmonton's main intersection has been enhanced with time.

The neighboring monolithic glass and concrete boxes which dwarf it, and the gathering dearth of traditional architecture in the downtown core can only reinforce that the architectural lines of the Canadian Bank of Commerce Building are of classic taste.

But whether the building's elegant east and south facades will continue to grace one of the downtown's most vital intersections was dependant upon a successful agreement between the bank and the Toronto-based developer Olympia and York Developments. In 1987, Olympia and York were due to begin construction of a multi-million dollar office and retail complex on the same block. Both the bank and the developer were optimistic at that time that the traditional facade could be retained.

The building opened in 1929 as the city headquarters of the Canadian Bank of Commerce, and was the last building of its style to be erected in the city. It was headquarters for the bank until 1962 when that bank amalgamated with the Imperial Bank to form the Canadian Imperial Bank of Commerce. At that time, the main offices were moved to larger quarters at 100th Street and Jasper Avenue.

The size of the 101st Street building was a tribute to the inherent cautiousness of bankers. The bank had been considering the erection of a 10-storey business block, but chose one half that size. The five-storey structure was designed by architect T. Horsbarch.

The building's east and south faces are of limestone from Tyndal, Manitoba, a common finish for government and financial buildings

McDougall United Church.

57

of the time, while the west side is finished in yellow brick. Paired Tuscan columns flank the front entrance supporting the entablature.

Three mock balconets line the south face, and four are found on the east face. There's an ornate stone cornice similar to that on the McLeod Building, and a one storey north annex.

The main banking floor, once the epitome of the solid austere image formerly desired by Canadian financial institutions, has yielded to the modernism of veneer counters and fluorescent lighting. In a 1964 renovation that saw the north wing demolished and rebuilt, the posh solid walnut counters were removed.

Prior to the renovation, CIBC considered demolishing the building and erecting a more modern structure. However, it would appear that conservative banking economics prevailed again.

Vestiges of the original interior design remain. These include the 20-foot high dentilled ceiling, strategically-placed plaster motifs, and columns with sculpted capitals highlighted in white paint in a 1984 refinishing.

When the 35,400-square-foot structure was built, the top four floors were rented. Among the original tenants were the Martha Silk Store, purveyors of "good class ladies hosiery and lingerie," and W.A. Ferguson Jewellers, "official timekeepers for the CNR." By 1985, about 3,000 square feet was unused on the upper floors. ■

McDOUGALL UNITED CHURCH • 1925

Roots of Church Go Back 114 Years
10025-101 Street

WHEN EDMONTON'S oldest-functioning Protestant church opened its present building in 1910, it drew a capacity turnout and rave reviews. McDougall Methodist Church, the congregation's third building since missionary George McDougall opened a simple log church in 1873, was filled for all three services on December 4, 1910.

The Edmonton Bulletin described in detail the oak pews in the sanctuary, the maple floors, the vaulted ceiling rising to a height of more than 22 metres (72 feet), and the encircling gallery supported by eight pillars. The church auditorium was the largest in Edmonton, "and without doubt one of the finest in Western Canada," the newspaper reported.

The brick structure was to become McDougall United Church in 1925 after the merger of the Methodist, Congregationalist and Presbyterian churches.

By the spring of 1911, the congregation had grown so big that oak pews were installed in the gallery, boosting seating capacity to 1,800. The church was considerably fancier and larger than its two predecessors, the first of which was a rough-hewn structure built largely by McDougall himself.

Called the Wesleyan or Methodist Church, in 1875, it laid claim to being the first building constructed outside Fort Edmonton in 1873. This original church was moved to Fort Edmonton Park in 1978 after being used as a boys' dormitory for neighboring Alberta College and then as a museum.

In 1892, a new frame church was built. It was demolished to make way for the present church. The cornerstone was laid by Mrs. E.V. Hardisty, McDougall's daughter. It was called McDougall Church after the much-loved missionary who had moved to Morley, west of Calgary, in 1875.

Major renovations were made to the church in the mid-1950s, but the sanctuary remains virtually the same as in 1910. During the renovations, the pulpit was extended slightly and enclosed. The original choir seats were replaced with wooden ones. An addition was also built and it contains the church offices and meeting rooms.

A Karn Warren pipe organ, in use since 1912, was rebuilt. It was replaced in 1976 by an electronic organ. On the ground floor of the older part is the Pioneer Chapel which contains the oak Communion table and pulpit, which have been in use since 1910.

There may be more drastic changes in store for the church. The congregation has discussed possible redevelopment of the site, but is adamant that the church sanctuary remain, in recognition of its historical significance for the city and for the United Church.

Church membership reached a high of 2,000 in the early 1950s, but a proliferation of neighborhood churches has seen it drop to about 650. Still, the numbers are stable and the congregation is faithful, coming from all parts of the city.

Jasper East

The greatest concentration of pre-World War I commercial buildings in Edmonton's downtown core is found along the Jasper East Block, west of 95th Street. Structures such as the Gibson and Ernest Brown blocks tell of Edmonton's economic boom just after the turn of the century, while the south wall of the Jasper House (Hub) Hotel dates back to Edmonton's emergence as a community during 1879 to 1881. Bordering the district are such landmarks as the old RCMP Barracks, Alex Taylor School and St. Boniface Church.

Over the years Edmonton's city centre moved westward and the Jasper East district declined in economic vitality. Some of the Edwardian buildings found alternative use, others went into disrepair, and many were demolished. However, the district now faces a resurgence with recent additions of the Citadel Theatre, the Convention Centre and Canada Place, and a potential to combine elements of Edmonton's elegant past with a dynamic future.

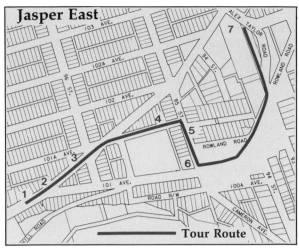

Jasper East

Tour Route

1. Hub Hotel
2. Ernest Brown Block
3. Gibson Block
4. Old RCMP Barracks
5. Hecla Block
6. St. Boniface Church
7. Alex Taylor School

Edmonton skyline looking north.

HUB HOTEL • 1882

Oldest Inn's Facade Revamped

9692 Jasper Avenue

THE HUB HOTEL was Edmonton's first and only brick edifice for nine years, and claimed to be the first brick building between Winnipeg and Vancouver.

Now three storeys with a dentilled cornice and shuttered windows at the front and two rear wings, the Hub began its life on June 30, 1882, as the simple rectangular two-storey Jasper House hotel.

The first five-day journey via stage coach to Calgary left Jasper House August 6, 1883. The Calgary and Edmonton Stage was operated by Donald McLeod, who charged $25 each way with allowance for 100 pounds of baggage.

Despite prohibition and the odd fine, a few million brew have been quaffed in the tavern since that time. But today, after numerous renovations and additions, the 49-room pioneer hostelry has faint resemblance to its original incarnation.

In fact a 1974 research paper by John Patrick Day says ''there is not much of the Jasper House left in the present building and the building is so far removed from the original as to be considered a different one.''

In 1882 it was built as a 24-by-30-foot frame building with a brick veneer by William West. There was a rear kitchen addition, and a 16-by-24-foot cellar. Outbuildings included a stable, wash house, outhouse, a 24-foot well with water at the 16-foot level, and a building for the production of four per cent beer.

Business was so good that a brick addition was built in 1884, filling out the frontage on Jasper Avenue. In 1907 a third storey was added, and in 1911 a rear brick addition constructed. In the 1940s more work was done inside and out.

James Goodridge, an avid hunter, managed the hotel until his death in 1900, when his son Leonard took over. For much of its early history it was said to be the haunt of the hunter and trapper.

Besides libation, sustenance, and accommodations, James Goodridge contributed much to early Edmonton. He was elected to the first town council in 1892, and again in 1893, and helped found the first school district. He was instrumental in founding the police and fire departments, including the first fire hall which doubled as the town hall until 1912.

Leonard Goodridge sold out for $55,000 in 1910. It went for $100,000 at the peak of the pre-war real estate boom in 1913. In 1920 it was renamed the Empress Hotel. Like other city real estate, its value went down and hadn't recovered when owner Mary Farme sold it for $35,000 to H.C. Pettet in 1940. Pettet changed the name to the Hub and spent another $20,000 in structural work.

Pettet sold the Hub for $49,750 to the Hub Hotel (Edmonton) Limited in 1945, a company owned by Mike Jerwak. After Jerwak's death in 1968, the company passed to his heirs and estate. ■

Photographer Ernest Brown, 1947.

ERNEST BROWN BLOCK • 1912

Central to Redevelopment Plans

9670 Jasper Avenue

IF ITS AESTHETICS have paled, it is still a photographic shrine: the pictorial history of Alberta was assembled on this site from 1891 to about 1920.

When this three-storey brick and stone structure was first erected, it housed the studio and historic photographic collections of some of Alberta's first photographers. It was built for the radical photographer, artist, and historian Ernest Brown. Across the pediment traces remain of the words "Everything Photographic. Ernest Brown Block 1912."

The Brown Block was built in two symmetrical sections and cost about $30,000. *The Edmonton Bulletin* of August, 1912, noted that Brown's structure was to be built of brick and steel with stone dressings on a 33-foot frontage, and was to extend back 107 feet. Offices were to be located on the top floors.

"The ground floor will be used by Mr. Brown for his business in connection with which he is having fitted up a marble studio which will be unique of its kind. The marble for interior furnishings will be brought from England. The ceiling will be supported by marble columns and the ceiling will be done in marble plaster."

The Brown Block is U-shaped in plan with two north/south wings at the rear. There's a central staircase, and traditional skylights on the third floor. The building's facade reflects the classical styling typical of commercial structures of that time. In typical commercial style, the entablature, with a decorated frieze and curved brackets that form the capitals of the pilaster strips, runs the length of the facade. The striated pilaster strips, shaped parapet and keystone voussoirs over the flat-arched windows highlight its classical scheme.

Ernest Brown Block, circa 1913.

While the block's architectural embellishments may fall short of awe, Ernest Brown's collection of photographs of the birth of the Canadian west—said to be 50,000 strong, may well constitute the visual backbone of the development of Alberta. ∎

63

The Gibson Block awaits a new sunrise.

Old RCMP Barracks now in disuse.

GIBSON BLOCK • 1913

Unique Wedge Shaped Building

9608 Jasper Avenue

UNIQUE in Edmonton because of its wedge shape, it has come to be called the Flat Iron Building. For many years it was a flop house for skid-row denizens, until it was shut down in the early 1980s as unfit for human habitation. Subsequent occupants of this four-storey block have been hundreds of pigeons and the odd vagrant seeking a night's lodging.

For much of the 1970s and 1980s, the building remained an enigma. Beloved by history and architecture lovers, politicians paid it lip-service, and the businessmen and investors it needed if it was ever to be restored, scorned it.

A developer was due to take title in the fall of 1987. Ambitious plans are rumored to be afoot to renovate the building and install a restaurant, shops, and offices.

Many cities across North America featured a triangular-shaped building similar to the Gibson Block by the 1920s. They are said to be modelled after the Flat-iron Building in New York City, constructed in 1902, and designed by Daniel Burham and Company.

Realtor William Gibson spent $40,000 constructing this building in 1913. He had purchased two parcels of land in 1913 for one dollar apiece and other unspecified valuable considerations, from the merchant brothers Samuel and Robert Williamson. One parcel was then valued at $9,000 and the other was valued at $11,000.

Gibson's building was designed for commercial use since the downtown core then centred around 97th Street. A year later, however, the upper floors were converted to suites when the block was purchased for $120,000 by the German firm of Schubert and Wenzel Real Estate Company. Schubert and Wenzel tried to change the building's name to—you guessed

it—the Schubert and Wenzel Block. The unwieldy tag never stuck, possibly due to anti-German sentiment which ran high in those years of the Great War, God, King, and Empire.

Among the original tenants was the Gibson Cafe. A racist sign, still visible on the west wall, notes ''Gibson Cafe. Open All Night. Best Service. Reasonable Prices. White Help Only.''

As well as the Gibson Cafe, the 1914 Henderson's Directory lists the Ross Hardware Company, Loptson Olafur and Sons Jewellers, and the Turkish Bath Parlor among the block's earliest tenants. The Eagle Pharmacy and the Farmer's Loan Company also opened for business shortly thereafter.

Upstairs in 1914, tenants were decidedly more upscale than in later years. They included a doctor, musician, electrical contractor, dressmaker, and a teacher. The last commercial tenants included a second-hand store and the enduring steam bath, which closed in 1978. ∎

Jasper Avenue East, from the Hotel MacDonald.

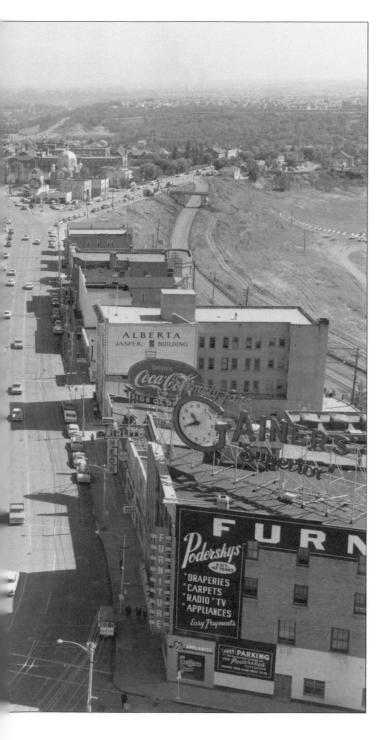

OLD RCMP BARRACKS • 1913

Building Faces Uncertain Future
9542-101A Avenue

IT WAS 34 years before the Royal North West Mounted Police would swallow their pride. After conducting operations from Fort Saskatchewan since 1875, the RNWMP—as the RCMP were then called—eventually accepted the pre-eminence of Edmonton. So in 1909, they packed up their kit-bags for the last time and rode up river to their new two-storey brick and stone regional headquarters at the top of Grierson Hill in the bustling City of Edmonton.

The first detachment of Mounties to arrive in these parts rode up 20-strong to Fort Edmonton under the command of Inspector W.D. Jarvis in the fall of 1874. They over-wintered at the fort where Hudson's Bay Company factor Richard Hardisty tried to convince them to stay.

Hardisty and other local settlers naturally desired the close proximity of the police. According to a 1937 account by W.A. Griesbach in the *Scarlet and Gold*, Hardisty had already picked out a location for the police fort—across the river where the University of Alberta stands today.

Scuttlebutt has it that Jarvis was adamant that any centre of settlement in these parts would naturally coalesce around Fort Saskatchewan. Jarvis reasoned that because the banks of the North Saskatchewan River were lower there, this would facilitate the building of bridges, the crossing of a railway, and the development of a city.

Despite or more likely because of the words Hardisty and Jarvis exchanged on the subject, the Mounties decided to show the factor just who really was the boss. The Mounties proceeded up river in the spring of 1875 to build what was first called Sturgeon Creek Post.

The now unused barracks in Edmonton serve as a testimonial to the Mounties'

erroneous assumption, which some say was exacerbated by a personality clash between Jarvis and the Hudson's Bay Company factor.

The L-shaped Edmonton barracks is part of a U-shaped formation, flanked by newer buildings on either side. The property is owned by the federal government, and the newer properties house prisoners on day-parole at what is now known as Grierson Centre.

The original fortress-like barracks with corner towers and crenellated parapets were designed by architect Roland Lines. Lines, who was killed in the First World War, was a most productive architect. The numerous buildings he designed or helped design, changed the face of the city in the prosperity that reigned here prior to the First World War.

When built, the barracks were complemented by another L-shaped building to the east, containing a 25-stall stable, storage space for hay and room for carriages and vehicles.

The barracks, which cost $70,000 to build, contained 10 cells for male prisoners and two for women on its first floor, as well as a kitchen, dining room, and offices. The basement contained a padded cell, cells for "refractory" prisoners and other facilities. A recreation room, five bedrooms for sergeants, and 20 cubicles for constables were on the second floor.

The moving of the RNWMP's "G" division headquarters to Edmonton—which in 1935 was to become "K" division—was naturally greeted with dismay in Fort Saskatchewan. "To speak frankly, the townspeople do not like it," *The Edmonton Bulletin* reported.

The building's future is uncertain. Officials say that if the barracks are sold, they will be protected by a Provincial Historical Resource designation. Alberta Culture has noted that the building has great historical and architectural significance, as there are no others of equal stature in the province. ■

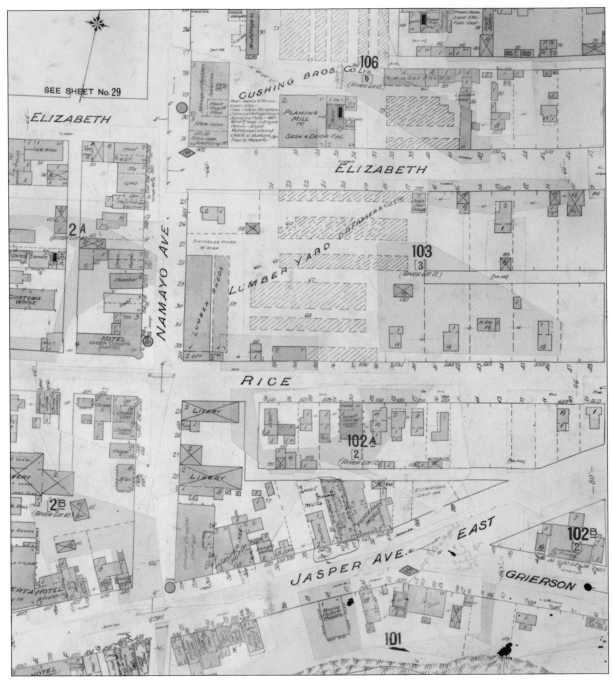

Insurance plan of Jasper East.

Sanctuary with barrel–vaulted ceiling, St. Boniface Church.

HECLA BLOCK • 1914
Building Named After Icelandic Volcano
10141-95 Street

JOHN JOHNSON'S investment in the Hecla was a venture which failed to pan out. Icelandic-born Johnson was the first owner as well as the builder of this handsome but modest three-storey brick building.

The L-shaped building can still turn an eye. Its dapper double facades are topped with rounded pediments. A roof-top flagpole stands behind the west pediment where Norse colors have flown.

The original stone canopy with period light fixtures still shelters the front entrance. A dentilled gable, tapestry brick facing, and stone accents complete an inviting and tasteful appearance.

Johnson also constructed the kitty-corner Riverview Apartments as well as about 60 homes in the east-central area of Edmonton during early boom days, prior to World War I.

Redevelopment was hardly an issue then—the Boyle Street area was being built up rapidly. Johnson along with many others considered it prime residential real estate, located as it was just east of the city's first business district along 97th Street.

Inside the building are all the trappings of another time. Original tilework in the foyer with the name Hecla inlaid, brass and glass vestibule doors, a skylight over the stairwell, brass door plates, and common water closets and bathrooms are found.

John Johnson was born in Skagafirde, Iceland, and moved to Gimli, Manitoba with his family in 1876. The Johnson family was part of a wave of Icelandic immigrants to Canada and the U.S. who were spurred by political upheaval, catastrophic weather, and volcanic eruptions in their homeland.

Johnson moved here to make his fortune. In 1906 he paid laborer Stefan Nivezez $2,025 for the two lots on which the building now sits. In 1913 he engaged architects David Hardie and John Martland to draw up the plans for the Hecla, to be situated on what was then known as Syndicate Avenue and Stewart Street. A building permit granted in April 1914 indicated the block's value at $40,000.

Martland went on to become City of Edmonton architect for 18 years. He also served as president of the Alberta Association of Architects.

Of the Hecla's classical revival design, Alberta Culture said that beyond its symmetrical plan, classical features included the decorated overhanging cornice and contrasting quoins, as well as ornamental keystones over the windows. One of the most interesting features of the building is its two facades.

But even on Hardie and Martlands' plans, there was no question that this was a building fit for Norsemen. The Icelandic flag is etched on the blueprints, as is the name Hecla. Throughout the Catholic world until the end of the 17th century, Mount Hecla was thought to be the largest volcanic mountain and Iceland's most celebrated volcano.

John Johnson and his company which owned the block, were foreclosed upon by the Molson's Bank in 1924. ■

ST. BONIFACE CHURCH • 1911

First Synagogue Now a Catholic Church
9510-101 Avenue

ST. BONIFACE Roman Catholic Church is the only German-speaking Catholic congregation in the city. But for more than 40 years it was Beth Israel Synagogue.

When it was constructed in 1911 at a cost of $12,000, the building became the first permanent synagogue for Edmonton's Jewish population.

Not only has the building's religious affiliation changed. One has to look carefully to recognize elements of the traditional styled synagogue building. Little was retained when the interior and exterior were renovated in the late 1950s and early 1960s.

Its contemporary lines belie its pre-First World War roots. An addition was built on the west face, the former front door and a south door sealed off, and offices and a second floor rectory added. The roof line was altered, and the entire exterior painted in white and yellow. The building is a far cry from the smaller brick and stone synagogue with its east-facing entrance—Stars of David on a front buttress and corners, a high pediment and corner ornaments.

Inside, fixtures and ornamentation are of modern design. The sanctuary has a barrel-vaulted ceiling, and a U-shaped gallery with a 100-year-old pipe organ at its centre. The altar is located at the former 95th Street entrance.

The organ was built for a church for German immigrants in Cincinatti, Ohio. When the building was about to be demolished for roadway construction, the organ was dismantled and moved to Edmonton.

The land for Beth Israel Synagogue—located at what was then known as Syndicate Avenue and Grierson Street—was donated by clothing merchant William (Boss) Diamond, one of the first Jewish settlers in Alberta and a pioneer Edmonton businessman.

Diamond arrived in Calgary in 1890 from New York, and opened stores there and in Edmonton, moving here in 1906. He was president of the Beth Israel congregation for 25 years. During his tenure, prominent city jeweller H.B. Kline served as vice-president.

The city's first rabbi was Hyman Goldstick, who came here in 1906. Goldstick left Edmonton for Edson in 1912, serving as the town's mayor for five years. Among his children was Cecil (Tiger) Goldstick, a legendary figure in Edmonton sports circles.

As Edmonton grew, so too did the congregation, and as a result the building became too small. A new synagogue was built for $150,000 near 119th Street and 102nd Avenue, and the old building was vacated in 1954.

It then served as Third Christian Reformed Church, and the Wells of Joy Gospel Centre. In 1958 the building was purchased for $33,500 by the Catholic Archdiocese of Edmonton. ■

Namayo Avenue (97th Street) looking north, 1913.

ALEX TAYLOR SCHOOL • 1908

A Mini-UN in the Inner City
9321 Jasper Avenue

UNDER THE TUTELAGE of an award-winning principal in the 1980s, Alex Taylor School is proving itself as versatile as the man for whom it was named.

The Edwardian three-storey brick structure is one of Edmonton's oldest schools. At the time, it was termed a "magnificent building" by school inspector G.E. Elles. The edifice was designed by architect Roland Lines and utilized pressed brick with sandstone detailings.

Lines incorporated classical architectural elements into his design. These include the solid, symmetrical appearance and its hipped roof. The enlarged voussoirs and keystone at the main entrance, along with the triple window and pedimented gable above, lend dignity and weight to the school's main facade.

By the 1980s, the school offered classes from kindergarten to Grade 6, and many other services. Its 140 students formed a miniature United Nations. Principal Steve Ramsankar lists 34 ethnic groups represented in the school at one time. The largest were Chinese, Vietnamese and Metis children.

The school operates a day care centre, English classes for immigrants, a drop-in center for senior citizens and a social centre for immigrant women. It provides breakfast and lunch programs and police liaison classes. It has held cultural celebrations and international field trips.

The programs have earned accolades for Ramsankar. He was awarded the Order of Canada in 1983 and was called honorary Chief Big Heart by the Cree Indians.

The school's flexibility and multiple purposes do justice to Alex Taylor, a pioneer giant in Edmonton. Taylor, who came here from Ontario in 1877 set up the city's first telegraph, telephone and electricity systems.

Overlooked by many is his partnership with Frank Oliver in co-founding *The Edmonton Bulletin*. Begun December 6, 1880 as a four-page weekly, *The Bulletin* ranks as Edmonton's and Alberta's first newspaper. First copy was recorded by the settlement's first telegraph operator—Alex Taylor.

Taylor purchased the printing press by mail in Minneapolis, Minnesota, and enlisted Frank Oliver's help in transporting it from Winnipeg to Edmonton. Oliver, who was to become a powerful federal politician in the future, was then but a humble general merchant who would make the Winnipeg trip by Red River cart in order to pick up supplies.

Because of Oliver's experience in the newspaper business, the two men agreed to a joint partnership in the publication of *The Edmonton Bulletin*. Early *Bulletin* copies duly note Oliver and Taylor as proprietors.

Taylor served as Edmonton's postmaster, and installed the first telephone system from his telegraph office to St. Albert in 1884. In a 1908 article, *The Bulletin* claimed that Taylor held the first long distance telephone conversation in Western Canada.

In an experiment in 1887, Taylor had all the telegraph equipment on the line from Edmonton to Battleford removed. Then he and Hugh Richardson at the other end, installed telephones and held the first 330-mile conversation in these parts, a feat which apparently left some locals agog. Like a good Scot, he repeated the experiment a few nights later, but this time transmitting the sweet sounds of the bagpipes and violin from the Edmonton office to Battleford.

Strathcona North

The first white man to settle in Edmonton south of the North Saskatchewan River was John Walter, whose 1874 house in Walterdale is the second oldest building in the city. Not until the arrival of the railway in 1891 did the thriving community called South Edmonton finally emerge. For 10 years, the Calgary and Edmonton Railway Station marked the end of the rail, and was the stopping off point for thousands of immigrants to northern Alberta. The station's original location south of Whyte Avenue also guaranteed a rapid growth for South Edmonton, which was incorporated as the Town of Strathcona in 1899 and as a city in 1907, finally amalgamating with Edmonton in 1912.

Unlike Edmonton, Strathcona did not become heavily industrialized. The Ritchie Mill near the end of the steel on Saskatchewan Drive was for years the most significant industrial structure. Rather, Strathcona assumed a more cultural and collegiate significance as the ''University City'', a role reflected in such buildings as King Edward School and, to the east, Faculté St. Jean. North Strathcona also came to feature some of the best residential architecture in Edmonton, with the homes of two former Strathcona mayors, J.J. Duggan and W.H. Sheppard being prime examples.

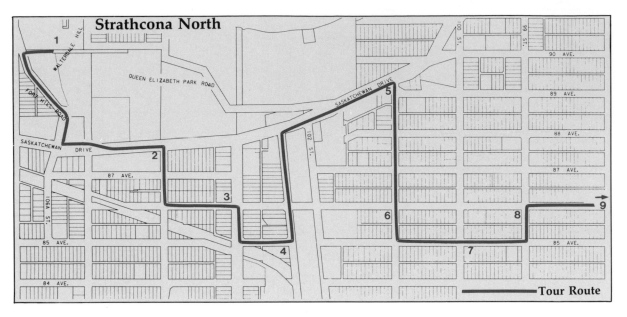

Strathcona North

1. John Walter Museum
2. Duggan House
3. Calgary & Edmonton Railway Station
4. Connaught Armoury
5. Ritchie Mill
6. King Edward School
7. Holy Trinity Anglican Church
8. Sheppard House
9. Faculté St. Jean

Tour Route

JOHN WALTER MUSEUM • c.1874

City's Oldest Surviving House
Walterdale Hill

WHEN THE BELLE of Edmonton plied the North Saskatchewan River, the toll was 10 cents per foot passenger, and five cents for farm animals.

Today, the murky waters are spanned by numerous bridges and the Belle of Edmonton has long since disappeared.

But two humble rough-hewn timber cabins—and a not-so-humble wood frame two-storey house—still stand at the foot of Walterdale Hill, marking the approximate location where John Walter's ferry once operated. If you look carefully, you may pick them out on your left, as you drive down the hill and over the 105th Street Bridge toward downtown. The buildings also mark the beginnings of the community that once dotted Walter's Flats. The three houses are collectively called the John Walter Museum, and they mark many firsts for our city.

Documenting the rise of John Walter—one of Strathcona's earliest pioneers and businessmen—the city-owned site includes the first building to be constructed on the south side, and one of the first to be built outside the palisades of Fort Edmonton.

Accounts differ on the year—it was built either 1874, 1875 or 1876. It served as the first telegraph office in 1880, as well as a general store and an office for Walter's ferry service.

The second log house was built in 1884 and Walter moved into it in 1886 with his new bride, Appia Elizabeth Newby. His two sons, John Jr. and Stanley, were born here.

Again, accounts differ on what year the third house was built—1899, 1900, or 1901.

The historic site, with the exception of the newest house, is used for student pioneer intrepretive programs. Inside, 19th century furnishings and artifacts provide a pioneer decor for such activities as butter churning, carding wool, and baking. Walter's last home has been headquarters for the Heritage Festival since 1982.

All of the buildings were moved from their original locations to where they now stand. Walter himself moved the first two houses from about a block east to their present site prior to 1900, after constructing his third and most imposing residence. The third house, which was built where the High Level Bridge now stands, was moved by the city in 1974. Ironically, its turn of the century interior was modernized as an office for the Fort Edmonton Historical Foundation. A 1985 fire caused $30,000 damage to this house, and repairs are now being completed.

John Walter was born in Scotland's Orkney Islands in 1849. He arrived at Fort Edmonton on Christmas Eve 1870 to build York boats for the Hudson's Bay Company and died Christmas Day 1920—50 years and one day after his arrival here.

After leaving the Hudson's Bay Company, he built the cabin across the river from the fort and staked his claim to River Lot Nine. He began his business career by operating the Belle of Edmonton, the first cable ferry west of Winnpeg. It ran until the opening of the High Level Bridge in 1913. He built the pleasure steamer, City of Edmonton, in 1909, and purchased Big Island, 22 kilometres upstream on the river, planning to turn it into a tourist resort.

Walter was also involved in the lumber business and operated a coal mine. But floods in 1912 and 1915 wiped out his lumber business, carrying away a large stack of lumber, destroying his mill, and ruining the previous winter's cut.

Walter, said to have been one of Edmonton's first millionaires, suffered devastating financial losses. But, undaunted, he was on a financial comeback when he died in 1920. ■

DUGGAN HOUSE • 1907

Former Mayor's Home Restored
10515 Saskatchewan Drive

DUGGAN HOUSE, an historic Strathcona residence once threatened with demolition, has been restored into graceful offices by the Alberta Association of Architects.

The three-storey brick building was once the home of John Joseph Duggan, who served as mayor of Strathcona between 1902 and 1910. Duggan purchased the land for $1,400 in January 1907 from Osborne Adamson. The association paid $140,000 to purchase the house from the city in 1982. By 1985, it had spent another $200,000 on the restoration.

The biggest single aspect of the restoration was rebuilding the front facade and verandah. In addition, the interior was refurbished and brought up to modern standards. Two rear corners were rebuilt and new cornerstones added. Remaining original features include the wood floors, two fireplaces, and the impressive Ionic columns with capitals and overhead dentils separating the foyer from the former drawing room. Duggan House was built in the Queen Anne Style, with restrained classical detailing.

The sills, quoins and keystones in the two round attic storey windows were of sandstone to contrast with the brick. Doric columns support the verandah roof and balcony, and the tall hipped roof has projecting gables.

Duggan, who was born near Fenelon Falls, Ontario in 1868, came to Alberta in 1891. He began the first lumber yard at 81st Avenue and 102nd Street in Strathcona. He operated this and another business until 1909 when he began a cattle ranch in the south side subdivision that now bears his name. He died in 1952. ■

Detail of capital, Duggan House.

One of three houses built by pioneer John Walter.

Above: Interior of old Calgary and Edmonton Railway Station.
Right: Replica of old Calgary and Edmonton Railway Station.

C & E RAILWAY STATION • 1891

Station Replica is Back on Track
10447-86 Avenue

AT FIRST GLANCE, it seems that somebody missed the point because this railway station, which comes with a front platform, has its back to the track.

Upon closer scrutiny, however, the rust-colored station proves to be none other than the relocated replica of the first Calgary and Edmonton Railway station. And its proximity to the tracks is only a coincidence.

The first train arrived at the original Calgary and Edmonton Railway station in Strathcona on August 1, 1891. More than 90 years later, in 1979, the first station arrived on skids at a city-owned lot that just happened to back on to CP Rail tracks.

The Junior League of Edmonton, a women's voluntary organization, agreed to restore the building in 1979 as its 20th anniversary project. Unfortunately, two years of deterioration—plus two moves, rotting floor joists and a remodelled interior, made the $250,000 restoration cost prohibitive, said Larrie Taylor, the architect who supervised the building of the replica.

The station was demolished and a replica constructed for $163,000 in 1982. The replica is known to differ from the original in some respects. For example, while the exterior is a "reasonable facsimile," the attached baggage room is about half the length of the original one because of city site requirements for a parking lot. Stairs are located on the interior of the two-storey portion of the building. In the original, they were probably located off the baggage room, Taylor noted.

Like the Strathcona Hotel, the first station and its replica are plain, solid-looking wood frame buildings. Simple tongue and groove siding is used for the exterior finish and a finial on the roof provides the only decorative touch. The use of different roof levels and types adds interest to the station's design. The stem of the building's T-shaped plan has one storey and a gable roof; finally, a shed roof canopy provides shelter on the platform.

The Calgary and Edmonton Railway Station is said to be a good example of the strong utilitarian architecture which was widespread in frontier areas before style and ornament became overriding concerns.

When the first station was built, there was twice weekly railway service between Calgary and Strathcona, with a one-way trip taking 12 hours. The arrival of the Calgary and Edmonton Railway, which CP Rail aquired in 1903, meant quick growth for the collection of clapboard shacks that constituted Strathcona.

The original building was used by the Calgary and Edmonton Railway until 1907, when it was replaced by the present structure near Whyte Avenue and 103rd Street.

Today, the building's main floor serves as a mini-museum, showing a typical turn of the century railway station with fir floors and trim. Historical photographs, mementoes and clothing are also displayed. On the second floor, the Junior League has its offices and boardroom. ∎

CONNAUGHT ARMOURY • 1911

Where Soldiers Once Toiled
10310-85 Avenue

THE CRACK of militia at firearms practice has since yielded to light beer, steak sandwiches and the beat of Top 40 artists, at the old Connaught Armoury.

The armoury, Alberta's oldest, is finished in orange brick with sandstone trim. The two-storey building was constructed in 1911 by the federal government to house the B Squadron of the 19th Alberta Dragoons.

By 1987 a snappy canopy and interlocking brick pathway extended from the arched entranceway which was topped by limestone cannonballs. Inside features such as a classy oak bar with a white onyx top, a stainless steel dance floor, chandeliers and mirrored blinds effuse the modern mind.

The restaurant sublets the building from the Old Strathcona Foundation, which in turn leases it for $3,000 a month from the city. The city acquired the building from the federal government in 1965 after the Dragoons were disbanded. The building sat idle for the next 14 years and was often vandalized. The foundation leased the armoury in 1976 because the building was considered an integral part of the old City of Strathcona. Three years later, it was given its historic designation by Alberta Culture.

In 1979 the foundation sublet the building to the Armoury Restaurant which spent $750,000 on renovations, including adding mementoes of the Dragoons and early Edmontonia. But the attempt at high-class gourmet dining failed to attract sufficient masses and the operation closed in 1983. In 1985, restaurant owners spent an additional $300,000 refurbishing the building.

To ensure that the dignity of the facade was maintained, the foundation and Alberta Culture monitored the renovations, which the foundation termed a quality job.

The armoury was named for the Duke of

Connaught, the third son of Queen Victoria and Canada's governor general from 1911 to 1916. The duke, Arthur William Patrick Albert, was born in 1850 and died in 1942.

The armoury which honored him included a 90-foot rifle range in the basement where continental cuisine would eventually be prepared. Other original features included a parade hall, reading room, mess room and regimental offices.

The Dragoons were the first Alberta regiment mobilized during the First World War, and saw action at Ypres, the Somme and Vimy Ridge. During the Second World War, they provided soldiers for various other units.

The Dragoons were reincarnated in several forms prior to reformation in 1954. They continued to use the armoury until they were disbanded a decade later, when the regimental colors were placed in Holy Trinity Anglican Church in the custody of the regiment's padre—Capt. T.L. Leadbeater. ■

Connaught Armoury with sandstone trim and limestone cannon balls.

RITCHIE MILL • 1892

Mill Faces Uncertain Future
10171 Saskatchewan Drive

FORMERLY KNOWN as North West Mill and Feed Company, the 17,000-square-foot building was located at the end of the Calgary and Edmonton Railway prior to the building of the High Level Bridge. The rail spur has since been removed.

The mill is believed to be the oldest existing flour mill in Alberta and one of the few remaining pre-1900 industrial structures, symbolizing the importance of agriculture in Alberta's early development. It was also one of the first mills equipped with steam-powered steel rollers.

With a valued river valley view, the aging mill was an easy mark for redevelopment in the boom of the late 1970s. Its previous owner—116640 Holdings Limited, a numbered affiliate of Qualico Developments, unsuccessfully sought a demolition permit. In 1982 the company donated the mill to the Strathcona Foundation, along with $150,000 for its restoration.

The earliest building—the flour mill in the centre of the structure—was built in 1892, by brothers Robert and John Ritchie. In 1895 the grain elevator was added.

In 1918 Robert Ritchie won the property back from Edmonton Milling Company in a successful foreclosure action, and turned around and sold it to broker Ernest Chauvin later that year for $28,000. Chauvin sold it in 1919 for the same sum to the North West Milling Company.

In 1967, the mill became the property of Donald Mercer Cormie of Principal Group fame, for $160,000. Cormie sold it for $1.1 million in 1978 to Mesza Holdings Limited. That very same day Mesza sold it to Qualico's numbered subsidiary and pocketed a $400,000 profit. ■

KING EDWARD SCHOOL • 1913

Design Resembles a Fortress
8530-101 Street

THE LURE of the suburbs in the face of an aging city core forced the fortress-like King Edward School to close its doors in 1984. Seemingly built to withstand almost anything short of a nuclear bomb, the barrack-style red brick building has bowed its head to the forces of social change.

Since the school was built in 1913 at a cost of $180,000, about 10,000 students have graduated. Its enrolment peaked at 862 pupils in 1926 as Edmonton's south side was rapidly expanding. The school was designed by the EPSB's staff architect George Turner who employed the same plans for the design of Highlands School.

King Edward was the first school in Edmonton built with reinforced concrete and a ground floor auditorium. The school's military air is enhanced by its central tower, and a false roof line punctuated with battlements and rifle slots as if for marksmen. Sandstone accents the brick with some ornate curvatures on the tower, and grape balustrade and other sculptured embellishments at the front entrance. In the tower, a bare concrete room has latticed windows and a trap door entrance.

The school has a striking front foyer, with oak-panelled walls, latticed windows and doors, and a terrazzo floor leading to the marble stairway. An old style bench for errant pupils is built into a corner by the principal's office.

Alberta Culture has observed that the style is more closely related to that of a monastery than to any building of military function. Its architectural heritage is derived from Collegiate Gothic institutions of higher learning in England, which became a popular style for North American schools and military academies. ■

HOLY TRINITY ANGLICAN CH. • 1913

Clinker Brick Exterior Design
10037-84 Avenue

FROM A SIMPLE frame building with makeshift pews and altar, the south side's first Anglican church has grown into a distinctive brick structure graced with magnificent stained glass windows.

The congregation dates back to 1892 when services were held in a railway station, with Reverend Charles Cunningham as minister. Cunningham was also minister of All Saints Anglican Church in Edmonton and made cross-river trips every Sunday.

In 1893, the first church was built at 81st Avenue and 100th Street. Two years later, Reverend Henry Allen Gray became the first rector. He was later to become the first Anglican bishop of Edmonton.

In the original church building, planks supported by chairs were used as pews, while the altar was a packing case covered in cloth. That's quite a contrast from the Holy Trinity that Edmontonians know today, with its clinker brick exterior, bell tower, and stained glass windows.

When the present structure was opened in 1913, an article in *The Edmonton Journal* said: ''None ever dreamed that such a beautiful building would occupy the site.''

The church initially had three stained glass windows above the altar on the east wall, and one at the back of the west wall. The east windows depict Jesus as the Good Shepherd, St. Peter and St. John the Evangelist. The Ascension window at the back draws the most accolades.

Through the years, more stained glass windows have been added in the chancel and along the aisles. Dedicated in memory of parishioners and former rectors, the windows show various saints and significant Biblical events—all in rich colour and detail. Reverend Christopher Carruthers, rector from 1912 to 1927, is credited with the quality of work.

Imposing grandeur of King Edward School.

Financial troubles forced the congregation to stop work soon after the basement was dug. Like St. Joseph's Basilica on the north side, the basement was roofed over and used. It became known as ''The Basement Church.''

The church was designed to accommodate 450 people, with room for an additional 150 in the tower, vestry and side rooms. There have been several additions over the years. A new hall was added in the 1940s and later expanded, while a new rectory was added in the 1950s. Holy Trinity's rich historical background is important to many members of the congregation, whose families have been involved in the church for many decades.

There are parishioners in their 90s who once attended the first wooden church. That first church was moved to University Avenue when the present structure was built. Known as Church of St. John the Evangelist, it was destroyed by fire in 1951.

The church was designated a Provincial Historical Resource by Alberta Culture in 1983. ■

SHEPPARD HOUSE • 1911

Old Mansion Restored for $70,000
9945-86 Avenue

CHILDREN'S VOICES again echo through the halls and bedrooms of Sheppard House, an historic mansion in Old Strathcona.

Built in 1911 by brewing magnate William Sheppard, the home is now a Provincial Historical Resource. It's also home to Judy Berghofer and her three children. Berghofer's interest in history also crossed into her work as a media consultant for Alberta Culture's historic sites service.

Sheppard, his wife Elsie and their seven children lived in the house from 1911 until Sheppard's death in 1944. But for three decades—from then until Berghofer purchased the mansion in 1974—it was subdivided into 13 suites and sustained a large amount of damage.

The three-storey house, faced with red brick capped by a hipped roof complete with a widow's walk (a walkway atop the building), has been an ongoing heavy-duty restoration project for the family.

When they bought the house, various hues and coats of paint, wood partitions, and other make-shift additions marred and obscured the Edwardian finish. They have spent more than 3,000 hours of labor and $70,000 on restorations since buying the 3,500-square-foot house for $60,000. Restoration has progressed to the point where the National Film Board used the house as a set in its 1984 film of Margaret Lawrence's *To Set Our House In Order.*

A reclaimed brick conservatory was added to the south wall in the back yard. Inside, restored fir woodwork predominates in panelling, moldings and a dining room plate rail. There is a fir and marble trimmed wood or coal-burning fireplace complete with built-in clock in the foyer.

Main floor features include a large foyer, study, parlor, dining room, butler's pantry and modernized kitchen. The second floor has five bedrooms and an old-style three-piece bathroom. A servant's stairwell at the rear of the house leads to the third floor which has a maid's room, plus an open ballroom with trap door access to the widow's walk.

The house was modelled in the Georgian Revival Style, popular in Alberta from 1900 to 1925. The style was seen as eminently appropriate for the sober and respectable, yet luxurious residence of a gentleman. Specific elements included plain brick work with classically-detailed quoins. The hipped roof was elaborated with side gables, the widow's walk and two gable-roofed dormer windows. While most windows are rectangular, a spoked semi-circular window punctuates the west side.

Sheppard, who spent $8,000 to build the house, was the founder of Edmonton Brewing and Malting Company, forerunner of Molson's Edmonton Breweries. He also owned three hotels, including the Strathcona, and was mayor of Strathcona. ■

FACULTÉ SAINT-JEAN • 1910

Roots of French College Date to 1908
8406-91 Street

ALTHOUGH THE INSTITUTION has undergone many evolutions since first seeing the light of day in Pincher Creek, Alberta in 1908, Faculté Saint-Jean remains an enduring symbol of ''la survivance'' in Alberta.

Once an independent educational institution, the school is now part of the University of Alberta. The college began as a bilingual institution primarily to prepare priests for the order of the Oblates of Mary Immaculate. The order wished ''to create an educational bilingual elite, in all walks of life.''

The college moved to the grounds of St. Joachim's Church in downtown Edmonton in 1910, before moving to its present location. By the late 1980s, only two of the original buildings remained—a three-storey students residence built in stages from 1910 to 1943, and a two-storey house built in 1910 and now used for offices. Both are constructed in traditional styling with brick and stone dressings.

A stone grotto at the southwest corner of the residence reflects the religious heritage of the faculty. It was built in 1942 by Polish Oblate Brother Anthony Kowalczyk, who died in 1947 and is now being canonized. When Pope John Paul II visited Edmonton in 1984, he made a point of praying at Brother Anthony's grave.

The west facing facade of the residence, which overlooks Mill Creek Ravine, is emblazoned with the Oblates crest at its centre. Arched windows on the first floor show the building's ecclesiastical heritage. Its charming vintage foyer has three-quarter dark wood panelling and leaded glass windows. Among the building's other features is an old chapel with a simply ornamented ceiling and dark wood panelled walls.

While the architecture is simplistic, given its history and association with Brother Anthony, Alberta Culture has indicated the building would make a good candidate for preservation.

The house—referred to as ''le chateau'' on campus—was a residence for nuns, the order of Les Soeurs de la charité d'Evron, from 1911 to 1968. They were responsible for cooking and the infirmary.

The house has a full-width front porch and a cross with the date of its construction (1910) at the front. An underground tunnel, now sealed, connected the house to the residence building. A popular story has it that the tunnel was sealed in order to quash rumors that the nuns and priests were using it to see each other surreptitiously.

When the college opened as the Juniorate of St. John the Apostle in Pincher Creek, it had but one professor, Reverend André Daridon, and three students. After moving to Edmonton, it served not only as a religious institution, but also as a private school for boys. Courses were taught in English until 1928. That year, French instruction began and the college became affiliated with the University of Ottawa.

Edmonton's Jesuit College closed in 1941 and two years later the Juniorate of St. Jean introduced a bachelor of arts program, and became known as Collège St. Jean. By that time, it had trained 79 priests.

In 1962, women were finally admitted to the university-level programs. A bilingual teacher training program had begun in association with Laval University. Its post-secondary programs became affiliated with the U of A in 1963 and, two years later, the college entered the Edmonton separate school system. In 1970 the academic program came under full control of the U of A although the Oblates retained ownership of the facility itself. The name was then changed to Collège Universitaire St. Jean. In 1972, the high school program was phased out.

With the religious character of the institution all but eliminated, the Oblates decided there was little reason for the order to continue financial support for the college. So, in 1976, the federal and provincial governments paid $3.5 million for the college. It was also in that year that the present name was adopted.

Original residence and grotto of Faculté St. Jean.

Sheppard House — fit for a brewing magnate.

Unrefurbished exteriors of Strathcona businesses, 1972.

Strathcona Central

The most noteworthy sight greeting thousands of immigrants to northern Alberta as they stepped out of the Calgary and Edmonton Railway Station in the 1890s was the imposing structure of Hotel Edmonton, later the Strathcona Hotel. Built in 1891 to accompany the arrival of the railway, this landmark was the first in a series of unique buildings along the north side of Whyte Avenue which attested to the thriving commercial centre Strathcona had become by the turn of the century. Among others, the Canadian Bank of Commerce building and the Dominion Hotel represent the economic boom that saw Strathcona evolve from a town to a city in the space of eight years.

Commerce however was not the sole preoccupation of Strathconians during the Edwardian period. To the immediate north of Whyte Avenue and 104th Street was the civic centre, much of which remains unaltered from its pre-World War I elegance. Knox Church, the Strathcona Public Library, Fire Hall No. 6 and the Orange Hall look as they did in 1914. Nearby, Holy Trinity Anglican Church and Old Scona High School, fashioned in harmonious orange and red brick, provided an architectural uniformity which underscored the deep sense of community that prevailed in Strathcona.

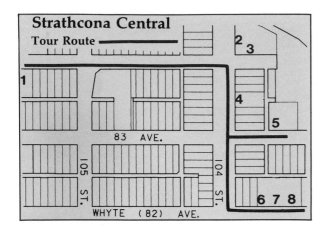

Strathcona Central

Tour Route

83 AVE.

105 ST.

104 ST.

WHYTE (82) AVE.

1. *Old Scona High School*
2. *Knox Church*
3. *Orange Hall*
4. *Strathcona Public Library*
5. *Fire Hall No. 6*
6. *Dominion Hotel*
7. *Bank of Commerce*
8. *Strathcona Hotel*

OLD SCONA HIGH SCHOOL • 1909

Renaissance Styling Featured

10523-84 Avenue

EDMONTON'S oldest-functioning secondary school was once slated for demolition to make way for freeway construction. But Old Scona Academic High School, built in 1909, was spared along with several other south side buildings when plans for a new 105th Street bridge and a connecting freeway were abandoned.

Old Scona was originally called Strathcona Collegiate Institute. From 1909 to 1911 some of the earliest classes of the University of Alberta were moved here from their first premises at Queen Alexandra School. In 1913, the name was changed to Strathcona High School. The latter name is still engraved on the front of the school, while the initials of the former are found in a crest above the main entrance.

The building's architecture is said to be English Renaissance in its primary inspiration. Alberta Culture also considers it significant as a key building in the development of education in Old Strathcona.

The school, which was designed by architect Roland W. Lines and built at a cost of $100,000, also has some Victorian influences, such as its domed central tower.

When it opened, the school was considered large for its time and had room for 400 students. Modern conveniences such as indoor plumbing, thermostatic controls, central heating system, and private telephone system were included.

The school was built with 600 tons of Alberta blue stone hauled from quarries 40 miles upstream on the North Saskatchewan River. Kootenay marble accents the front entrance. ■

KNOX CHURCH • 1907

Gothic Revival Style

8403-104 Street

THIS WEATHERED brick church in Old Strathcona stands as testimonial to the enduring faith of early south side pioneers.

The building, now home to Knox Evangelical Free Church, was built in 1907 as Knox Presbyterian Church under the inspiration of Reverend D.G. McQueen. It succeeded the original church built in 1892 after parishioners tired of services in ad hoc premises ranging from warehouses to the kitchen of the Strathcona Hotel.

Another church was begun in 1894, but before a spire could be put on the tower, plans were made to build a bigger church of brick. Those were the days when the blast of a Calgary and Edmonton Railway locomotive whistle would regularly jolt nodding parishioners during the Sunday sermon.

The church was designed by Magoon, Hopkins and James of Edmonton, and built by Thomas Richards of Strathcona.

In 1911, large organ pipes were installed and in 1949 a brick hall was added. A new pipe organ was installed in 1950, and stained glass windows added in 1957.

The building was designated a Registered Historical Resource by Alberta Culture in 1976. Alberta Culture notes that its Gothic Revival architecture "exhibits the asymmetrical bell-tower, perpendicular tracery on windows and crockets on top of the tower, and other features typical of Presbyterian churchs."

The church's exterior style reflects the retention of Scottish traditions. On the other hand the interior plan is "Akron American," and features a serpentine-shaped balcony, an arched dome, and an "in the round" sanctuary design. ■

Striking facade of Old Scona High School.

ORANGE HALL • 1903

A Humble Clapboard Hall

10335-84 Avenue

TUCKED between the Strathcona library and an Edmonton Transit garage stands a white clapboard frame hall. One of the south side's oldest buildings, the Orange Hall was home to the Loyal Orange Order, Chapter 1164.

The small building still accommodated monthly meetings of various lodge groups, and manifested another destiny as the home for the South Side Folk Club. The building was also used by the Fringe Theatre Festival and for other private events, but deep inside it remains true orange.

In dusty locked cupboards in the hall basement lie some of the order's oldest documents. These include a 1915 black leather Bible with LOL No. 1654 inscribed on the cover, and the first minute book with meetings carefully noted as early as 1895. It was in that year the lodge began, with the first meetings held in the home of founding member and treasurer H.W. Nash, a Strathcona grain buyer.

Another founding member—and the order's first recording secretary—was R.W. Pettipiece, who was editor of the weekly *South Edmonton News*, predecessor of *The Strathcona Plaindealer*. Some accounts say that noted south side pioneer Robert McKernan was the order's first worshipful master, but the lodge's incorporation charter—dated 1895 and mounted on the wall left of the stage podium—noted that Reverend Robert A. Munroe occupied that position.

McKernan, whose signature is liberally inscribed in the ancient minute book, was a subsequent worshipful master. McKernan came to Edmonton in 1877. He then purchased a farm on the south side for $10 from a Cree Indian. It is found where the neighborhood that bears his name is located today. The elder McKernan, who died in 1908, built the Dominion Hotel in 1903 on Whyte Avenue, while his son John was responsible for building the Princess Theatre.

The first Orangeman's parade was held on the ''Glorious 12th of July'' 1895, when the flags of the British and King William III were strutted down Whyte Avenue by 60 Orangemen to the accompaniment of fifes and drums. The biggest parade was held in 1904, when 2,500 Orangemen assembled. By the later part of the 20th century, parades were seldom held, except on special occasions.

The hall was constructed about 1903 on a lot purchased for $150. Members built much of the hall themselves to reduce labor costs. The interior is said to have been plastered and painted for $240. The basement was added later.

The building is of a simple design with an unembellished clapboard exterior, and lacking the elaborate detailing which later became prevalent. It features an assembly hall with hardwood flooring, wood wainscotting, and a stage with a centre podium and a carved wooden arch. The Queen's photograph overlooks the hall over the lodge's unfurled banner, while historic photos and charters decorated the walls.

By the mid-1980s, the lodge had about 90 members and operated primarily as a benevolent association, raising funds for various children's charities. ■

STRATHCONA LIBRARY • 1913

New Page Opens For Landmark

8331-104 Street

BUILT IN 1913, Edmonton's first library was given a $250,000 interior restoration and reopened in 1985.

The Strathcona Public Library is a two-storey English Renaissance Revival Style structure. The renovations restored this earliest sanctum of Strathcona culture to its former austere but tasteful decor.

Money for the renovations came from a trust fund set aside from the sale of the old main library on MacDonald Drive, which was demolished in 1968 to make way for the AGT Tower. The Old Strathcona Foundation also contributed $15,000.

This well-known library is finished in weathered orange brick with limestone embellishments. The brick was probably manufactured from clay in one of the many brickyards which flourished in the North Saskatchewan River valley at the turn of the century.

It was completed at a cost of $30,000, and was designed by the prominent Strathcona architectural firm of Arthur G. Wilson and David E. Herrald, who also drew up the plans for numerous other early south side buildings. Their works included the University of Alberta campus home of Alberta's first premier, Alexander Cameron Rutherford, First Presbyterian Church, as well as the Douglas Block at 10442 Whyte Avenue.

Strathcona townsfolk had petitioned their council for a library as early as 1907. But the matter was put on hold due to Strathcona's pre-occupation with building a city hall and market. In 1910, the City of Strathcona purchased the land for $6,250 from farmer James Edmund Smith and liveryman Douglas Edward Cameron.

Negotiations began in earnest that same year for a grant from Andrew Carnegie, the

American philanthropist and industrialist. E.L. Hill, inspector for the Strathcona school district, led the negotiations. He had earlier helped develop libraries in Guelph, Ontario, and Calgary. However, Carnegie only offered $15,000 and this was turned down by the City of Strathcona as inadequate. Shortly after Strathcona's amalgamation with the City of Edmonton, debentures were sold to raise $25,000 for the library building.

The library proved to be an instant success and more than 53,000 books were circulated in its first 9 months of operation. Books were stored only on the main floor. The basement was devoted to a men's reading room, while the second floor was used as an auditorium.

While the City of Strathcona officially turned over its properties to the City of Edmonton after amalgamation, its name remained on the property title until 1916, when the Edmonton Library Board took title. No sum of money changed hands, but pursuant to land titles regulations, the library's real estate value was duly noted at $37,800. The building has remained in the board's possession to this day.

It saw renovations in 1948, and was closed in 1984 to make way for the latest facelift in which the exterior was left untouched. The remodelling job was designed by R.R. Roberts Limited, an Edmonton architectural firm.

The Strathcona Library was designated as a Registered Historical Resource by Alberta Culture in 1976 because of its age and imposing architecture. It was described as ''an integral unit'' of Old Strathcona. ∎

Strathcona Library is city's oldest.

Left: Knox Presbyterian Church was home to early south side congregation.
Opposite page: Insurance plan of Whyte Avenue.

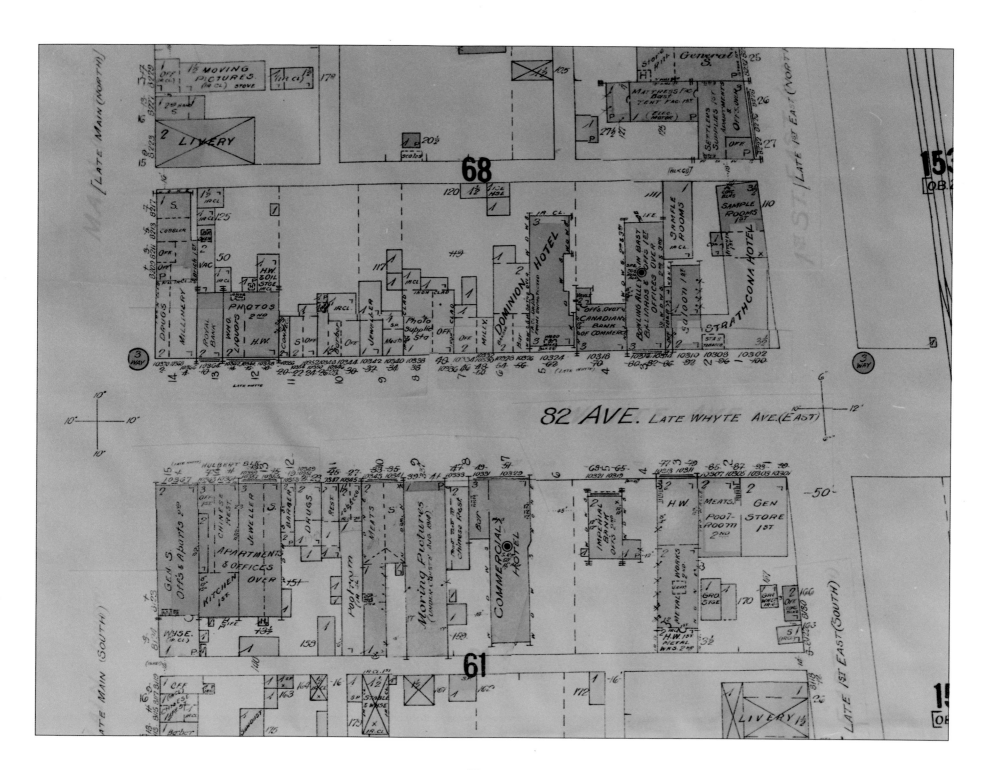

82 AVE. LATE WHYTE AVE.(EAST)

68

61

Fire Hall No. 6 as it appeared in 1920.

FIRE HALL NO. 6 • 1910

Reborn As Walterdale Playhouse

10322-83 Avenue

THE THEATRE-BOUND now flock where horse-drawn fire wagons were once launched on errands of mercy in Old Strathcona.

Fire Hall No. 6 was first known as Strathcona Fire Hall Number One. After Strathcona amalgamated with its successful cross-river rival in 1912, the building's name was changed.

The home of the Walterdale Playhouse amateur theatre group, the exterior of this vintage fire hall was restored to its original 1910 condition. Trees sprout from the base of the building and an interlocking brick patio sports a concrete sign indicating the hall's new use—a lofty elevation from its days as a deteriorating furniture warehouse.

The fire hall was built in 1910 by contractor J.M. Eaton, who submitted a tender for $13,715, the lowest of five received. Heating and plumbing cost $998. Another $2,000 was required to finish the hall due to structural cracks in the walls and an embarassing lean in the bell tower. At the time, *The Edmonton Bulletin* termed the design "unusually commodious and handsome."

Designed by south side architects Arthur G. Wilson and David E. Herrald, the fire hall contained stables in the rear for nine horses, with loft and feed bins overhead. The area behind the Walterdale stage is used to build and store theatre sets. The garage area, once used to house fire wagons, has been converted to the theatre proper and a curved lobby area. Two of the front bays are closed with cedar partitions, while the third is used as the patron's entrance.

An 11-foot-square bell and hose tower was erected to a height of 77 feet with a rack to accommodate firehose. The original town bell of Strathcona was installed and remains there today. The second floor was divided into a chief's office and a bedroom, a firemen's band room, general hall, five bedrooms for firemen, and bathrooms with showers. There were two sliding poles to the main floor.

The poles are now gone and the holes covered. Walterdale also converted the upstairs to a lighting and sound room, furnace room, wardrobe and set rooms, and actors change areas.

The building was used as a fire hall until 1954 when it was leased to Strathcona Furniture as a warehouse. It narrowly avoided destruction the previous year. The building was used for storing furniture until 1974 when it was renovated and leased to Walterdale Playhouse for $1 a year and taxes.

The hall is constructed of brick with stone quoins, cornices, and oversized voussoirs in the large arched garage doors, which provides some ornament. Alberta Culture noted that the exterior is almost completely original.

The province designated the fire hall a Registered Historical Resource in 1976. It was then the oldest remaining fire hall of its vintage in Edmonton and Calgary. ■

DOMINION HOTEL • 1903

Strathcona Hotel Reborn

10324 Whyte Avenue

ROBERT McKERNAN'S once-dandy Dominion Hotel died of neglect in 1983. But its ornate facade was reborn in 1984—ersatz history some have termed it—disguising a modern $1.2 million four-floor office building home to Athabasca University and the Edmonton Board of Health.

In 1983 the hotel's new owner—The Old Strathcona Foundation—was forced to tear the original structure down. The foundation's plans to restore it were scuttled by a city inspection which found the building in violation of a number of fire and health regulations.

Beyond its restored facade with charming gingerbread trim and centre cupola, inside it is nothing like the hotel of yesteryear. A three-storey atrium topped with a skylight greets bewildered visitors who may have thought they were about to return to the beginning of this century.

Modern offices, meeting, storage, and computer rooms bristling with word-processing technology are packed behind new brick walls. About 4,000 students a month were being served by Athabasca University's offices here in the 1980s, through seminars, registration, counselling, tele-conferences, and computer labs.

In a 1984 interview the foundation's property director, Wes Candler noted that "it's really not a historical building in the normal context—its a brand new building in every respect."

The foundation, with approval and a grant from Alberta Culture, reconstructed the Dominion Hotel as a new building with a recreated front facade because "it forms a very important part of the old street. Filling that site with a modern office building would have been completely out of context," Candler said.

Fire Hall No. 6 finds new life as theatre.

The Dominion Hotel first opened in October 1903, a business venture of prominent south side pioneer Robert McKernan. McKernan's first holding—a large farm near 110th Avenue and 76th Street paid him handsome profits, and he diversified into the hotel trade.

Unfortunately McKernan, who helped build and operate the first telegraph line into Edmonton in 1877, did not enjoy the fruits of the hotel business for very long. He died five years after the Dominion opened its doors.

Accounts of its facilities vary—likely due to its short life in the accommodation business. The advent of prohibition in 1916 forced the closure of a successful beer parlor, and then the hotel itself. Its rooms were then converted into rental apartments.

When finished, one account says the Dominion Hotel had 33 rooms plus a formal dining room and of course, the beer parlor. Yet a 1911 special feature in *The Bulletin* said the hotel had 50 rooms and 20 employees.

In 1921 the building was sold to Len Pheasey, who began the Acme Meat Market in the hotel's former beer parlor. Acme occupied the premises until 1981. The year previous, the building was purchased by the Old Strathcona Foundation from Dolly Pheasey for $100,000. ■

Facade of Dominion Hotel replica.

BANK OF COMMERCE BLDG. • 1908

One of City's Oldest Bank Buildings
10318-82 Avenue

IT'S CHANGED hands and names, but it's more like its original self than it has been for some time. In fact, few can remember when the three-storey building ever looked better. Renamed the Griffith Block by owners Bill and Carmine Griffith, it was known as the Bank of Commerce Building for most of its years.

But in 1983, it was sold to Rivendell Management Group Limited for $270,000. With hands-on labor, the Whyte Avenue edifice was graciously reappointed and graced with the name of the firm's president and sole shareholder Bill Griffith.

The street facade is finished in brown brick with stone trim. A white dentilled cornice separates the second and third storeys, and stone pediments are found over the entrance and third storey windows.

Inside, brown onyx flooring is found in the foyer and banking hall. There are working fireplaces in the banking hall manager's office and on the third floor, and the original vaults are still in use on the first and second floors.

All the oak moldings and railings have been restored throughout, as well as the fir trim on the third floor. A 60-year-old traditionally-styled carpeting was custom-ordered and installed in the stairwell and hallways. Original lath and plaster work was restored and embellished.

The original windows were put back in working order and all transoms remain intact. No air conditioning is required due to the good air flow throughout with the pulley windows and transoms. The original vintage boiler and hot water heater continue to labor away as efficiently as ever in the basement.

While the 5,800-square-foot building was in good structural condition when purchased, it required clean up work, painting and new

Dominion Hotel in its heyday.

wiring. Holes in walls and ceilings were repaired, missing moldings and doors were milled and replaced, and custom marbled glass panes were ordered for interior doors and offices. The restoration cost $75,000, but would easily be double that had the Griffiths not done much of the work themselves.

As a result of their efforts, Rivendell received an honorable mention from the Alberta Historical Resources Foundation in 1985. The firm was also engaged by the Old Strathcona Foundation to administer the store front program and manage the restoration of another 18 store facades on Whyte Avenue.

The old banking hall was a focal point of business on the south side and played a significant social and commercial role in the community. The site was owned by the National Trust Company in trust for the Bank of Commerce as far back as 1906, when the bank's first office there consisted of a modest two-storey frame structure with a boomtown front. However the bank had conducted business in Strathcona as early as 1901. In 1908 it constructed the edifice in question for $30,000.

A banking hall was planned for the first floor, four office suites for the second, and accommodation for bank staff including a sitting room and two bedrooms on the third floor. A furnace room, cellars and concrete vaults were located in the basement.

The building was designed by the bank's in-house architect, a Mr. Cawston, in consultation with the manager, G. W. Marriott. Cawston took up residence in the Strathcona Hotel to supervise construction.

The May 5th, 1908 edition of *The Strathcona Plaindealer* noted that "four tall pillars of stone will rise to the top of the second storey giving the front a rich and classic appearance." Cawston obviously modified his plans, for the pillars were constructed of brick and capped with stone. ∎

STRATHCONA HOTEL • 1891

The Lap of Luxury
10302 Whyte Avenue

IN 1913, *The Edmonton Journal* described the Strathcona Hotel as an historical landmark having "an eye to comfort and refined good taste, both in arrangement of offices, lounging room and sleeping quarters.

"It was here the big men of yesterday gathered to execute some of the largest land deals made on the American continent," *The Journal* extolled in its 10th anniversary issue.

The Strathcona Hotel is the oldest wood frame building on the south side. Today, rooms are rented at $13 per night to a "working class" clientele, and the hotel also serves as home to long-time residents.

The south side hotel caters to a walk-in trade in its tavern—students, baseball teams and old-timers. Its longevity and prominent location have earned it a special place in the city's heart.

The Strathcona Hotel opened in December 1891 as the Hotel Edmonton, to serve passengers off the Calgary and Edmonton Railway. It is believed to have been renamed the Strathcona after the town of Strathcona was incorporated in 1899. It was built at a cost of $5,000, and in its original plan, the front entrance was on First Street (now 103rd Street), with an office entrance on Main Street (now Whyte Avenue).

At that time, the ground floor housed an office, billiards room, bar room, kitchen and two pantries. There is no longer a kitchen or restaurant on the main floor, simply a lobby, offices and a tavern, as well as a small shop.

The site was originally owned by Thomas A. Anderson, who sold it to Winnipeg real estate brokers Augustus Nanton and John Henry Munson in 1890. Nanton and Munson assembled much of the land in Strathcona for the Calgary and Edmonton Railway, in order to build up a thriving end-point, and profit, for both parties.

While Nanton and Munson's name remained on the land title until 1906, some say it was held in proxy for the Calgary and Edmonton Railway. In 1906 the property was sold to brewing magnate William Henry Sheppard for $6,500.

In the hands of later owners, prohibition pushed the hotel into foreclosure. From 1923 to 1928 it was owned by the Presbyterian Church, and was known as Westminster Ladies College.

Construction of the building began August 5, 1891, a few days after the first train rolled into the South Edmonton station from Calgary. The hotel was originally stained in dark wood, but was painted a cream-color with maroon trim around 1910. In 1978 the hotel was given a major facelift. Its stuccoed exterior was removed and replaced with stained cedar siding. It was restored to its 1910 colors in 1982, and plastic cornices replaced the former wooden ones.

A two-storey brick annex was erected on the western side in 1903 to house an expanded bar, and in 1907, a concrete extension designed in keeping with the original structure was built to the north at a cost of $18,000. In its heyday, the hotel had 54 rooms, now there are 46.

In 1915, with the onset of Prohibition, the bar annex was leased to a fruit store and a bank. It was later registered under a separate title, and is home to another business.

Although described as simple architecturally, the hotel forms an integral part of the historic facade of Whyte Avenue. It was designated a Registered Historical Resource by the province in 1976.

The Strathcona Hotel endures.

Strathcona South

Long after the City of Strathcona amalgamated with Edmonton, Whyte Avenue continued to function as the major commercial artery on the south side. Unlike Jasper Avenue however, the southern counterpart did not undergo extensive redevelopment, and between 103rd and 105th Streets many of the pre-World War I buildings still remain, and are now protected by legislation. Collectively, they provide a unique opportunity to view the commercial core of a Canadian prairie city during the pre-war period.

Along the south side of Whyte Avenue, structures from the 1890s such as the Ross Block and the Hub Cigar building were complemented after the turn of the century by such buildings as the Tipton Block, the Gainer Block and the Chapman Brothers Store, which reveal the commercial importance of the district. In 1908, the increased transportation demands necessitated the replacement of the old Calgary and Edmonton Railway Station with the CP Station which is still standing. Other varieties of activity in the area are reflected in the Princess Theatre, and in 1913, the presence of the federal government was felt with the construction of the Strathcona Public Building, later the South Side Post Office.

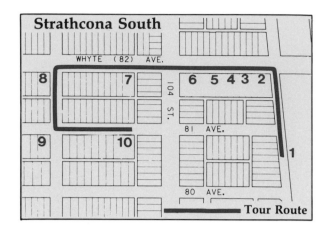

Strathcona South

WHYTE (82) AVE.

8   7   6 5 4 3 2

104 ST.

81 AVE.

9   10

1

80 AVE.

Tour Route

1. *C.P. Rail Strathcona Station*
2. *Ross Block*
3. *Princess Theatre*
4. *The Gainers Block*
5. *Hub Cigar*
6. *The Tipton Block*
7. *Chapman Bros. Ltd.*
8. *Strathcona Post Office*
9. *Scona Garage & Apartments*
10. *Malone Block*

CP RAIL STATION • 1907

Reminder of Glory days in Rail Travel
8103-103 Street

THE CP RAIL Strathcona Station was not much more than a shell of its former self by the 1980s. But the station, just south of the site of the original—albeit more humble—station, stands as a reminder of the historic importance of the railway to the south side.

The station also serves as a tombstone marking the demise of rail passenger service between here and Calgary. The last VIA Rail Dayliner made its run in the fall of 1985.

Built in 1907 at a cost of $30,000, the two-storey station sports a traditional brick and Tyndal stone facade, including Tyndal stone quoins and sills. It has a bellcast hip roof, irregular roof lines, stone roof brackets, and an octagonal tower with a pyramidal roof, pilasters and decorative stone trim.

Inside, the station was remodelled and by 1986 served as CP Rail's city freight centre, with administration and yard offices occupying the once classic interior. Employees now work in renovated offices on two floors. A former freight room at the south end of the station was transformed into a modern lunch room and locker room for yard crews.

The waiting room was converted into a storage area. New wood panelling, drywalling, linoleum flooring and carpeting are everywhere save for the basement. From the inside, only transoms over outside doors remind one that this is not a modern building.

While no one knows for certain, it is likely that hardwood flooring once graced the original waiting room, station agent's office, and living quarters. The second floor offices were built in the 1950s, usurping space that formerly served as a dance hall and bunkhouse. CP Rail's investigation department, yard-master's offices and a board room were located here by 1986.

Once again the station is as busy as a beehive, but its incoming traffic is often manufactured parts and machinery, and the outgoing traffic is largely comprised of petro-chemicals. In 1985, CP Rail shipped 18,000 carloads from the station, while 5,000 carloads came in.

The station measures 134 by 38 feet and was originally steam heated. The heating system was upgraded in 1984. The main floor originally contained an express office, women's waiting room, general waiting room, agent's office with wickets, and ticket and telegraph offices opening to the east side platform. Other facilities included a conductor's room, gentlemen's smoking room and lavatories on the main floor.

Alberta Culture described it as representative of the vital role of the railway in the development of northern Alberta. It is architecturally unique and one of four larger remaining urban stations in the province—the others being in Lethbridge, Medicine Hat and Red Deer. ■

Whyte Avenue and 103rd Street looking west.

The architecturally unique C.P. Rail Station was built in 1907.

ROSS BLOCK • 1894

Oldest Brick Building on Whyte Avenue

10313 Whyte Avenue

WERE HE ALIVE TODAY, William Edward Ross might well be pleased that his old two-storey building is once again a going concern on one of Strathcona's most enduring streetscapes.

Ross, who died in September 1903, built the Ross Block in 1894. It is the oldest brick building on Whyte Avenue, and is considered a pioneer structure because wood was the dominating material of the time.

Ross's first wife Lizzie purchased the land where the building now stands for $150 in 1894, and the family moved here from Canmore to begin their hardware business. In 1898, Ross purchased the title from wife Lizzie for $4,000. He bequeathed the building to his second wife, Muriel, and his son, Charles. Charles was killed in France in 1916.

Muriel Ross managed the hardware business until she could no longer afford the mortgage payments, and turned the property over to the City of Edmonton for $200 in 1926. The city held title for 20 years, until the block was purchased by Adolph and Bertha Minchau. It subsequently passed through a number of hands, until Serge Caldararu purchased the property.

In addition to housing a hardware store from 1894 to 1926, and then again from 1933 to 1957—under a variety of names—the Ross Block has been the home of a feed store, a restaurant, a clothing store and a night club. The upstairs was used for a Masonic lodge in the early days and then converted into apartments. As a result, the early south side building has received the protection of a Registered Historical Resource designation from Alberta Culture. ■

Princess Theatre: Old Strathcona's grande dame.

PRINCESS THEATRE • 1914

First South Side Theatre
10335-82 Avenue

THE GRAND old dame of silent films and vaudeville flourishes with class and profitability once again, thanks to the efforts of the Old Strathcona Foundation.

As well, the historic and quaint facade of the Princess Theatre has become a flagship of sorts—an integral part of the revived Old Strathcona business district.

The Princess was built by John McKernan in 1914 for $75,000. It incorporated the first marbled front of any building west of Winnipeg. It has approximately 4,000 square feet on the main floor, and 420 seats, though it once had 600.

The Princess is a visual treat with its white marble facade with copper cornices and parapet. There is an arched and sculpted ceiling with ornate plaster frieze work in rust and white, as well as a rebuilt balcony in the theatre. Marine cherubs dance in sublime embrace above the screen. The lobby is elegant with red carpeting, oaken doors, and a large crystal chandelier.

The theatre was designed by the architectural firm of Wilson and Herrald, and constructed by contractors Brown and Hargraves, both Edmonton firms. It has a third floor of rooms no longer in use, and a full basement, once home to Spike's Poolroom and a barber shop. It was the only south side theatre until the Garneau opened in 1939.

"So elaborate has been the nature of the theatre finish and decoration that the work took three months more time than scheduled," *The Edmonton Journal* reported in 1915, while its competitor *The Bulletin* said the building "shows a particular advantage with its mass of solid marble and copper cornices and the high standard of material and workmanship is carried over into every corner of the building."

While the first private opening reception featured tub-thumping First World War films, the first commercial showing was "The Eagle's Mate", starring Mary Pickford. Advertising promised "the main program of entertainment will be high-class moving pictures varied occasionally with high-class vaudeville or unusual concerts." Pianists or three-piece bands would accompany the silent films.

The first talkie movie feature was "The Canary Murder Case" around 1930. Television competition is said to have helped close the Princess in 1958 and it was used as a shoe store and sewing machine shop.

The building was purchased by Towne Cinemas in 1970 and given a $270,000 facelift to reopen as the Klondike. But the Klondike struggled and the Old Strathcona foundation stepped in. Since 1980, the Princess has succeeded under a bill of fare termed "classic and repertoire" film. The theatre generates traffic of 125,000 patrons annually into Old Strathcona while the Princess Theatre Club has 5,000 members at $10 each per year.

The building was repainted and replastered in 1982 for $15,000. ∎

THE GAINER BLOCK • 1902

Second Home of Meat Packing Empire
10341 Whyte Avenue

SANDWICHED between the Princess Theatre and the Hub Cigar Store stands the Gainer Block, built by meat packing magnate John Gainer.

Hanratty's trendy eatery is now esconced in the 5,000-square-foot brick and stone building featuring multi-paned front windows and four semi-circular brick arched second-storey windows. A honey-combed brick parapet adds height and decoration to the facade.

The block was built as the second store for John Gainer's butcher shop as his business ballooned with the growth of the Town of Strathcona.

Despite its small size and the simplicity of its design, Alberta Culture gave it the highest level of historic designation because it typifies the old business core of Whyte Avenue, and because of its association with a well-known Strathcona and Edmonton business.

The philanthropic Devonian Foundation assisted the Old Strathcona Foundation in purchasing the building for $125,000 in 1978. The OSF was responsible for the subsequent renovations.

The facade and upper west wall were water blasted to remove cream and green paint. New mortar was installed and the bricks repointed. The interior was completely gutted save for the first and second floors. The main floor was raised two feet, wooden window frames installed, and new electrical, mechanical and plumbing systems put in place. On the upper floor, the original hardwood was refinished.

The Gainer Block was originally owned by John Gainer and his family, who came here via the Calgary and Edmonton Railway in 1891. Gainer was born in Perth, Ontario, in 1858, and spent time in North Dakota and

Manitoba before moving to Strathcona.

At the age of 36, Gainer started John Gainer and Company in his home behind the Strathcona Hotel, killing and dressing his own meat in the back, while his wife Amy supplemented their income by selling baked goods.

He also took his wagon on the road, slaughtering animals on clients' property. Business prospered and he built a slaughter house near the Canadian Pacific Railway before constructing the Gainer Block.

Gainer purchased the site for $200 in 1893 from Calgary and Edmonton Railway brokers Augustus Nanton and John Munson. He resold the site for the same sum a month later, to grain merchant Henry William Nash. Nash transferred it to his wife's name two years later.

In 1899, the lot came back to Gainer for $550. Thirty-seven years later John Gainer transferred the title to his wife, Eulalia. The Gainer Block was owned by his family until 1943, when it sold for $6,000 to barber Nils Christenson.

In 1911, John Gainer closed the retail shop to concentrate on his abattoir and packing house, near Mill Creek Ravine. ∎

HUB CIGAR STORE • 1894

City's Oldest Newsstand
10345 Whyte Avenue

THE GAILY-PAINTED orange and white facade of the Whyte Avenue institution puts a brave face on the aging structure of the Hub Cigar Store.

Wedged between the Gainer Block and the Bagel Tree, the wood frame store has zero insulation levels and is in such bad shape that it should be levelled and rebuilt, store owner Ken Knowles said. In the dead of winter a glass of water on the floor will freeze in two hours due to its 19th century construction.

There is a retail area stuffed with magazines and paperbacks, a small video arcade area, and a rear storage room. A 1960s sign for the now-defunct Star Weekly is still found over the main magazine area.

According to Alberta Culture, the store is particularly significant because it is one of the few remaining examples of wood frame buildings from the earliest period of construction in Strathcona. The Hub is also significant as the only remaining cigar store and newsstand operation which continued to operate as it did in the historic era. When the Hub opened in 1910, there were about 10 in existence. By 1987 it was the city's last remnant of an earlier age.

The one-storey building has a false-front which extends the facade upward to create a two-storey illusion. The facade above the front windows was originally pierced by two fake windows.

"Wooden molding enriched with balls and finials rises in a decorative peak suggestive of a pediment to cap the facade," an Alberta Culture research paper noted. "Behind this pretentious facade is a low flat roofed structure, likely constructed as warehouse space at the time of the store's construction."

The building was constructed by Cornelius

Hub Cigar still going strong.

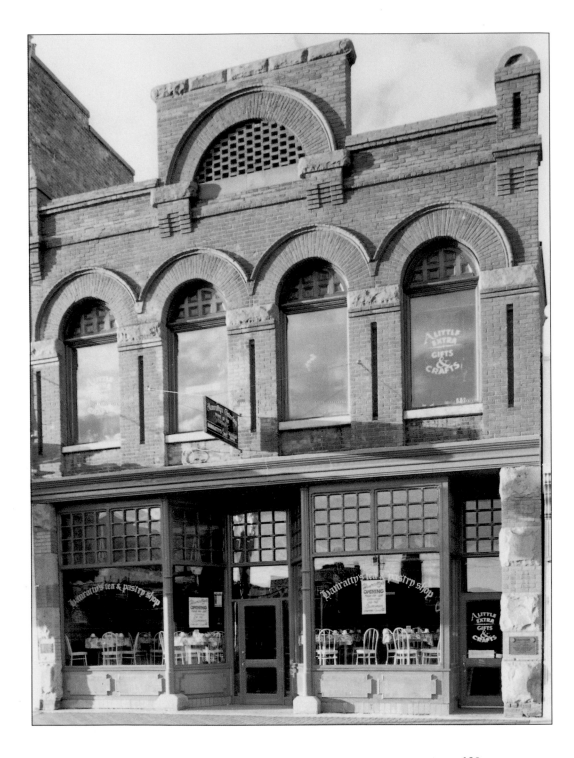

J. Duggan and, in 1895, was rented to Arthur Davies for use as a general store. Davies, who later became mayor of Strathcona, operated the store until 1904 when it was taken over by former Strathcona and Edmonton alderman Thomas P. Malone, who continued the business until 1910. That's the year when Charles Fisher and a Mr. Bell opened the Hub Cigar Store. Malone subsequently purchased his own building nearby.

An article in *The Strathcona Plaindealer* on September 16, 1910 observed: ''The new Hub Cigar Store, on Whyte Avenue, was opened this week by the proprietors Fisher and Bell, with an accommodation and equipment equal to any establishment of its kind in the two cities.''

In 1914, the building became the property of Roman Catholic Bishop Gabriel Breynst of Fort Providence and, later that year, title was transferred to the Roman Catholic Episcopal Corporation. The building was owned by the church until 1960, when it was purchased by the Bleviss family. ∎

Gainer Block serves up tea and pastries.

TIPTON BLOCK • 1911

A Success for Foundation
10355 Whyte Avenue

THE TIPTON BLOCK is a thriving success story for the Old Strathcona Foundation. The three-storey brick building was one of the first renovation projects for the publicly-funded foundation devoted to the restoration of Old Strathcona.

The classical detailing of the building's early 20th century commercial facade was maintained, including the bracketed cornices, concrete keystones, and pilaster strips. However, the interior was completely rebuilt. The renovated building has 12,000 square feet of commercial space.

Greenwoods Bookshoppe has occupied the main floor since the building reopened. There's a refinished brick feature wall, white-washed walls and new oak moldings. The high ceiling is trimmed with plaster moldings.

The block was built in 1911 by Russell Albert Hulbert, an implement dealer who also owned the Hulbert Block next door. Hulbert came to Alberta from Nova Scotia in 1893, and was a member of the first village council of Strathcona.

Hulbert sold the building for $40,000 in 1912 to lawyer John G. (Judge) Tipton. He also used the block as offices for Tipton and Sons Investment Company, a real estate and insurance firm.

Tipton, who came here from Kansas in 1893, also established a homestead near Big Island and developed a coal mine. He served as a city councillor in Strathcona prior to its amalgamation with Edmonton, then on Edmonton's council.

When he died in 1914, *The Edmonton Daily Capital* called him "a moving factor in the amalgamation of the twin cities ... during his last term, 1912-13, he was one of the most popular alderman." ∎

Tipton Block is Old Strathcona success story.

CHAPMAN BROTHERS LTD. • 1907

Store Dates Back to 1900s
10241 Whyte Avenue

SADDLES and western wear can still be purchased at the Chapman Brothers turn of the century store. But the harnesses that were hand-made in the back room by Buster Chapman and that made up so much of the original business have long since disappeared—another casualty of the age of the automobile.

Work clothes, jeans, coveralls and boots are the store's contemporary mainstays. In fact, Chapman Brothers received an award in 1984 from GWG for selling its products since 1912, one year after the clothing manufacturer began operations. Archibald Benjamin Chapman and his sons Buster and Lang are no longer alive, but the store is still owned and managed by the family. The historic building and its business are owned by Buster's children, Jack and Darlene Chapman. Their son, Matt, has managed the store since 1982.

The interior and exterior of the building were renovated in 1984 and 1985 with the assistance of Alberta Culture and the Old Strathcona Foundation. The facade was restored to its original color and style after three arduous weeks in which 20 to 30 coats of paint were removed.

Inside, new shelving and cedar panelling were installed and the old oiled wood floor was covered with carpet. Still, many original fixtures remain.

The store was designated a Registered Historical Resource by Alberta Culture in 1967, but Matt said that Buster, who died in 1973, was not all that keen about it.

"My grandfather did not think it should be ated as a historic site because he in change himself. He said if he was he would have had it torn down something bigger."

lture designated the site as an

Chapman Brothers store in 1919. James C. Chapman is in the centre.

excellent example of the 1900s harness goods shop. The building is also one of the few left which employed imitation brick tin siding—a turn of the century construction method. The building is described as a frame building with a boomtown facade, step parapet, and recessed symmetrical double entrance. Well-maintained and in good condition, the store represents an important aspect of early Strathcona commercial history.

The store was built without a basement about 1907 by Robert Ritchie, a one-time mayor of Strathcona. It was home to the south side branch of the Great West Saddlery Company managed by Matt's great grandfather, A.B. Chapman, who came here

with his family in 1903 from Port Elgin, Ontario. He bought the business in 1912 and started Chapman Brothers.

In 1917, Buster began minding the store, along with his brother Lang. The Chapmans didn't buy the building until 1949. ■

STRATHCONA POST OFFICE • 1912

"Capacious" Edifice Reopens
10501 Whyte Avenue

WITH THE REJUVENATION of the Old Strathcona Post Office in 1986, another block was laid in the redevelopment of Whyte Avenue's historic streetscape. After 10 years of cobwebs, dust, and boarded windows, the old post office emerged as Strathcona Square.

Inside the two-storey edifice there is a merry assortment of merchants peddling everything from food to flowers to art. It's all a far cry from the lack-lustre digs last occupied there by the post office in 1976. The cleansed facade of Tyndal stone with red stretcher bond bricks is set off with green accents, oak doors, canopies, and etched and stained glass windows.

The building was purchased from the city by Clarion Hospitality Industries in 1985. The redevelopment bill was tallied at $5 million, plus another $3 million in leasehold improvements.

A new roof caps off the old clock, a skylight extends to the north sidewalk and provides light for basement vendors, and a glass wall provided elevator passengers and passersby with views of each other. The wings were elevated to two storeys. The 27,000-square-foot interior sported white and green ceramic tiling, and pink, green, and white plaster embellishments.

Times were more economically promising when the building first opened as the Strathcona Post Office in 1912. The size and style of the building is said to reflect the confidence of the expansionist period prior to the First World War.

It was designed by department of public works architects under the direction of David Ewart. The design was a compromise between stone structures in Lethbridge and Vancouver, and plain brick editions built in smaller towns.

The two facades are divided into five bays by stone pilasters which support stone entablatures and the parapet. The stone clad clock tower dominates the north west corner with its pyramidal roof while its eaves form a semi-circle around the clock face. The south wing was built in 1911, while the west wing was built in 1948.

It is considered a departure from the usual attenuated Romanesque Style of post office architecture, with the clock tower being the only motif shared by this building and the more common Romanesque variety. The decorative detailing follows the symmetrical, logical classicism of the Beaux-Arts Style, and the building is considered a nationally-significant example of the transition towards the Beaux-Arts Style.

Strathcona citizenry and their board of trade started earnest lobbying for a new post office as early as 1908. Construction finally began in 1911. *The Strathcona Plaindealer* called it "handsome and capacious" upon its opening. *The Edmonton Bulletin* noted that "it is also most becoming that the first day for business in the new office will be July 1st, 1912, the occasion of the first grant annual amalgamation celebration." For it was on that date the fair city of Strathcona joined Edmonton.

The clock was made by the Midland Clock Works in Derby, England. It finally arrived in February 1913, but caused quite a commotion when the clock wouldn't fit the space. Another 10 feet were added to the tower to accommodate the clock.

It was eventually installed by Whyte Avenue jeweller M. Reynolds. The clock's displacements were impressive enough at the time to warrant blow-by-blow description: overall weight of 4,200 pounds, a 350-pound striker, a dial with a diametre of four feet, six inches, an 800-pound bell, and seven-pound hands.

The building was designated a Provincial Historical Resource by Alberta Culture in 1985. ∎

SCONA GARAGE AND APTS. • 1912

Car Hospital Now Restaurant
10505-81 Avenue

OTTO EDINGER was a victim of Alberta's perennial boom and bust economy.

While Edinger's name was familiar to those active in Edmonton's construction industry prior to the First World War, contemporary city residents are likely more familiar with his once classy garage and apartment building. The Scona Garage and Apartments is also known to the dining and drinking set, having served as the Keg Restaurant since 1974.

The two-storey rectangular brick building has terracotta trim and was erected by Edinger for $40,000 in 1912, just before the collapse of the local real estate market and a subsequent economic downturn. With his businesses floundering and real estate values in a tailspin, he lost the building in a foreclosure action seven years later.

The Keg occupies the first floor—once used as a garage—while the second floor is sealed off except for storage purposes.

The structure has a crenellated roof line with crest embellishments. Canopies have been erected over its entrances, and while the former apartment entrance is closed off, it features an arched stone entrance with the year of its construction above.

With the pre-war economy at its peak, Edinger doubtless saw good business prospects in the arrival of the horseless carriage, and the great population influx into Edmonton and Strathcona. But the history books show us that Edinger failed to make his payments to J.B. Little and Sons, a Riverdale brickyard that is still in operation. In a 1919 foreclosure action, he lost the property to J.B. Little, which still owns the building.

During its construction in 1912, *The Edmonton Capial* reported that Edinger was considering turning the building into a hotel.

The Strathcona Post Office now houses a festival market.

But *The Strathcona Plaindealer* said the top flat was being used for apartment purposes and office suites.

"The structure furnished as it is with steam heating, room telephones and all modern conveniences has cost close upon $40,000, while the machinery is valued at $8,000.

"The first storey, which is devoted to the needs of ailing automobiles is probably one of the finest motor hospitals in Canada, and certainly the finest in the west. There is storage for 65 automobiles and efficient and experienced engineers minister to their needs."

The newspaper went on to say that "the second storey of this palatial building is designed as an apartment house on a modern flat system. The accommodation is arranged in suites and single rooms and the scheme will satisfy a long-felt want."

The building continued to house tenants on its second floor and a garage below until 1974 when it was leased to The Keg after being condemned on fire and safety grounds. Extensive renovations were made by the restaurant. A rustic atmosphere, complete with stained cedar and photo murals of life in early Strathcona are found within. Further renovations in 1979 expanded the lounge. The building is said to be in good shape. ■

Old Scona Garage and Apartments is now a popular restaurant.

MALONE BLOCK • 1912

Strathcona Alderman Owned Block

8123-104 Street

TRAGEDY, politics and accomplishment lurk behind the dapper facade of the Malone Block. The 1912, two-storey edifice is named for Thomas P. Malone, the building's second owner. Suffering from a serious disease, Malone shot himself while undergoing treatment in a Vancouver hospital in 1926.

Malone, a former Strathcona and Edmonton alderman, purchased the block in 1920 from Isobel Mills. The wife of Nelson Darius Mills, Strathcona mayor from 1908 to 1909, she bought the lot in 1909, presumably constructed the building, and called it the Mills Block.

Malone ran a general store here from at least 1912 until 1925. At that time he sold the store and the building to Alberta's first premier, Alexander C. Rutherford. Rutherford, who practiced commercial and corporate law after he was defeated in a 1913 election, assembled a number of Whyte Avenue properties over the years, presumably for investment or revenue purposes.

Thomas Malone came to Alberta in 1901 and began his mercantile business in Strathcona in 1905 after disposing of a similar business in Olds. His first location was in what would become the Hub Cigar Store, where he stayed until 1910.

Malone had plans to construct a three-storey building to house the business. In a story that ran in July 1912, *The Edmonton Daily Capital*, itself a short-lived creature of the city's pre-war economic boom, said:

"Realizing that the High Level Bridge is to make the south side one of the most thickly settled portions of the City of Edmonton, it is the intention of this enterprising merchant to provide conveniences that must place his establishment here on a competing basis with any in the city."

Possibly due to the economic recession of 1914, Malone never proceeded with his plans, instead he leased space in the Mills Block and eventually purchased the building.

As well as serving on city councils, Malone was a separate school trustee and was the first president of the federation of community leagues. His wife Sara was the first separate school teacher in Regina, Saskatchewan where she taught in a log house. They had two sons and two daughters. Joseph became a Catholic priest and served as a chaplain overseas during the Second World War. Afterwards, he contributed in the completion of St. Joseph's Basilica.

The Malone's daughter, Anna, became head librarian at the University of Alberta. Paul became a reporter and a diplomat.

Rutherford, who died at age 84 in 1941, transferred his interest in the building back to the mortgager, Northern Trust Company, the year previous. The building changed hands several times until Hank Hendricks purchased it in 1971.

The commercial space was first used for Malone's department store, then for a furniture store. Hendricks later used the space for his flower shop. After he retired from active business life, he leased it to the Bank of British Columbia.

The bank completely renovated the basement and main floor. New heating, ventilating, electrical and plumbing systems were installed. After the bank left in 1986, the space was sub-leased to yet another furniture store. A one storey annex at the back houses Greenwoods Small World Bookstore.

Only the second floor retains its traditional trimmings. The building is in excellent structural condition. The facade was cleaned, and the bricks repointed in 1985 as part of the Strathcona storefront program.

University of Alberta

In 1906, the Alberta Legislature established that a University of Alberta would be created. Amid some controversy, the Garneau district of east Strathcona was chosen as the site. By 1915, a series of buildings were constructed which provided the central facilities of the university and established the architectural character of the campus for years to come. However, by the 1960s, the harmony of design was disrupted by the erection of numerous modern buildings, nevertheless, many of the older structures remained intact and the original features of the university can still be seen.

Various architects designed the early university buildings, and as a result, different architectural styles exist. For example, the Tudor elements of St. Stephen's College, the first building to be occupied on campus in 1911, contrasted with the Neo-classical elements of the Arts Building built in 1915. Overall however, a sense of uniformity, as is found in the three student residences, prevailed and was later complemented by such additions as the Dental Sciences Building, St. Joseph's College and Corbett Hall. This is also true of the early homes surrounding the campus, such as the residence of Arthur C. Rutherford, Alberta's first Premier and the university's first president.

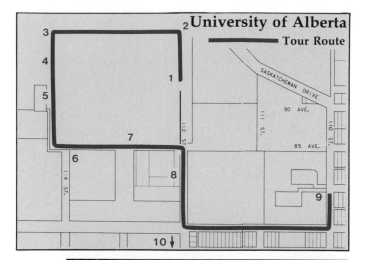

ARTS BUILDING • 1915

Arts Restoration Project
112 Street & 89 Avenue

A SYMBOLIC stone carving—chiselled from the 1914 construction budget—may finally grace a second-storey pediment on the Arts Building in the near future. The carving of an old man with a scroll and a young woman with a book symbolizes the old and new ways of teaching.

An $11 million restoration project finished in 1987 on the winsome campus edifice, will see the old and the new brought together.

Once a prominent campus landmark, the Arts Building is now hidden behind modern brick and concrete structures of eclectic design and questionable taste. It was just such an architectural jungle that the Arts Building designers—Montreal architect Percy Nobbs and George Hyde—intended to avoid. They prepared extensive plans for the entire university campus and wrote papers on how this university could avoid the creation of a disjointed amalgam of conflicting architectural styles.

The university's board of directors agreed, and decreed in 1912 that "the materials employed should be brick and stone, the proportion of stone to brick being increased in the more important buildings," and also that "the buildings generally be carried out in an elastic free classical style in accordance with modified English traditions."

Referring specifically to the Arts Building, the board said: "When executed this building should be architecturally one of the most important elements of the scheme."

Had their dream come to pass, it would have provided an architectural Mecca for Edmonton. However, the war and recession which slowed construction of the Arts Building and the flow of architectural fees to

Craftsmanship of Arts Building

116

The stately Rutherford House is now a museum.

Nobbs and Hyde, would also crimp the university's ambitious construction program until after the Second World War.

The three-storey Arts Building made of brick and sandstone trim, was described by its architects as being of the "elastic free classical" style. Built on a sandstone and granite foundation for $829,000, it features a balustrated roof line and is embellished with various crests, including a sculpted owl embracing the university crest immediately over the front door.

Other highlights include a circular central dome above a ceramic tiled corridor, terracotta tile walls along with first and second floor hallways, numerous skylights and traditional transoms and inner windows.

Highlighting the second floor is the Senate Chamber, with its wood wainscotting, ornate sculpted moldings, plaster relief sculptures and a two-storey oval ceiling with decorative plaster trim.

The renovations were approved in 1985 and supervised by the city architectural firm of Bouey, Auld, Faling and Shaw. The building will continue to house classrooms and language laboratories. Convocation Hall, attached to the west face of the Arts Building will not be affected as it has already been restored. ■

Ceiling of elegant Arts Building foyer.

RUTHERFORD HOUSE • 1911

Home of First Premier

11153 Saskatchewan Drive

DWARFED by the grey monoliths of modern architecture, Rutherford House seems at odds with its surroundings. Ironically the home of Alberta's first premier—Alexander Cameron Rutherford, both belies and belongs.

The three-storey house visually contradicts its companion buildings. Yet its historic roots here are much deeper than those of its neighbors, thriving as a historical and physical rejoinder of the beginnings of the university and this province.

Rutherford purchased a 1.25-acre parcel from southside pioneer Lawrence Garneau in 1909, and had the house built for $25,000 in 1911 by Strathcona contractor Thomas Richards. The bricks were made from river valley clay by the now-defunct Pollard's Brickyards.

He named the house "Achnacarry" after the ancestral home of his mother's clan—the Camerons, in Scotland.

The house was designed by the firm of Arthur G. Wilson and David E. Herrald. Its style is said to be eclectic, incorporating many styles—the most predominate is Jacobethan Revival—popular in Rutherford's home province of Ontario at that time. Yet there is a Georgian style pillared balcony at the front, and the windows are said to be Palladian Style, generally recognized as an architectural symbol of the British Empire.

Achnacarry's central theme was ample room for entertainment befitting a Premier. The large oak-panelled central hall and foyer with rooms emanating on either side is influenced by British architecture.

The impressive stairway splits into two wings and is lighted by a stained glass skylight. Ceilings are 11 feet high, most wood panelling is fir except for the central staircase and foyer, and flooring in public portions of the house is maple, while fir is found in the private rooms.

When built it had the most up-to-date conveniences of its time—a telephone, central steam heating with a coal-fired boiler, electrical outlets in every room, interior toilet and lighted walk-in closets.

The main floor includes a 350-foot formal dining room, Rutherford's library, a drawing room, a den, breakfast room, kitchen and pantry area.

Upstairs there are three family bedrooms, a guest room, a crafts area which was used by Rutherford's wife Mattie, maid's quarters, a bathroom and a water closet.

The Rutherford family lived in Achnacarry from 1911 to 1940. A daughter—Hazel, was married in the drawing room in 1919, and Mattie died here in 1940.

Many large gatherings were held here. Rutherford sponsored tea parties for university graduates right up until 1938 when 500 were said to have attended. The same year 200 guests attended the Rutherford's golden wedding anniversary.

Restoration began in 1971, and the house opened as a public museum and historic site in 1973. It was officially opened a year later. It received Provincial Historical Resource designation in 1979—the highest level of protection under provincial legislation. ∎

ASSINIBOIA HALL • 1912

Housed Offices of First President

89 Avenue & 114 Street

ASSINIBOIA is the northernmost of the three almost identical early university buildings, the others being Athabasca and Pembina Halls.

All of the buildings are U-shaped with four levels, three above grade. They have crenellated roof lines, and a buttressed front entrance.

Alas, beyond the Jacobethan Revival Style facade and its arched entry-way with bevelled glass doors and spindled transom, nothing remains of the genteel traditional decor in Assiniboia. Instead of wooden trim, fireplaces, and other heartwarming appointments, bright modern offices accommodate various university departments. University officials agree that due to its remodelling, it is in very good shape.

Like its comrades, Assiniboia was first built as an all-purpose building in 1912. For most of its history, Assiniboia functioned as a student residence, with all the attendant sufferings, pleasures and hijinks. Prior to its closure for renovation in 1978, the building housed the department of English.

Assiniboia was built by the provincial department of public works. It is reported that 100 men with shovels, horses and wagons excavated Assiniboia's basement. The granite base was laid in April and the building was partially occupied in October of that year.

In 1913 it housed the offices of university president Henry Marshall Tory, as well as those of the registrar, and bursar, the university library, and the extension department. The second and third floors were devoted to accommodations for married staff, the south wing for lecture rooms and laboratories, and the north wing for student accommodations.

Portrait of Alberta's first premier hangs in his library in Rutherford House.

R.K. Gordon described the flavor of the early life and times in Assiniboia Hall from 1913 to 1919 in a 1946 article published in *New Trail*, the university's alumni magazine. Gordon noted that the staff corridor was not at all times an abode of scholarly peace:

"From a room in the east end came long drawn mournful strains from C.A. Robb's clarinet. In a neighboring room A.L. Burt of the history department had found space for a piano by shoving his desk of drawers into a cupboard. He was a masterful player with a preference for a resounding marche militaire. To its soul-animating thunders Douglas Killam, who was going to be married in the spring of 1914, rehearsed a triumphant wedding march down the corridor, after which he would dance Turkey in the Straw."

With the completion of the Arts Building in 1915, it functioned solely as a residence, and Gordon wrote that it was quite empty, for many students had enlisted for service in the First World War.

Nurses lived in the north wing for awhile, and in 1916 the Alberta Company of the Western Universities Battalion (196th) moved into the south wing before departing overseas. When the 196th departed, their space was taken by the Red Deer Ladies College, who Gordon noted, filled the air with the sound of piano practicing. Between the wars it became a student residence for men only. ■

Athabasca Hall. Renovated residence now houses chancellor's offices.

ATHABASCA HALL • 1911

New Interior Rejuvenates Hall
89 Avenue & 114 Street

SAVE FOR old St. Stephen's College, in 1911 all of the University of Alberta could be found in Athabasca Hall.

While the three-storey building retains its original brick and sandstone exterior, most of the interior was given a new look in 1976. The 47,500-square-foot building now houses the chancellor's office, as well as various university services.

When it opened, Athabasca Hall was located in a virtual wilderness. It contained accommodation for 50 students, seven classrooms, five laboratories, a library, administrative offices, a gymnasium, a dining room and a kitchen.

The Jacobethan Revival style building was designed by provincial architect Allan Merrick Jeffers from recommendations made by Professor Percy Nobbs of McGill University. Jeffers also worked on the Legislature Building, Government House and the Civic Block.

Life at Athabasca Hall in its early days was not without its high points. One of these included the daily formal dinner, complete with a Latin grace recital by the building provost.

During the Second World War, Athabasca Hall was used by the Royal Canadian Air Force as a training school. It became a residence after the war, serving this purpose until 1971 when it was deemed unsafe.

In 1976, a crane removed the roof and the interior was gutted. Inside the brick walls, a modern building was installed, retaining some facets of the original. Total cost of the renovation was about $2 million. ■

PEMBINA HALL • 1914

Residence Upgraded
89 Avenue & 114 Street

CECIL SCOTT BURGESS would have been proud. When the University of Alberta contemplated the demise of Assiniboia Hall, Athabasca Hall and Pembina Hall—only Pembina seemed solid enough to save. On-site architect, Burgess, insisted that the interior structural framework be of steel and concrete.

Pembina's 1975 upgrading cost was $800,000, considerably less than the $2 million for Athabasca and $3 million for Assiniboia, both originally built with wood frame interiors. Under the direction of Bittorf, Holland, Christianson Architects, Pembina's woodwork was restored and new wiring, ventilation and plumbing systems installed. The pains to retain the building's character are reflected throughout, and resulted in an award for restoration from Heritage Canada.

Space was at a premium when Pembina was begun in 1913. Student nurses were moved into the south wing in 1914, a year before the building was finished. Upon completion, Pembina also had 20 classrooms, along with offices and the "stiff" lab— otherwise known as the anatomy laboratory—in the north wing. Pembina served as an all-purpose building until 1919, when it was converted into a women's residence. The same year, Pembina became a temporary hospital for victims of influenza—80 people died in Pembina before the epidemic passed.

From 1941 to 1945, the building was requisitioned as headquarters for the RCAF's No. 4 Initial Training School. In typical forces fashion, a wall was demolished and a bar installed. ■

ST. JOSEPH'S COLLEGE • 1926

Catholic Education Centre
89 Avenue & 114 Street

THE BUILDING of St. Joseph's College as an affiliate of the University of Alberta in 1926, represented a triumph for the Roman Catholic Church. After struggling for many years to raise the necessary funding, the construction of the college established a beachhead for the church in its quest to provide higher Catholic education in the west.

In the 1980s, the college, which is owned by the Catholic Archdiocese of Edmonton, continued to fulfil its original role as a residence for university students, as a teaching centre, and as centre of the Catholic campus ministry.

About 1,500 students received instruction in Catholic history, ethics, scripture, thought and doctrine this academic year. Courses are recognized as university credits.

The four-storey building features a Jacobethan design with a 300-seat Gothic style chapel on the southwest wing. The structure was designed by city architect Edward Underwood, who also served on the executive committee of the college's fundraising foundation. Other examples of Underwood's work include the Archbishop's residence south of St. Joseph's Cathedral, St. Albert Church and St. Alphonsus and Mt. Carmel Schools.

The brick and Tyndal stone facade features three sets of triple-stacked bay windows. The roof line features stone finials, triangular gables, and a cross over the peak. Ionic pilasters flank the main entrance.

In a 1986 interview, college rector Father P.W. Platt said the building was in good structural condition. "It is a remarkable construction for its time, considering its flexibility for making offices and open areas," he said.

Its flexibility has made for many changes

over the years—most of them in the 1960s. In fact, little remains of the original interior, save for the student residences which have been heavily painted over. Classrooms have been renovated and fire exits added. The original gymnasium has been converted into a library and the original library is now a faculty lounge.

Built for $212,401.03, the college building is now insured for $5 million. When its original organizer, Reverend John MacDonald, withdrew, Archbishop Henry O'Leary commissioned Brother Alfred of the Christian Brothers to continue fundraising efforts.

The Carnegie Corporation of New York had granted the college $100,000, providing an equal amount could also be raised. Brother Alfred raised the remainder of the money from the parishes and towns of Alberta.

Prominent Albertans, including men of other denominations supported the fundraising campaign. Some of the college's patrons were then premier Herbert Greenfield, university president Henry Marshall Tory and Reverend D.G. McQueen of the First Presbyterian Church.

While some could surmount religious differences, others could not. Tory received at least one critical letter, signed only as ''not a pseudo-Protestant.''

Its kinder remarks included: ''We did not know you were a Papist till reading in *The Journal* of your heartiness to the proposed campaign for the erection of a Popish college in proximity to the university and you have with traitors now McQueen besides all those hypocrites who pose to be Protestants one day and next day Roman toe kissers.''

The first college rector was Brother Rogatian. The Christian Brothers, who administered the college until 1963 when the Basilian Fathers took over, contributed much to the university. ∎

Ionic pilasters flank entrance of St. Joseph's College.

Above: Chapel of St. Joseph's College.
Left: Pembina Hall.

125

DENTAL PHARMACY BLDG. • 1921

Classical Features Highlight Facade
89 Avenue & 112 Street

AMIDST CRASS behemoths masquerading as architecture, the imposing facade of the Dental Pharmacy Building is a classical rejoinder of fine design.

Alas, function and form were no longer equal partners when the University of Alberta built four additions to the original building after the Second World War. The additions, while providing highly-sought facilities, were mercifully hidden behind the front of the building. While built of similar materials, they are distinctive only in their unremarkability.

Finished in Redcliffe brick and Tyndal stone, the building's English Renaissance Revival style of architecture is distinguished by the central cupola, pilasters, and the finialed roof line. When completed in 1921, the well-proportioned university edifice was called the Medical Sciences Building, first home of the faculty of medicine. It was then U-shaped with east and west wings extending half as far as present.

The structure was designed by the Montreal architectural firm of Percy Nobbs and George Hyde, in conjunction with university staff architect Cecil Burgess.

Now in the shape of an enclosed E, there are two central courtyards devoted to parking and a seven-storey north wing towering over the remainder of the four-storey building. It is home to budding dentists and the shrill cries of some of their patients as they hone their skills on the parsimonious.

Other departments include pharmacology and the Edmonton Radiopharmaceutical Society, which manufactures radio-active drugs for city hospitals with the aid of a $300,000 nuclear reactor encased in the basement.

Besides the enchanting facade, its original features do not extend much past its magnificent foyer, with an oak and leaded glass vestibule with built-in clock, ceramic tile flooring, marble stairs, barrel-vaulted ceiling with plaster indentations and terracotta tile walls.

University building officials have called the structure one of the soundest on campus. The building will be maintained but a future renovation will update the ventilation and heating system.

When first built, the building doubled the available instructional space on campus. It housed the faculty of medicine, of which dentistry was then a part, the provincial laboratory and all the science classes. Its facilities included twin lecture theatres flanking the entrance as well as classrooms, laboratories and offices. The faculty of medicine moved out in various stages to newer buildings from 1968 to 1973, and the space was absorbed by dentistry and pharmacy.

The seven-storey north wing was built in 1961, while the east, west and central wings were constructed from 1946 to 1951. Alberta Culture has noted that if a historic designation tag were applied, it would only cover the original classically-inspired building. ■

Dental Pharmacy medical library, 1929.

OLD ST. STEPHEN'S COLLEGE • 1911

First University Building
8820-112 Street

IT IS SAID that William Aberhart was born again as a disciple of Social Credit within the hallowed halls of Old St. Stephen's College. The future premier of Alberta was in his room at the college in 1932, where he was staying while marking examination papers. Aberhart's ear was bent by fellow teacher Charles Scarborough, who insisted Aberhart read a book on the meaning of Social Credit. The book, *Employment or War*, by Maurice Colbourne, was a popularized version of the theories of Major Clifford H. Douglas, a Scottish engineer.

Thus began the rise of Social Credit which was to rule Alberta for 36 years. All this and more in a building twice threatened with demolition in the 1970s to make way for a parking lot.

The five-storey T-shaped red brick structure, built in 1910, was the first completed building at the University of Alberta. Its facade is now largely obscured by trees, but its twin octagonal turrets, distinguished roof line and crenellated parapets are still visible.

The building now houses offices and laboratories for Alberta Culture's Historical Resources Division and its archaeological services branch. It was designated a Provincial Historical Resource in 1983.

The design is "eclectic" and springs from the English Collegiate Gothic Style based largely on English Tudor Style precedents such as Trinity College at Cambridge University and St. James Place in London. Designed by Edmonton architect H.A. Magoon, the college was built for $130,000.

It was first known as Alberta College South. Its role was that of a theological learning centre as well as a dormitory with dining and recreation facilities, meant to serve the needs of both the university and the Methodists.

The site was part of land assembled by the department of education for the university. Known as River Lot Five, it cost $150,000 in 1907. A portion was leased to the Methodists for 99 years.

The building features a five-storey centre, four-storey north and south wings, and a three-storey west wing. Two more storeys, complete with dormer windows, were added to the west wing in 1912. A chapel, noted for its stained glass windows, was added to the main floor in 1935.

From 1917 to 1920, other quarters were used by the college as the building became a convalescent hospital for soldiers wounded in the First World War. At that time tube fire escapes were added to the end of each wing. Students later used the tubes to initiate freshmen. The unlucky souls were dumped down the tubes and followed up by buckets of ice cold water as they slid past every floor.

Even faculty members were not immune to such stunts. One morning after Halloween, principal Riddell arrived to find his buggy perched precariously on one of the college's towers.

In 1925, when the Methodist and Presbyterian churches joined to form the United Church of Canada, the name was changed from Alberta College South to United Theological College. It was renamed St. Stephen's in 1927. ■

Above: Dental Pharmacy Building with classically styled facade.
Right: Old St. Stephen's College featuring towers.

Aerial view of University and Garneau community.

EMILY MURPHY HOUSE • 1912

Home of Social Activist
11011-88 Avenue

THIS BROWN and white Garneau two-storey isn't distinguished by its architecture, as much as by the social contributions of a former owner. This is where Alberta social activist and suffragette Emily Murphy lived until her death.

With the exception of the brass plaque on the house front commemorating the home's one time resident, Emily Murphy House appears at first sight to be an unremarkable older house.

Though designated a Provincial Historical Resource in 1977—Emily Murphy House was awarded the honor chiefly because the well known Albertan lived there. Alberta Culture described its design as a frame house with a typical Arts and Crafts-influenced style of the early 20th century. It was built with materials that were neither unique or unusual.

Emily Murphy, born Emily Ferguson in Simcoe Country, Ontario in 1868, is best remembered as one of the five Alberta women who won the Persons Case. In 1929, Murphy and her four colleagues—Henriette Edwards, Nellie McClung, Louise McKinney and Irene Parlby—presented their case to the English Privy Council that women were legally "persons" and as such should be able to sit in the Canadian Senate.

Much of the preliminary planning and organizational work took place during meetings at Emily Murphy's home. Today their victory is marked with a plaque outside the doors of the Senate chamber in Ottawa. And, while it is perhaps the most famous of Emily Murphy's contributions, the Persons Case was but one accomplishment in her lifetime of social activism.

Emily Ferguson married Reverend Arthur Murphy in 1887. They moved to Edmonton in 1907. The mother of two daughters, she soon found herself active in community concerns. She joined with other community members to push for more playgrounds in Edmonton. She started a movement for medical inspection of Alberta schools. She organized the first Alberta-Saskatchewan branch of the Canadian Committee of Mental Hygiene.

Murphy advanced the registration of women for war work, was a founding member of the Edmonton Equal Franchise League and prompted women to run for political office. In 1916, Emily Murphy was named the first woman magistrate in the British Empire.

Besides her social activism, Murphy also wrote a variety of books and magazine articles under her pen name Janey Canuck. During the 1920s she campaigned ardently against narcotics, and her book, *The Black Candle*, won international acclaim for alerting the world to the phenomena of drug addiction. ■

CORBETT HALL • 1929

Named After Faculty Director
82 Avenue & 112 Street

CORBETT HALL—formerly Edmonton Normal School—is a classically designed building on the southeastern tip of the University of Alberta. Since 1929, the ornamental block and Tyndal stone edifice has served the needs of higher education, albeit with interruption.

Its lengthy devotion to academic pursuits was twice disturbed—first during the 1930s when it was closed for two years due to government fiscal restraint, then during the Second World War when No. 4 Initial Training Squadron of the Royal Canadian Air Force occupied the building.

Other than that, the building was a centre for teacher training from 1929 until a new education building was built in 1963. Since that time, Corbett Hall has been home to the faculty of extension, drama department, and faculty of rehabilitation medicine.

The east facade maintains its pristine Jacobethan Revival styling, with a projecting rotunda flanked by bay windows. Twin arched entries feature leaded glass windows above their traditional wood doors, and ornamental finials project skyward from the balustraded roof line.

Inside the hall, bits of traditional styling remain, especially in the twin foyers, and the rotunda with its ornate plaster ceiling complete with gold and white dentilled frieze. Other than the gumwood and birch doors, panelling, and woodwork, the classrooms and offices have been overhauled through the years and present a contemporary appearance.

The middle wing of the building contains an auditorium and, behind that, a gymnasium with a skylight. The gym is now divided into art studios, while the auditorium is used for drama productions.

The building is two storeys high with a

raised basement. It was designed in an E-shape with a 259-foot long facade by architects D.E. McDonald and George Heath MacDonald.

In 1945, the University of Alberta assumed responsibility for teacher training. In 1965, after the education faculty moved to its new building, the original quarters were renamed in honor of Edward Annand Corbett, director of the faculty of extension from 1928 to 1937. Corbett, who died in 1964, helped found Radio Station CKUA and the Banff School of Fine Arts. He was also the author of a

biography on Henry Marshall Tory, first president of the U of A.

The palatial Corbett Hall is home to the Faculty of Extension.

Oliver

In 1883, the Hudson's Bay Company sold several blocks of land north of the North Saskatchewan River and just west of 109th Street to the Oblate Fathers of Mary Immaculate and the Grey Nuns to build their church and hospital, and settle their people. After the completion of St. Joachim's Church in 1898, the community later to be known as Oliver began to emerge and develop a distinctly Francophone character. Bylaws assured that the community west of 109th Street would remain residential.

A West End Community League was organized in 1922, and in 1937 it was re-named the Oliver Community League in honour of the former Edmonton M.P. and Minister of The Interior, Frank Oliver. He had never lived in the community, but had given his name to the Oliver School on 117th Street. Elements of the original Francophone character of the neighborhood still remain in St. Joachim's Church and LeMarchand Mansion, and in the homes of A.V. Bouillon, P.E. Lessard and Joseph Daigenault. Other non-Francophone landmarks to appear in later years were mainly churches such as the Wesley Methodist Sunday School and St. Joseph's Basilica, and schools such as Oliver and Grandin.

GRANDIN SCHOOL • 1914

Eclectic Style for Bilingual School
9844-110 Street

IN THE SUMMER of 1914, John Cormack got out of bed each day and headed for "work" right next door to his house. There was a school to be built and John, then four years old and now a retired judge, was determined to help speed up the process.

The object of his dedication was Grandin School, named for Bishop Vital Grandin. And even with John's help, it still took a year to build.

Edmonton Catholic school trustees acquired six lots from Bishop Grandin, added five more and then voted to have the school face 111th Street. But soil tests showed the east side of the site had better supporting quality so it was built facing 110th Street.

The brick three-storey school has an arched entrance. Its eclectic style is based on classical English Renaissance motifs. A number of progressive ideas went into the design of Grandin, including pipes in the walls for intercom phones and vacuum cleaning.

The original school had 10 classrooms when it opened—and no school office. "I guess they didn't need one in those days," mused principal Dennis Landreville in a 1986 interview.

The halls are 15 feet wide—certainly tempting for kids of any age to use as a playing field for any number of games—and the gymnasium was probably downstairs on the lower floor. The blackboards were built up a step from the rest of the classroom and each classroom had its own cloakroom.

The original reserve tank for hot water was in use until recently when it was replaced by a modern hot water heater. The original two boilers are still there, but they haven't been used in several years. Two additions—one in 1954, the other in 1962—saw eight more classrooms and a gymnasium added.

1. Grandin School
2. St. Joachim School
3. St. Joseph Basilica
4. LeMarchand Mansion
5. Wesley Sunday School
6. Oliver School
7. Christ Church

Grandin has been a French-immersion school since the early 1970s, but Landreville said it has always been bilingual. "The first school register shows there were English classes and French classes," he said. "In the 1940s and 1950s, those that wanted to take French had to study during the noon hour and recess."

A number of notable people attended Grandin. They included John Ducey, Edmonton's Mr. Baseball; Red McCarthy, who later became an international ice show celebrity; Murray Murdock, who became a hockey player with the New York Rangers; and Cecilia Chochen, who became a top tennis player. And Walter Benn, the school's first assistant principal, led the school system's first teacher's strike in 1919.

An elementary school for the last seven years, Grandin was also a junior high school for most of its history. ∎

Grandin School was named after Bishop Vital Grandin.

ST. JOACHIM CHURCH • 1899

City's Oldest Catholic Church
9920-110 Street

YOU DON'T have to be a believer to feel a certain reverence in St. Joachim Church, one of Edmonton's oldest buildings. A sense of awe is triggered by the subtle yet majestic Old World sights and smells of this Provincial Historical Resource built in 1899.

The smell of aging wood and prayer books combined with the arched fir ceiling, elaborate woodwork, religious icons, and sculptured altars could overwhelm even the most hardened atheist.

St. Joachim is Edmonton's oldest Roman Catholic church. It was constructed of red brick with a 120-foot high central tower and flanking pinacles. Other features include a galvanized steel roof, a 31-foot high arched ceiling, arched stained glass windows, and imported Italian marble and plaster altars with built-in electrical lighting. There is a carved octagonal oak pulpit with a base that tapers to a diameter of eight inches. A sacristy was added in 1912.

The 500-seat treasure remains much the same as when it was built for $15,000. Reverend Father Maurice Beauregard estimated its value at more than $2 million in 1986, with the three altars alone accounting for half that amount.

Beauregard said that the details make the church a magnificent setting for a wedding—''when they play the bass on the pipe organ, the windows shake.'' Creaky wooden steps lead to the original pipe organ in the choir loft, which affords a commanding view of the sanctuary and altar.

Patterned after Quebecois-style churches of the 19th century, St. Joachim is Edmonton's historical link with the colonization and missionary efforts of the order of Oblates of Mary Immaculate in Western Canada. As the Oblate's city beachhead, it is the mother church of all Edmonton Catholic parishes.

For this reason, there was no negative response to its historical designation by Alberta Culture in 1978.

St. Joachim's roots date back to 1854 when the parish was started by the legendary Father Albert Lacombe inside the confines of Fort Edmonton. The parish moved outside the fort some 22 years later when a church was built on Stony Plain Road between 121st and 123rd Streets. Another church, a white frame structure, was built in 1886, near the site of the present building.

When the current St. Joachim opened, Edmonton's Catholic population was largely French, Metis or Native, but when the city experienced its economic boom prior to the First World War, the size of the English-speaking congregation grew correspondingly.

As a result St. Joachim served both French and English-speaking congregations until after the First World War when Archbishop Henry Joseph O'Leary commissioned St. Joseph's Cathedral for English-speaking Catholics.

St. Joachim was the centre of a Catholic enclave which included the first Misericordia Hospital, a convent, seminary and a Catholic school. Only the church and Grandin School remain. ■

Right: Stained glass window in St. Joseph's Basilica.
Opposite page: Exterior and interior of St. Joachim, Edmonton's oldest Roman Catholic Church.

ST. JOSEPH'S BASILICA • 1925

Prize Place of Worship
10044-113 Street

THE BASEMENT of St. Joseph's Basilica was one of Edmonton's first English-speaking Catholic churches. Built in 1925, the basement served as the cathedral for 38 years, though that wasn't the original idea. Through the Depression, the Second World War and the early years of Edmonton's post-war economic boom, parishioners worshipped in the unimpressive crypt church.

Not until the early 1960s did Archbishop Henry Joseph O'Leary's dream of an impressive Gothic Style cathedral come to fruition. O'Leary, the city's first anglophone archbishop did not live to see the awesome structure officially opened—fittingly enough on May 1, 1963, the Feast of St. Joseph the Worker.

The building is the first designated basilica west of Manitoba. It was so named in honor of the 1984 visit of Pope John Paul II.

St. Joseph's began as an outgrowth of the heavy population influx into the city during the years prior to the First World War. Archbishop Emil Legal formed St. Joseph's parish in 1917, but church-goers used the facilities of St. Joachim's Church until 1925. At that time, O'Leary designated St. Joseph's as his cathedral church—meaning throne of the archbishop.

The land was purchased in 1924 and church plans were designed by Frank Underwood. The crypt church was opened on March 19, 1925—feast day of St. Joseph, husband of the Virgin Mary. Elaborate plans were designed for a Gothic cathedral to be built on top, but funds were not forthcoming.

A building fund established in the 1940s provided the impetus for the cathedral's completion. But due to the basement's erection on a former swamp, the foundation walls had to be reinforced and the floor underpinned to carry the present-day structure's great weight.

The finished building was designed by Montreal architect Henri Labelle, who noted that its architecture ''will be contemporary, but will preserve a distinct note of Gothic ancestry.'' Edmonton architect Eugene Olekshy was also engaged in the design.

The finished architectural masterpiece incorporated $300,000 of stained glass windows and $15,000 of gold inlaid Stations of the Cross, all imported from Germany. Oak woodwork is from eastern Canada, a pipe organ from Casavant Frères of Quebec, and a 1,500-pound gold tabernacle from Dublin, Ireland. The cathedral is finished in Tyndal stone as was the crypt.

A fire set by an arsonist in 1980 caused about $500,000 damage. During the repairs, parishioners retreated to the original basement church. The basilica is now closed at nights and sophisticated electronic surveillance detectors have been installed to guard Edmonton Catholics' prize place of worship.

St. Joseph's has been called more than just a place of worship. Its classic lines and interior decor make it a piece of art erected to the glory of God. ■

The grandeur of St. Joseph's Gothic-influenced interior.

St. Joseph's Basilica is the first designated basilica west of Manitoba.

LeMarchand Mansion reflects Old World charm and elegance.

Stained glass panel dominates the foyer in LeMarchand Mansion.

LeMARCHAND MANSION • 1911

A Touch of Paris in Edmonton
11523-100 Avenue

RENE LeMARCHAND wanted to make a lasting contribution. His vision was an apartment complex which would reflect the cosmopolitan luxury of Paris and London, one which would take advantage of this city's most endearing natural feature—the lush and meandering North Saskatchewan River valley.

LeMarchand came to Edmonton from Paris in 1905. Already in his late 50s, LeMarchand had saved a sizeable sum in an extraordinary way. For years he worked as a butler to a Parisian gentleman who insisted on using a new razor blade just once. This was at a time when most men would own but three or four blades in a lifetime. Upon his employer's death, LeMarchand was bequeathed the collection of once-used razor blades which he immediately sold. Those funds and the investment he secured from the Union Garçons de Café (Paris Waiter's Union) provided the financial foundation for his Edmonton building.

In 1906 and 1907 he assembled the land for about $4,300. The building was designed by Alfred Marigon Calderon. Construction began in 1909 and the building was completed in 1911. Estimates of its cost range from between $140,000 and $200,000.

For rents of $40 to $100 a month, tenants could live in the city's first natural gas heated building. Since natural gas wasn't yet available, LeMarchand built a coal degasifer plant on site. Tenants used one of the first elevators installed in the city, enjoyed spacious five to seven-room suites that boasted at least one fireplace if not two, and enjoyed the natural light provided by the window found in every room of the suite. This was an uncommon touch, for most apartments of the time used lighting shafts to brighten interior rooms.

And of course there was the building's style—Beaux-Arts, a French classical architecture popular in France at the turn of the century, featuring recessed entranceways with towering columns and triangular pediments on top of the columns.

Alberta Culture has noted that the combination of style and use of materials in the mansion is unique to Edmonton and possibly all of Alberta. Through its imposing stature, luxurious design features and elaborate architecture, it is a striking symbol of the spirited economy of the boomtown era. Its style reflects the French heritage of the community and is a good example of Late Victorian, French classical influence.

LeMarchand is said to have returned to Paris about 1916. He maintained his interest in the building until his death in 1921. The Montreal Trust Company took title in 1923 as administrators of LeMarchand's estate.

The building remained in the hands of LeMarchand's estate until 1949. That year it sold for $150,000 and passed through numerous hands in the years to come. Although some suites remained until 1977, many of the lower floor apartments were converted to offices following the Second World War.

Restored in 1977 at a cost of $4.5 million, it once more reflects the elegance of Old World style in this prairie oasis. During the renovation, the mansion's interior was restructured, but its former elegance had returned. The doors feature elaborately-designed bevelled glass. The foyer has marble flooring, a brass-hooded fireplace surrounded by oak-panelled walls and a large stained glass panel dominates the ceiling. The refurbished corridors continue the charm with oak panelling, hardwood oak floors, wool carpets and brass fixtures.

Designated a Provincial Historical Resource on July 13, 1977, the red brick LeMarchand Mansion continues to command architectural attention and aesthetic appreciation. ■

WESLEY SUNDAY SCHOOL • 1915

Former Sunday School Home to Natives
10176-117 Street

THE BUILDING is showing signs of its age and a 1979 fire. It has been home to the Canadian Native Friendship Centre since 1971—a non-profit society dedicated to elevating the life style of the urban Indian.

Buildings of this vintage usually identify their function by their form, but the casual passerby may be excused for confusion at this structure, possibly construed as a Tudor manor with ecclesiastical touches. Close examination reveals its original use. The title Wesley Sunday School, etched into a stone slab, is discernible above the former main entrance.

In 1912, a group of church elders purchased the property at 117th Street and 102nd Avenue from The Governor and Company of Adventurers of England Trading into Hudson's Bay. In the 1980's that firm was known simply as The Bay.

The group included such prominent citizens as William John Magrath. Land titles records the property's worth at $6,025. The Wesley Methodist Sunday School, which opened in 1913, cost $40,000 and seated 600.

Built of Redcliffe brick with a wood shingle roof, the two-storey building had an auditorium with U-shaped gallery and a raised platform in the centre built from timbers of the original church.

Alberta Culture has called the design a modest version of the Late Gothic Revival Style. Design characteristics include a less complicated roof line than High Victorian Gothic designs, more simplified applied ornamentation, smoother wall surfaces and less emphatic vertical thrust than in other Gothic Revival Styles.

Originally intended as a Sunday School, various interior changes were made to beautify the building for use as a church—a role it performed until the end of 1970. ■

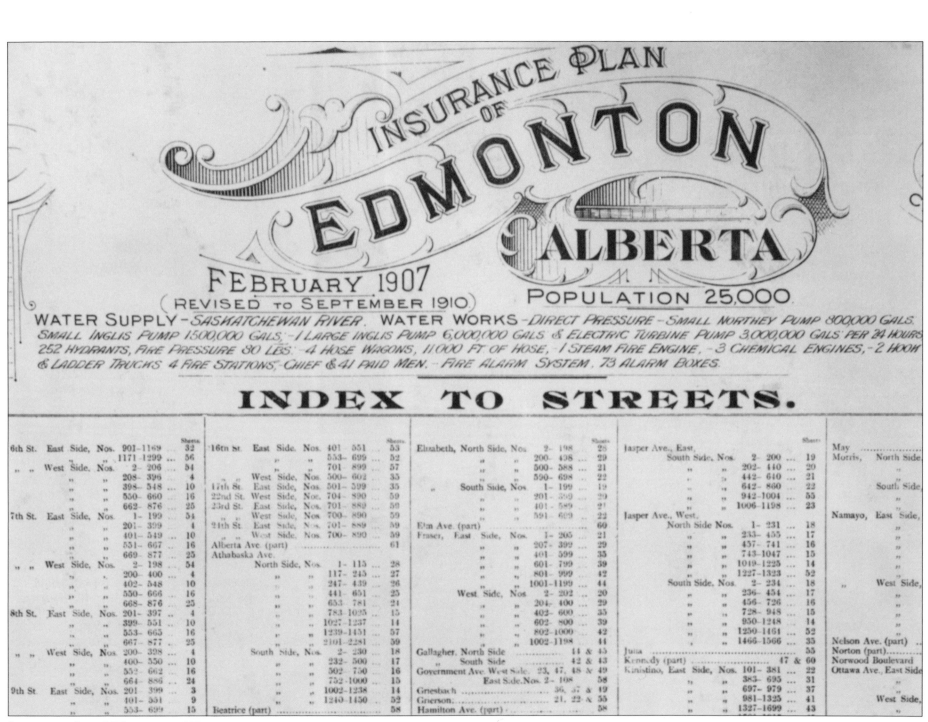

INSURANCE PLAN OF EDMONTON ALBERTA

FEBRUARY 1907 (REVISED TO SEPTEMBER 1910)

POPULATION 25,000

WATER SUPPLY - *SASKATCHEWAN RIVER*. WATER WORKS - *DIRECT PRESSURE - SMALL NORTHEY PUMP 800,000 GALS. SMALL INGLIS PUMP 1,500,000 GALS; - 1 LARGE INGLIS PUMP 6,000,000 GALS & ELECTRIC TURBINE PUMP 3,000,000 GALS PER 24 HOURS. 252 HYDRANTS, FIRE PRESSURE 80 LBS; - 4 HOSE WAGONS, 11,000 FT. OF HOSE, 1 STEAM FIRE ENGINE, - 3 CHEMICAL ENGINES, - 2 HOOK & LADDER TRUCKS, 4 FIRE STATIONS, - CHIEF & 41 PAID MEN. - FIRE ALARM SYSTEM, 73 ALARM BOXES.*

INDEX TO STREETS.

			Sheets
6th St.	East Side, Nos.	901–1169	32
" "		1171–1299	56
" "	West Side, Nos.	2– 206	54
" "		208– 396	4
" "		398– 548	10
" "		550– 660	16
" "		662– 876	25
7th St.	East Side, Nos.	1– 199	54
" "		201– 399	4
" "		401– 549	10
" "		551– 667	16
" "		669– 877	25
" "	West Side, Nos.	2– 198	54
" "		200– 400	4
" "		402– 548	10
" "		550– 666	16
" "		668– 876	25
8th St.	East Side, Nos.	201– 397	4
" "		399– 551	10
" "		553– 665	16
" "		667– 877	25
" "	West Side, Nos.	200– 398	4
" "		400– 550	10
" "		552– 662	16
" "		664– 886	24
9th St.	East Side, Nos.	201– 399	3
" "		401– 551	9
" "		553– 699	15

			Sheets
16th St.	East Side, Nos.	401– 551	53
"		553– 699	52
"		701– 899	57
"	West Side, Nos.	500– 602	35
17th St.	East Side, Nos.	501– 599	35
22nd St.	West Side, Nos.	704– 890	59
23rd St.	East Side, Nos.	701– 889	59
"	West Side, Nos.	700– 890	59
24th St.	East Side, Nos.	701– 889	59
"	West Side, Nos.	700– 890	59
Alberta Ave. (part)			61
Athabaska Ave.	North Side, Nos.	1– 115	28
"		117– 245	27
"		247– 439	26
"		441– 651	25
"		653– 781	24
"		783–1025	15
"		1027–1237	14
"		1239–1451	57
"		2101–2281	59
"	South Side, Nos.	2– 230	18
"		232– 500	17
"		502– 750	16
"		752–1000	15
"		1002–1238	14
"		1240–1450	52
Beatrice (part)			58

			Sheets
Elizabeth, North Side, Nos.		2– 198	28
"	"	200– 438	29
"	"	500– 588	21
"	"	590– 698	22
"	South Side, Nos.	1– 199	19
"	"	201– 399	29
"	"	401– 589	21
"	"	591– 699	22
Elm Ave. (part)			60
Fraser, East Side, Nos.		1– 205	21
"	"	207– 399	29
"	"	401– 599	35
"	"	601– 799	39
"	"	801– 999	42
"	"	1001–1199	44
"	West Side, Nos.	2– 202	20
"	"	204– 400	29
"	"	402– 600	35
"	"	602– 800	39
"	"	802–1000	42
"	"	1002–1198	44
Gallagher, North Side			44 & 45
"	South Side		42 & 43
Government Ave. West Side.		23, 47, 48 & 49	
"	East Side. Nos.	2– 198	58
Griesbach			36, 37 & 49
Grierson			21, 22 & 55
Hamilton Ave. (part)			58

			Sheets
Jasper Ave., East,			
"	South Side, Nos.	2– 200	19
"	"	202– 440	20
"	"	442– 640	21
"	"	642– 860	22
"	"	942–1004	55
"	"	1006–1198	23
Jasper Ave., West.			
"	North Side Nos.	1– 231	18
"	"	233– 455	17
"	"	457– 741	16
"	"	743–1047	15
"	"	1049–1225	14
"	"	1227–1323	52
"	South Side, Nos.	2– 234	18
"	"	236– 454	17
"	"	456– 726	16
"	"	728– 948	15
"	"	950–1248	14
"	"	1250–1464	52
"	"	1466–1566	35
Julia			55
Kennedy (part)			47 & 60
Kinistino, East Side, Nos.		101– 381	22
"	"	385– 695	31
"	"	697– 979	37
"	"	981–1325	41
"	"	1327–1699	43

May	
Morris,	North Side
	South Side
Namayo,	East Side
	West Side
Nelson Ave. (part)	
Norton (part)	
Norwood Boulevard	
Ottawa Ave., East Side	
	West Side

Insurance plan of Edmonton, 1907.

Canadian Native Friendship Centre, formerly Wesley Sunday School.

Tudor Style Christ Church was built in 1921.

OLIVER SCHOOL • 1911

Elite Academic School
10210-117 Street

OLIVER ELEMENTARY, one of Edmonton's oldest schools, was built for $100,000 and opened in 1911. The school was named after Frank Oliver, who co-founded *The Edmonton Bulletin* in 1880 with telegraph operator Alex Taylor.

In his book *Looking Back*, a history of Edmonton public schools, EPSB archivist, Mike Kostek wrote that Oliver was noted for winning more governor general's medals than any other school. The medals were awarded for top achievement in Grade Nine

departmental examinations. In addition, Oliver held a record for staff tenure and longevity. Robina McMillan taught there from 1919 to 1962, as did Helen Raver from 1922 to 1946.

Some of Oliver's more illustrious alumni include Justice Tevie Miller of Court of Queen's Bench, city publisher and Canadian nationalist Mel Hurtig, former Alberta cabinet minister Lou Hyndman, former federal cabinet minister Judd Buchanan, marksman John Primrose, and boxer Ken Lakusta.

When Oliver opened, its 280 students enjoyed all the modern conveniences in what was then very much a rural setting. There were indoor toilets, electric lights, even a miniature rifle range.

The first principal was J.A. McGregor. His staff consisted of nine single women, since married women were not then allowed to teach. But when 25 city teachers left to serve in the First World War, and four paid the supreme sacrifice, a teacher shortage prompted the board to bend its rules and married women were temporarily hired. One of them was Grace Martin McEachern, who celebrated her 107th birthday in 1987. Grace Martin School in Mill Woods was named in her honor.

A west wing addition was built in 1928 at a cost of $136,000 and served elementary students, while junior high pupils were housed in the original building. The school continued to offer junior high classes until

1979, when declining enrolment forced abandonment of the program. Enrolment peaked at more than 700 in the 1950s and a gymnasium was built in 1957. The number of students reached a low of 130 in the early 1980s. By 1987 there were about 200 students.

The school, designed by public school board building commissioner George Turner, has distinctive elements of the Jacobethan Revival architectural style, popular in educational architecture around the turn of the century.

The design, compounded from Jacobean and Elizabethan styles, combined elements of both periods, which in themselves are often difficult to distinguish between. Styling characteristics include steep-sided triangular gables, tall chimneys, brick and stone facing materials, quoins, ornaments and rectangular windows.

When the school was built, *The Bulletin* said: "Externally the design of the building is well-proportioned and with its grouped windows and battlemented and buttressed entrance porches will prove a handsome addition to the public buildings of our city." ∎

Opposite page: School day at Oliver elementary.

CHRIST CHURCH • 1921

West Edmonton Anglican Church
12116-102 Avenue

THE QUAINT Tudor Style church in the Oliver community looks as if time has passed it by.

Built in 1921, Christ Church seems a lonesome survivor in an area now dominated by apartment and office buildings. Many of the single-family homes which once surrounded the Anglican church have tumbled in the face of urban pressures.

The church is finished in white stucco with a red asphalt tile roof. Matching buildings contain the parish hall, offices and a rectory.

The church's present low profile belies the stature of some of its parishioners. They included its architect, William Blakey, and H.M.E. Evans, the former city mayor and financier who was the logical choice to spearhead the church's building drive.

The parish was actually started in 1909 by members of the Anglican church in west Edmonton. At that time, west Edmonton was anywhere west of 109th Street. It is said that few civilized folk would venture that far because most of the area was still bush and farm land. However, the provincial government had just purchased land further west to construct the official residence for the lieutenant governor and plans for the affluent Glenora suburb were under way.

The parish purchased two lots from the Hudson's Bay Company in 1909 and a plain wood frame church was built at 116th Street and 102nd Avenue.

The diamond jubilee history of Christ Church notes that "the records impress one with the faith, courage, and resourcefulness of the members of the first Christ Church, for at that time there were more blocks of woods than blocks of homes within the boundaries of the parish."

The first rector was Reverend John Robinson. In 1921, with the old building outliving its usefulness, the parish built the present structure, when Reverend J.M. Comyn Ching was rector. At that time, the land was being used as a skating rink and tennis court.

"With a high board fence around the grounds and a shabby clubhouse on the northeast corner, it required great imagination to picture what our new rector could see," the historical account notes. The clubhouse was refurbished as a rectory, although a new rectory was built in the 1930s. The parish hall was built in 1925.

The first service in the new church was held October 9, 1921. In 1985 the building— including its fixtures, stained glass windows and the Casavant Frères organ—was valued at almost $600,000. The parish hall was said to be worth another $455,000 and the rectory more than $90,000.

Features of the church include dormer windows and a two-storey open beam roof featuring dark stained Douglas Fir with ceiling fans and hanging light fixtures. Various stained glass windows were added in later years as dedications by parishioners.

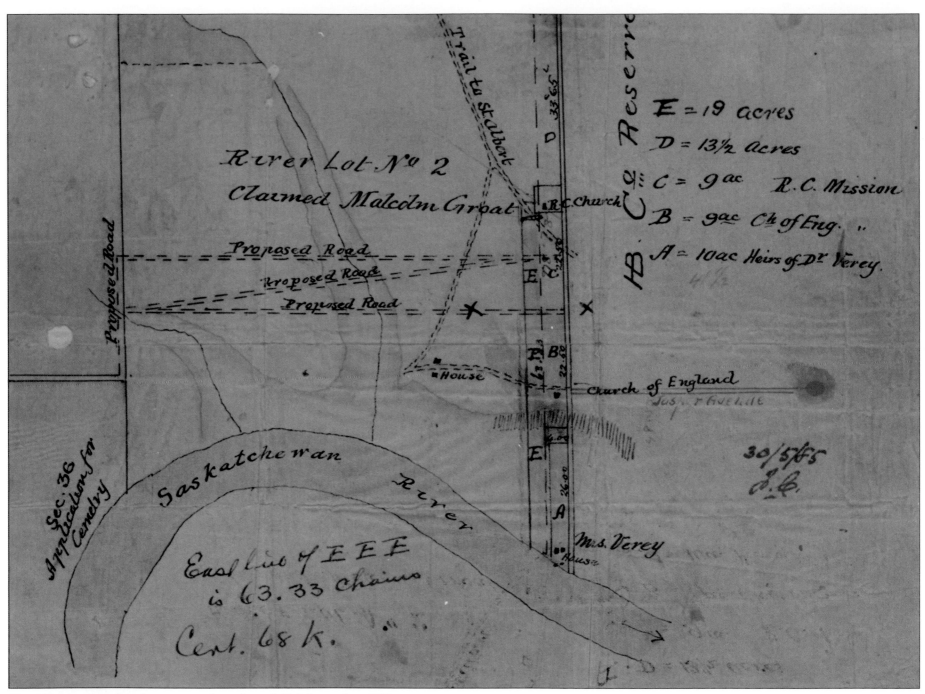

Groat Estate map showing proposed roads and divisions, circa 1885.

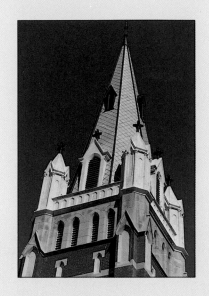

Groat Estate

In 1870, the land between 121st and 142nd Streets north of the North Saskatchewan River was acquired from the federal government by Malcolm Groat. Sporadic settlement, including Groat's farm, occurred there over the next 40 years. However, the area known as Groat Estate, and especially the ravine, was used mainly for recreational purposes. In 1908, the area west of 124th Street was acquired and subdivided by the Montreal entrepeneur James Carruthers, who was intent upon turning it into an exclusive upper class neighborhood for the burgeoning metropolis of Edmonton. Carruthers financed a bridge across the ravine, brought an extension of the Edmonton Street Railway to the area, and placed a caveat on the properties, thereby ensuring only homes of certain value would be built.

In 1909, Carruthers sold the point of land west of the ravine and south of 102nd Avenue for a modest sum to the provincial government to build a home for the lieutenant governor. The completion of Government House in 1911 virtually assured the exclusivity of the neighborhood surrounding it. Although the north-east portion of the Estate did develop into an industrial area with the extension of the Edmonton, Yukon and Pacific Railway in 1905, most of the community continued as an elegant suburb. Between Chief Justice J.B. O'Connor's ''Graenon'' to the west on St. George's Crescent and Robertson Presbyterian Church, stood the homes of some of the most prominent men in Edmonton, such as architect George Heath MacDonald, journalist John Imrie, James Cornwall and William Griesbach.

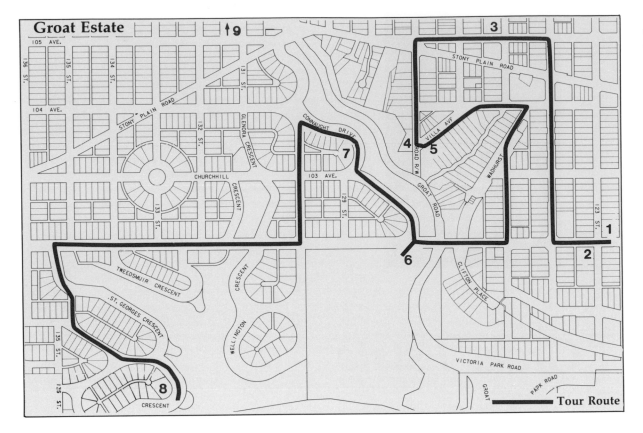

Groat Estate

1. **Robertson Wesley United Church**
2. **Buena Vista Apartments**
3. **The Gibbons House**
4. **The Villa**
5. **McIntosh House**
6. **Government House**
7. **The White House**
8. **The Graenon**
9. **Westmount High School**

ROBERTSON WESLEY CH. • 1914

Music and Architecture Marks of Church
10209-123 Street

ROBERTSON WESLEY United Church, built in 1914, is as imposing as ever. Of High Victorian Gothic Revival architecture, it was modelled after First Baptist Church in Calgary, when the recession forced its congregation to economize.

The church was built of Radcliff pressed brick with stone dressings. Interior woodwork is of quartered oak. The gracious interior features curved pews, a barrel-vaulted ceiling with bronze chandelier, a full complement of stained glass windows and a U-shaped gallery.

The church was named in honor of Reverend James Robertson, superintendent of all Presbyterian mission operations for Manitoba and the Northwest Territories from 1881 to 1902.

In 1925, Robertson joined the United Church of Canada—the union of the Methodist, Presbyterian and Congregationalist churches. In 1971, Wesley United Church and Robertson merged. Wesley's memorial windows were installed in Robertson.

Memorial Hall was designed by architect George Heath MacDonald. The hall featured a chapel dedicated to those who gave their lives during the Second World War. There were 297 enlistings from Robertson—28 never returned. A window was dedicated to Squadron Leader Reverend J. Gordon Brown. Brown was a much loved minister who was killed at Antwerp Belgium in 1944 while serving as a chaplain with the RCAF.

The first organ, built by Casavant Frères of St. Hyacinthe, Quebec, was installed in 1914 for $7,000. It was renovated in 1956, and replaced in 1979 by a newer organ built for $200,000 by Gabriel Kney of London, Ontario. ∎

BUENA VISTA APARTMENTS • 1913

Investment Dreams Shattered

12327-102 Avenue

ACROSS FROM the Buena Vista apartments, steam engines of the Canadian Northern Railway chugged through the 20-acre estate of Malcolm Groat. Downstairs, the Merchants Bank of Canada, druggist Charles A. Mooney, and City Grocery No. 2 administered to tenants' culinary, health and financial needs. The year was 1913, and the Buena Vista Apartments had recently been completed at the southeast corner of Athabasca Avenue (now 102nd Avenue) and 124th Street.

The three-storey building finished in brick with stone trim still carries its original gastronomical appeal: "We make our own sausage, corned beef, head cheese, and pure lard. Quality goods. Good Service."

The Buena Vista was not the city's first brick tenement house, but it was one of the most westerly. Although not overly embellished, the structure did provide the standard visual relief so often overlooked in later times. The west and north faces feature a dentilled cornice, windows accented by radiating voussoirs and balconets with black wrought iron ornamentation.

According to Alberta Culture, the building's design was popular in Canada in the early years of the 20th century. The design recalls those buildings which housed the commercial aristrocracy in renaissance England.

The city's population zoomed upwards before the First World War, from 25,000 in 1911 to 70,000 in 1913. Given those heady and innocent days, it is not surprising that a group of investors purchased the property for $11,000 from the estate of Malcolm Groat in September 1912.

The group formed Riverview Land Company. Its shareholders were Dr. Edgar Allin, a noted surgeon and a resident here since 1909, Dr. Harry R. Smith, two real estate men—Martin Runnalls and James H. Smith, florist Walter Ramsay and Norman B. Peck of Vancouver.

Flowers and real estate investments were not Ramsay's only accomplishments. He came to Alberta as a teacher prior to the turn of the century, and served as a principal at McKay Avenue and Queen's Avenue Schools, before moving on to chair the Edmonton Public School Board from 1912 to 1914. Dr. Harry R. Smith was a city alderman in 1913 and eventually became superintendent of the Royal Alexandra Hospital.

The Riverview Land Company had great plans for Groat's old real estate. Runnalls ran his own firm, M. Runnalls Real Estate and Insurance, established in 1907. In 1912 he was trying to market lots in the upscale burg of Buena Vista, which *The Edmonton Bulletin* described as "a most desirable residential property in the west end."

If the truth be known, Buena Vista was best known then as an abode for eccentric gold panners, a gravel pit and a wilderness area frequented by moose and beaver.

When the economy went bust one can only surmise that Runnalls suggested the name Buena Vista be applied instead to a more marketable commodity. That was an apartment building within easy physical and financial reach of Edmonton citizenry who suddenly found their pocketbooks a little thin.

The Buena Vista's plans were drawn up by Edmonton architects R. Percy Barnes and C. Lionel Gibbs in December of 1912, and a building permit was issued in January of 1913.

Hard times interfered with their investment dreams. The City of Edmonton foreclosed on the Buena Vista Apartments in 1930 for non-payment of taxes after filing a caveat on the property two years earlier.

As Riverview Land Company had taken out a $24,000 mortgage with Credit Foncier in 1912, the firm was anxious to recover some of its investment. In May 1930, Credit Foncier paid out the $5,656.77 in taxes and penalties to the city and assumed title. The building is now owned by Francana Real Estate Limited which, along with Credit Foncier, was purchased by Montreal Trust Company. ■

Robertson Wesley United Church is noted for its architecture and organ recitals.

Dedicated stained glass window in Robertson Wesley United Church.

The U-shaped gallery flanks choir loft and altar area of Robertson Wesley United Church.

GIBBONS HOUSE • 1911

Built by Soldier of Fortune
10534-125 Street

THE ORANGE BRICK two-storey in Groat Estate was among the last resting places of ''soldier of fortune'', James Gibbons.

Gibbons built this five-bedroom home in 1911, after a varied career in the American Army, as a miner, explorer, fur trader, scout, freighter, trapper, homesteader, Indian agent and businessman.

More recently, his property became home to Richard and Gillian Caldwell, their son, two cats, and a dog. It is one of few brick buildings on a mature Groat Estate street mainly consisting of large wood frame two-storey homes built for those of gentrified aspiration prior to the First World War.

The house features a wrap-around verandah on the east and south faces with a second-storey balcony. Numerous renovations ''of good workmanship but poor taste'' were done over the years. Hence the Caldwells' ongoing restoration of the interior to its traditional glory, assisted by the consultative services of Alberta Culture.

The home is modelled after Georgian Revival residential designs popular in Canada and the U.S. from the 1880s to 1915.

As was typical at that time for the home of a person of stature, the foyer was large enough to accommodate the comings and goings of numerous guests. In fact Gibbons married off his daughter Alice in the adjoining living room in the 1920s.

Major general William Griesbach, a close friend of Gibbon's, wrote down Gibbon's verbal account of his life. Perhaps his most controversial action was his participation in a massacre of Native women and children southwest of Salt Lake City in 1863. In Gibbon's words:

''The Indians were causing a good deal of trouble on the road from Salt Lake City to California and Connor was raising a force to deal with them so I volunteered for service in the cavalry. We had a big fight with the Indians at Bear River in 1863—with the Pokatellish band, who were Utes and Piutes from the Humboldt River.

"We lost about 30 men before we saw an Indian. Finally however, we got the better of them. One of our scouts discovered that in a concealed position, there was a large camp of squaws and children belonging to this band, and the question arose what should be done with them.

"This question was submitted to General Connor, whose answer was: 'Nits make lice,' so we finished them all off."

Gibbons made his way to Edmonton in the spring of 1865, seeking to make his fortune in North Saskatchewan River gold. In the summer of 1866 Gibbons harvested $800 in gold—not a lot compared to the $500 a week he made in one of his U.S. claims, but better than many for these parts. For four years, he panned in a number of locations, including Miner's Flats, now known as Laurier Park. He later purchased land and homesteaded in the Miner's Flats area.

Gibbons went on to become an Indian agent, and later a wholesaler in the liquor business. He met his wife in Edmonton. Born Mary Isabel Gouin in Manitoba, she spoke only French when she arrived here at the age of three in 1863. She married Gibbons a scant 11 years later, and bore him 13 children. She died, at age 96, in 1956.

Gibbons purchased the 125th Street lot and the one immediately south for $3,000 in 1911. He built his home on the northern lot at a cost of $7,000 and then built another house on the southern lot in 1913, for the same price.

After Gibbons' death in 1927, the property remained part of his estate until the sale of his residence alone for $6,000 in 1934 to public accountant Roland Sladden. Gibbons' wife moved to their farm at Miner's Flats. ∎

THE VILLA • 1912

Elegant Tudor Revival Home
10330-127 Street

WHEN COLONEL James Kennedy Cornwall built the 10,000-square-foot Villa on the east bank of the Groat Ravine in 1912, deer, bear, and the odd moose wandered here. Indians would come to the door of his unfinished library to trade in furs.

The Tudor Revival Style brick and stucco house that now stands above the city's hustle and bustle was built for $20,000 by F.W. Ward and designed by the prolific city architect Roland W. Lines. Its design was an outgrowth of the Queen Anne Style of the late Victorian era. Varied roof lines, grouped chimneys, eccentric placement of windows and a generally picturesque sensibility were already present in the Queen Anne version. So in a sense, all that was needed to create a Tudor Revival house was to apply timbering, Alberta Culture observed of this home.

Elegant as it was, it was foreclosed upon in 1926 and then purchased for $16,000 in 1927 by city lawyer Jeremiah Wilfrid Heffernan. It was purchased by Jim and Cody Murphy in 1968.

The mansion features oak panelling and flooring, silver light fixtures and a bank of stained glass windows in the dining room. There are vintage built-in burglar, intercom, paging and central vacuum systems.

Peace River Jim, otherwise known as Col. J.K. Cornwall, was born in Brantford, Ontario in 1869. Cornwall went to sea and sailed around the world before settling in the U.S. He bankrupted himself speculating on the Chicago Grain Exchange and joined the Yukon Gold Rush in 1897.

He came to Alberta, set up a number of northern trading posts and helped settle the Peace River area. He promoted the development of a postal service to the Peace River district, and when the federal government failed to sponsor it, Cornwall himself began his own mail service with horse and dog sled. He also provided several paddle wheel boats on the Peace River and Lesser Slave Lake.

He was said to be a friend of the Natives and spoke Cree, Slavey, Chippewyan, Dogrib and Inuit languages. He introduced wheat, oats and swine to the Peace River area, and was acclaimed Independent MLA for Peace River in 1908.

He was a friend of Twelve-Foot Davis, the first free trader in the Peace District in 1873. When Cornwall heard of the aged and near-blind Davis' death in 1900, he had the body exhumed and reburied on a projecting point of hill overlooking the Peace River. It had been one of their favorite camping spots.

If Cornwall didn't initiate western regionalism, he added vociferously to it. In a 1964 article in *The Journal*, Jim Coleman wrote that while in the lobby of Toronto's Royal York Hotel, Cornwall would announce "in a booming voice that the east was full of cranks, fakers, and political stuffed shirts."

He resigned as an MLA in 1912, and went on to encourage and survey the Alberta Railway system into the north. Several years later he was instrumental in developing the oil resources at Norman Wells discovered in 1920.

He was awarded the Distinguished Service Order during the First World War, where he had organized and commanded the 218th Battalion of the Irish Guards. He was on the first airplane to fly over the Arctic Ocean and with his partners in the Northern Transportation Company, began the first air service to the north originating from Edmonton.

In 1934, he was in Ottawa, pleading the case of Native rights before the federal government. In 1945 he was back advocating an Arctic tanker route for oil. Cornwall died in Calgary in 1955. ∎

Left: Interior of McIntosh House.
Opposite page: The Villa atop Groat Ravine.

The Groat Ravine, circa 1915.

McINTOSH HOUSE • 1912

Mansion Restored to Former Grandeur
10325 Villa Avenue

A THREE-STOREY brick mansion on the east bank of the Groat Ravine has been restored to its traditional grandeur.

The house is in an area once known as "Robbers Roost" due to the large number of monied residents with lavish homes. From 1920 to 1978, the house was known as the Ravina Apartments, due to its proximity to the Groat Ravine.

Built in 1912 on two lots for real estate tycoon John Robert McIntosh, the house was subdivided into seven one-bedroom suites in 1920 by McIntosh and his wife, who continued to live there until 1927. They then moved to a smaller house across the street.

McIntosh, who came to Edmonton in 1902, had the house designed by architect Alfred Marigon Calderon who also counted LeMarchand Mansion and Sheriff Robertson House among his credits.

McIntosh later speculated on a 320-acre farm in what was to become Calder. Until his retirement in 1946 he was a land agent for the Hudson's Bay Company. As land agent, he helped promote the fateful company land sale of 1912, which contributed to the depreciation of real estate in the recession following the First World War.

McIntosh house was last purchased by Alex and Anne McPherson in 1978 for $95,000. About $250,000 later, the McPhersons and their four children were living in a refurbished six-bedroom house with about 5,500 square feet.

Most of the renovations were carried out from 1980 to 1982. New wiring and plumbing were put in, some 100 window panes replaced and the brass light fixtures, fittings, moldings and trim restored. Alberta Culture designated it a Provincial Historical Resource in 1982 at the McPherson's request.

The main floor features oak flooring, panelling, sculpted trim and a combined living and dining room, with three cathedral-style windows. Original oak French doors abound, complete with bevelled glass panes which split the sunlight into rainbows of color. The second floor has maple flooring, five bedrooms and a rear sundeck. The walls of the house are made of 24 centimetres of brick plus another 10 centimetres of exterior brick veneer, which Alberta Culture describes as displaying high quality craftsmanship. ∎

GOVERNMENT HOUSE • 1913

Former Vice-Regal Residence
102 Avenue & 128 Street

THE STATELY sandstone mansion overlooking the North Saskatchewan River has had many lives since it was first used as a vice-regal residence.

Erected in 1913, Government House was home to Alberta's first six lieutenant governors before being padlocked by the government of the day. It was then a home to employees of the North West Airlines and Second World War veterans. Today, the mansion is used as a centre for government conferences and for state receptions. Its gleaming hotel-like kitchen prepares more than 10,000 meals for 300 functions a year.

Government House was designed in Jacobethan Revival Style by Richard Palin Blakey, and Allan Merrick Jeffers, who was the chief architect of the Legislature Building. Two-storey bay windows, raised gable ends and grouped double-hung windows lend character to the building. It cost $350,000 and originally had an adjoining conservatory, long since demolished. The 28-acre grounds also include a building once used as combined quarters for the servants and horses. It is now used for maintenance purposes.

The mansion's elegant original furnishings included silverware and china engraved with the Government House crest. Most of the furnishings have disappeared, having been auctioned in 1942 for a total of $19,642—a fraction of their original cost of $75,000. Only a few items have been recovered and are on display. After serving for 25 years as the lieutenant governor's residence, accommodation for visiting royalty and the scene of many grand social occasions, the gates to the grounds were padlocked in May 1938. The Social Credit administration of the time closed the building, ostensibly for reasons of economy. However, around that

Above: Government House library maintains original look.
Right: Detail of front entranceway embellishment.

time Lieutenant Governor J.J. Bowlen had refused to sign several bills passed by the government believing them to be *ultra vires*. When Premier William Aberhart withdrew funding for Government House, Bowlen moved to a suite in the Hotel MacDonald before finding a new residence.

In 1964, the federal and provincial governments chose the site at 102nd Avenue and 128th street as the site of the Provincial Museum and Archives of Alberta, which opened in 1967. The mansion was also returned to the province in 1967, for the sum of $350,000.

Several years later, more than $2 million in renovations were carried out. They may well have been expedited when the drawing room chandelier and sculptured plaster ceiling caved in shortly after then Soviet Prime Minister Alexei Kosygin visited the building in 1971. The building was officially reopened in 1976 as a government conference centre.

Renovations were extensive. Sandstone taken from the demolition of Edmonton's Old Courthouse was used to match the original finish. Its current facilities include six meeting rooms, each named after one of the resident lieutenant governors. The third floor has a large conference room—known as the Alberta Room—with an overhead dome. A reception area with a decorative ceiling made from 7,428 pieces of stainless steel is on the second floor. A dining room with seating for 100, a library and music room are on the main floor.

Various works by Alberta artists adorn the mansion walls. Some original areas remain with few alterations, including the library and music room, the central oak staircase and the second floor den. ■

Opposite page: Regal exterior of Government House.

THE WHITE HOUSE • 1913

Home of Architect and Journalist
10360 Connaught Drive

THE ARCHITECTURE may not be overly remarkable, but the house was home to a remarkable architect, not to mention a remarkable newspaperman.

All but obscured by mature foliage, this Georgian Revival two-storey has come to be called the White House, possibly due to its white wood siding. It was built by the prodigious early Edmonton architect George Heath MacDonald, as a wedding present for his wife Dorothea, about 1913.

Sagging economic conditions after the First World War forced the MacDonalds to sell the Glenora house to *The Edmonton Journal*'s managing director, John Mills Imrie and his wife Lizzie Anne (Beth) in 1921. After Imrie's death in 1942, his widow continued to live here until she died at age 99 in 1984.

The present owners have undertaken numerous renovations, including the construction of an architecturally compatible southwest addition. The restoration has been most tasteful.

The social and cultural contributions associated with this piece of real estate are indeed noteworthy. As well as being a prominent city architect who began his practice here in affiliation with Herbert Magoon in 1904, MacDonald has been cited by the Edmonton Historical Board as being among the first to show interest in reconstructing Fort Edmonton. While MacDonald died in 1961 before the fort was rebuilt, he laid much of the groundwork in lobbying governments, undertaking the necessary research, preparing plans and writing two books *Fort Augustus—Edmonton*, and *Edmonton—Fort House, Factory*.

Among the hundreds of buildings he planned or helped to plan, the "crown of his career was designing the federal building," his son Ian MacDonald recalled in a 1986

The White House built by architect George Heath MacDonald.

interview.

MacDonald built his bride, Dorothea, a home that was definitely upscale. Dorothea, known as a "first class" pianist, played at the Alberta provincial inauguration program in 1905 and occasionally at services in Robertson Wesley United Church.

Heath and Dorothea built another home nearby after selling the White House to the Imries. John Imrie was managing director (the then equivalent of publisher) of *The Journal* from 1921 to 1939.

In 1937 Alberta's first Social Credit government introduced Bill No. Nine, the Accurate News and Information Act. The proposed law would force reporters to reveal their sources, make it mandatory for newspapers to publish government prepared statements and allow officials to stop any news story they didn't want to see published.

To his credit, Lieutenant Governor J.J. Bowlen, refused the bill royal assent. For his impertinence, Bowlen was shown the door at Government House. He was the last lieutenant governor to live in that splendid official residence.

Imrie and his associate editor Balmer Watt, led the campaign against the bill and together they secured the 1938 Pulitzer Award for *The Journal*, the only Pulitzer given outside the U.S. ■

THE GRAENON • 1914

Early Glenora Home a "Sunny Place"
36 St. George's Crescent

"THEY SAY a house isn't a home until someone is born in it, married in it, and died in it. I guess this house qualifies according to that." So mused Peggy O'Connor Farnell, author of the book *Old Glenora*, as she reminisced about her residence—The Graenon.

Not only was Farnell born in the house, but her wedding reception was held there and her parents died there. Also, the late J.J. Bowlen took his oath of allegiance to the Queen in the house when he was Alberta's lieutenant governor.

The Tudor Style brick and stucco house was built in 1914 by Farnell's father, George Bligh O'Connor, who became chief justice of the Alberta Supreme Court.

Farnell said the home was named The Graenon by her mother Margaret after the Irish word meaning "sunny place." Yet as she noted in her book, "The trees planted when the house was built now tower over (it), making the yard more of a shady place!" Glenora was largely bush when the house was built, Farnell recalled, and even by the 1920s there were only three homes on St. George's Crescent.

Her father came to Edmonton in 1905, shortly after winning the silver medal and graduating from Osgoode Hall law school in Toronto. He later recalled that his voyage west was auspicious in that his prized silver medal was lost en route.

Soon afterward, he began a law practice with William Greisbach, an association which lasted until 1940, when Greisbach left to take up duties with the army. Their partnership and friendship was somewhat of an anachronism, as Greisbach was a devoted Conservative and O'Connor a devoted Liberal.

In fact, O'Connor was campaign manager in the 1911 and 1917 federal elections for Frank Oliver, publisher of *The Edmonton Bulletin*, who had been Minister of the Interior in Prime Minister Sir Wilfrid Laurier's government. Oliver's competitor for the seat was none other than Greisbach.

O'Connor met his wife, a journalist from Kingston, Ontario in 1913. After their marriage, they lived in LeMarchand Mansion while The Graenon was built. Mrs. O'Connor later became a theatre critic with *The Edmonton Bulletin*.

Before being named a judge in 1950, O'Connor was the first chairman of the Canadian Labor Relations Board as well as president of *The Edmonton Bulletin*. He died in 1957.

The two-storey Graenon with three main bedrooms was built by Mrs. O'Connor's brother, W.A. Fairlie, and another man named Morrison. It incorporated a gabled roof with dormer windows, latticed windows, a screened verandah and oak panelling, flooring and overhead beams. Among its luxuries were central vacuum and intercom systems, neither of which is still in use. It had two stairwells, the rear one for use by servants as was customary at that time. Except for the kitchen which has been remodelled, the house remains as it was in 1914. Among the highlights are the living room and library, which integrate oak woodwork and flooring, as well as brick fireplaces.

Farnell said the house is known to neighborhood children as the house with the cat on the roof, referring to a porcelain cat brought back from Normandy and installed by her mother in 1928. ■

WESTMOUNT SCHOOL • 1915

Example of Edwardian Gothic
11125-131 Street

WESTMOUNT Junior High School was almost strangled financially before it got off the ground. The economic downturn that came with the advent of the First World War thwarted its completion for seven years. Construction began in May of 1913 and ceased two months later.

The next seven years were marked by intermittent construction, court battles and garnishees between the contractor, the EPSB and the numerous subcontractors and laborers involved in the building.

The school was occupied at Easter 1915, but the second floor remained unfinished until 1920. The final cost of the building reached $227,830.

When completed however, the edifice was striking. In 1986, EPSB archivist Mike Kostek called it one of the best examples of Edwardian Gothic Style architecture in Edmonton. Alberta Culture calls it a very good example of the late Gothic Revival Style, first introduced in the U.S. in the early 1890s.

Said *The Journal* in April 1915: It "embodies the latest ideas in school planning. Its exterior design represents a free treatment of late Gothic ... which is more or less traditionally associated with collegiate work."

The two-storey building, with central tower and smaller towers over each wing, was another design of George Turner, EPSB building commissioner, who also prepared the plans for King Edward and Highlands schools.

Westmount is built of bricks, at least some of which were supplied by J.B. Little's Riverdale brickyard, and of Indiana Bedford stone, sent from Chicago, Illinois. The facade features a crenellated roof line with crest embellishments. Stone carvings including wolves' heads flank the former front

Porcelain cat high-steps The Graenon.

entrance, no longer in use.

Inside the main entrance there is oak panelling, terrazzo flooring, and oak doors inset with leaded-glass windows. The oak and leaded-glass door treatment is also found in the second-floor library in the central tower, which served as a gymnasium until 1970.

Despite its striking architecture, Westmount Junior High School remains unprotected by historic site designation.

The site, part of the old Norris farm, was purchased by the EPSB in 1909 for $3,200. The first Westmount school was a two-storey frame building at 128th Street between 100th and 111th Avenues. It opened in November 1909 with an enrolment of 19 students from Grades One to Three, under the tutelage of Miss Adelle Bremner. By the end of 1913 there were eight rooms to the school, scattered over various Westmount locations.

The first principal of the permanent school in 1915 was John Scoffield. When it became the first junior high school in the city in 1918, Mr. P.S. Bailey was principal.

Tragedy struck in 1918 when the influenza epidemic closed the school from October to December, and the building, like many other city institutions, was pressed into service as a relief centre.

By 1936, Westmount was an elementary, junior high, and high school, all at once. It reverted to a junior high in 1950.

Edmonton North

Although the turn of the century saw Edmonton's industrial core centralized in the river valley, the arrival of the Canadian Northern Railway in 1905 and the Grand Trunk Pacific several years later gave great impetus for the northern district of the city to emerge as the industrial section. The Canadian Pacific continued to facilitate rail traffic southward, however as most of the city's commerce flowed east, it was along the CN arteries that the greater industrialization occurred, from the factories in the north-east to the warehouses in the north-west. In between were primarily the homes of working class citizens.

Aside from the industrial structures, Edmonton north central today contains a variety of residential, religious, scholastic and public buildings which reflect the lifestyle of the area in the early 20th century. Sacred Heart Church is but one of many along 96th, or ''Church'' Street. Nearby are such landmarks as St. Josaphat's Cathedral and the first mosque in Canada, Al Rashid. The schools to serve the district in the early years included Norwood, McCauley, John A. McDougall and H. Allen Gray, while the Glenrose Hospital was for years the major medical facility on the city's north side.

JOHN A. McDOUGALL SCHOOL • 1913

Women Had Starring Role

10930-107 Street

THE WORLD'S most successful women's basketball team, and the much-lauded first female principal of a large city school are found among the annals of this elegant inner city edifice.

John A. McDougall Elementary/Junior High School, built in 1913, heavily damaged by fire in 1929, and restored in 1930, is not as prominent a building as it once was. Newer and larger structures now surround it.

But from 1919 to 1943, the building, specifically the third floor gymnasium, was home to that fabulous Edmonton legend, the Edmonton Commercial Grads Basketball Club. No other Edmonton amateur team has ever come close to the world records established by those who did it for love of game alone under the leadership of their coach ''Papa'' Percy Page.

When McDougall School threw open its doors in 1914, city fathers may well have knit their eyebrows in incredulity, for the school board had seen fit to appoint Miss Kate Chegwin as its first principal. While female teachers were nothing new at this time, female principals were relegated to three-room temporary schools or, when lucky, perhaps appointed to an acting role in something bigger.

''If there ever was a teacher that symbolized good teaching in the Edmonton Public School Board, it was Kate,'' said EPSB archivist Mike Kostek in a 1987 interview. Unfortunately public honor eluded her upon her retirement in 1929. An all-male school board drew the line at naming a city school in her honor.

McDougall School was designed by EPSB staff architect George Turner in a Collegiate Gothic Style, abbreviated somewhat by changes to the roof line after the 1929 fire. The style was especially popular on buildings

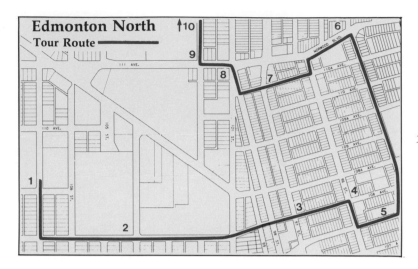

Edmonton North
Tour Route

1. John A. McDougall School
2. Prince of Wales Armory
3. St. Josaphat's Cathedral
4. Sacred Heart Church
5. McCauley School
6. Norwood School
7. Lambton Block
8. Al Rashid Mosque
9. Glenrose Hospital
10. H. Allen Gray School

of an academic nature around the turn of the century. Inside, the foyer has oak panelling and terrazzo flooring. Traditional-style classrooms have the separate cloakroom and built-in corner cabinets.

The Grads' former drill hall on the third floor became a library when the new gymnasium annex was built in 1972. It still has its oak doors and leaded glass windows.

In 1916 the city's first commercial high school courses were transferred here from neighboring Victoria High School, and the commercial section functioned as McDougall Annex on the second floor, separate from the public school below.

A 29-year-old Percy Page came along with the commercial courses and began as the girls basketball coach. Page eventually became principal of the commercial school. Page went on to become a Conservative MLA and Alberta's lieutenant governor from 1959 to 1966.

The rest, as they say is history—18 years of national championships, 17 years of international championships, 516 wins out of 540 games played over 25 years and the winning of all 51 Olympic exhibition games from 1924 through 1936. Women's basketball was not then a recognized Olympic activity.

The inventor of basketball, Dr. James Naismith, called them the greatest basketball team in the world.

The school was named in honor of John Alexander McDougall, a pioneer merchant who arrived here in 1879 when there were only 40 whites living in the tiny settlement above Fort Edmonton. In 1881 McDougall was one of the 10 citizens who banded together to guarantee the $500 salary of our city's first public school teacher.

He was mayor of the town in 1897 and mayor of the city in 1908. From 1909 to 1913 he was a Liberal Member of the Legislative Assembly. ■

PRINCE OF WALES ARMORY • 1915

Awaits New Lease on Life
10440-108 Avenue

BATTERED by the vagaries of public policy, recession, depression, and advancing age, the Prince of Wales Armory still awaits a new lease on life.

The armory was declared excess by the department of national defence in 1977 and was transferred to the public works department for disposal the following year. It was obtained by the City of Edmonton in a land swap for city lands assembled for the Canada Place project.

The armory was first known as the Edmonton Drill Hall and this name is inscribed in stone flanked by stone cannonballs over the front entrance. A number of regiments called it home, including the 101st Regiment, the Edmonton Regiment, the Loyal Edmonton Regiment and the Edmonton Fusiliers.

Built in 1915, the armory cost $280,000. It was constructed of brick with a concrete foundation and steel structural work. Architects D.E. Ewart and E.C. Hopkins designed it in typical military style—a fortress-like design with a crenellated roof line and corner towers and turrets.

The city described the 65,000-square-foot structure as a basic two-storey rectangular building organized on four sides around a central drill hall. The hall is covered by a longitudinal saddle-back roof supported by arched steel trusses. The building sits on a 17-acre site—one of the largest single parcels of underdeveloped land in the inner city.

The armory has shooting galleries, armories and jail cells in the basement. Offices, lounges and storage rooms adjoin the drill hall on the main floor. An officers club on the second floor includes an elegant dining room. The armory was designated a Provincial Historical Resource in 1979. ■

ST. JOSAPHAT'S CATHEDRAL • 1943

Ornate Place of Worship
10825-97 Street

ST. JOSAPHAT'S CATHEDRAL is among Alberta's youngest historic buildings.

The seven-domed Ukrainian Catholic church wasn't completed until 1943. Normally, a building must be at least 50 years old to be designated a Provincial Historical Resource but, in 1983, Alberta Culture made an exception for the church largely because of its architecture.

St. Josaphat's is considered Alberta's best example of the Prairie Cathedral architectural style developed by Reverend Philip Ruh. Additionally, the church is regarded as one of the most ornate places of worship in the province.

While the cathedral is not the largest Ukrainian Catholic church in the city, the brown-brick building is distinguished by its imposing architecture and the unique colorful tempera religious frescos decorating the interior.

The cathedral replaced another church named after St. Josaphat—the only Ukrainian saint. The original church was built in 1904 on the same site under Reverend Sozont Dydyk, whose dream was to build a monumental church in Edmonton.

When construction began the parish had only $13,000 in funds. Volunteer labor was largely employed and it took four years to complete the church at a cost of $250,000.

Ruh, who studied architecture before becoming a priest, came to Canada in 1911. He first did missionary work among the Ukrainian immigrants who settled in northern Alberta. Ruh, who died in 1962, designed about 30 other churches including the Holy Trinity Ukrainian Catholic Church northwest of Leduc. Most of his designs were for churches in Alberta, as well as a monastery in Mundare.

St. Josaphat's was designed as a traditional Ukrainian Catholic Church, with the sanctuary located at the east end—a repudiation of the pagan tradition of installing the apse at the west end.

Ruh's design incorporated a number of architectural styles. Cornices on part of the facade and the drum supporting the domes are of the Roman Style. The cupolas are of Renaissance Style, while the columns in front of the facade are in a pseudo-classic style.

Only the largest dome, which signifies Christ as head of the church, is open. The others are simply decorative and have no religious significance.

Among the interior highlights are the bright tempera frescos on the walls and domes. The paintings were completed over five years in the 1950s by the late Julian Bucmaniuk who came to Canada in 1950 after teaching at several European art schools. He also designed the elaborate iconostasis separating the tabernacle area from the church proper.

The frescos are painted in the Baroque Style with neo-Byzantine influences, using tempera prepared by Bucmaniuk. The dominant colors are blue for heaven and serenity, and yellow for brightness and tranquillity.

The artist used parishioners as models for the saints and prophet and a young priest as a model for Christ. He painted the faces of Hitler, Lenin, Stalin and Khruschev into Hell, and himself into Heaven in his rendition of Judgment Day. However, Ukrainian Catholic Bishop Demetrius Greschuk did not appreciate Bucmaniuk's artistic licence, saying that only the Lord can judge.

A large chandelier descends from Bucmaniuk's painting, God the Father, on the hemispheric ceiling of the large dome. The painting originally inspired so much dread that it had to be toned down. ■

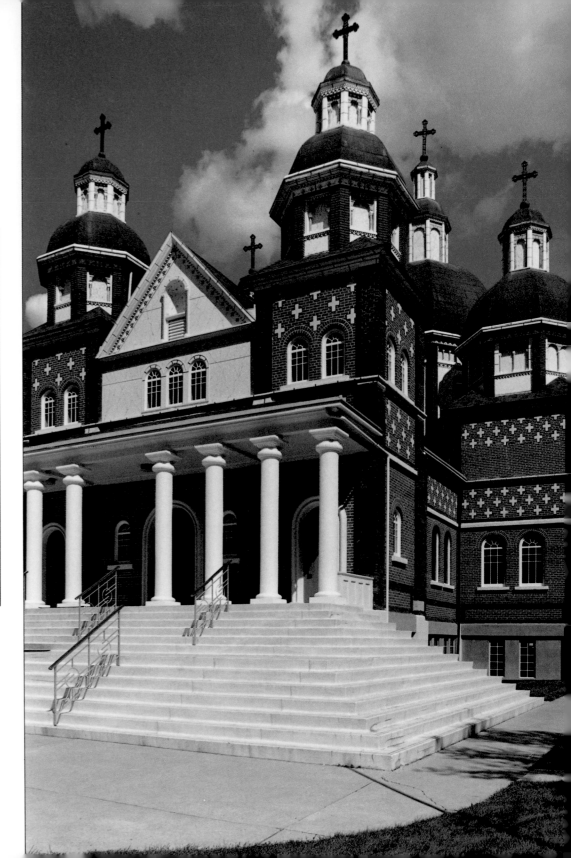

Above: Judgment Day fresco, St. Josaphat's Cathedral.
Right: Multi-domed St. Josaphat's Cathedral, Edmonton's 'youngest' historic building.

SACRED HEART CHURCH • 1913

Spires Tower Above Gothic Church
10821-96 Street

MINISTERING to the inner city's spiritual and material needs has been an enduring role for Sacred Heart Roman Catholic Church.

The Gothic Style brick structure was built in 1913 to accommodate growing numbers of English-speaking Catholics. By 1986, one of the three Sunday masses was celebrated in Spanish for the large population of refugees from Chile and Central America.

Serving immigrant needs is nothing new to Sacred Heart. Prior to the Spanish group, the largest ethnic group was Croatian and before that Native Indian—all in a span of six years.

In addition to adapting to fluctuating waves of immigrants, the church operates a food bank out of the adjoining rectory. Some 600 hampers a month are dispensed to destitute transients, Natives, and outpatients from Alberta Hospital. Sacred Heart is also known in the Boyle Street area for its annual Christmas dinner for the less fortunate. It attracts about 1,000 people annually.

Unfortunately, little if anything remains of the building's original interior. The church was devastated by a 1966 fire, which caused $160,000 in damage. The reconstruction saw the interior remodelled in more modern materials. There is vinyl tile flooring over the original hardwood, new wood panelling, a cedar finished ceiling and a contemporary flair to the wood-covered pillars. The U-shaped gallery was dismantled and replaced by a gallery which runs straight across the rear of the church. And in keeping with the new liturgy of the Catholic church, the altar was moved to the middle of the congregation, from its former place at the head of the church.

The church architecture is Gothic Revival with French influences. Some of its characteristics include the two-tower plan and the centre stained glass window with its pointed arch on the west face.

Despite or perhaps because of the fire and subsequent work, the church is in solid structural condition. In 1980 the deteriorating north tower was reinforced and the brick exterior repointed and cleaned.

Sacred Heart was erected for $75,000 on what was then the corner of Syndicate Avenue and Ross Street. When built, the church could seat 1,000 people and its 130-foot north tower was the highest spire in the city.

Features of the face include buttressed walls, windows with pointed arches and the stained glass windows which were largely unaffected by the fire. The church was built on a 62-by-90-foot concrete foundation and a brick superstructure with stone dressings.

The first parish priest was Reverend Maxim Pilon. He lived in a rectory to the south, which was also built in 1913 at a cost of $8,000. A furnace in the rectory basement heats both buildings, with pipes running through an underground pedway to the basement hall of the church.

The church was designed by local architects David Hardie and John Martland. While little is known of Hardie, Martland was later to become the City of Edmonton architect and a president of the Alberta Association of Architects. He also designed the Hecla Block apartments. ■

Norwood School detail.

McCAULEY SCHOOL • 1911

A Link to Our Educational Beginnings
9538-107 Avenue

THE NAME of Edmonton's first mayor and public school board chairman lives on in one of the city's oldest schools. McCauley Junior High School is named after Matthew McCauley. He headed the school board from 1881 to 1884 and was mayor of Edmonton, then a town, from 1892 to 1894.

The three-storey school was opened in 1911 and was then the city's sixth-largest school with 12 classrooms. Its first principal was Hector Kennedy, who served only one year.

Designed by school board architect George Turner, construction costs totalled $93,800. The brick-faced school is accented by stone mullions and has a crenellated roof line. There are shield embellishments on the east and west abutments.

The building features separate arched entrances for boys and girls, each with leaded glass windows. Hallway floors are of polished terrazzo and the original fire-proof· metal staircases are still in use. Washrooms feature molded granite slab cubicles while hardwood floors in classrooms have been covered with linoleum. Classrooms feature traditional cloak rooms.

The third floor was used as a gymnasium until 1961, when a red brick addition was built on the school's west end. The top floor was then converted to a library and classrooms.

In the 1980s the school was a microcosm of inner city life and new wave immigration. Its duty was to instruct 195 students from kindergarten to Grade Nine, more than two-thirds of whom are Oriental.

McCauley was one of the 500 people present at the school's official opening in 1912 and according to *The Edmonton Bulletin*, "the consensus of opinion of all present was that McCauley School is the best institution of its kind in the northwest and the equal of any in Canada."

McCauley organized the fundraising efforts of the fledgling community outside Fort Edmonton. In 1881 he sold subscriptions to raise necessary funds for the first school house. In so doing, some might rightly accuse him of having had a vested interest—his two wives bore him a total of 12 children.

McCauley, who also became a Northwest Territories and Alberta MLA, arrived from Ontario in 1879 and established a livery stable and cartage business on the site of the present AGT Tower, then part of the Methodist Mission estate, in 1883. He was also responsible for bringing the first radial railway system to the Northwest Territories in 1893.

McCauley is another one of those towering figures of early Edmonton. In addition to his many exploits, he held office as warden of Edmonton Penitentiary from 1906 to 1911. Along with Frank Oliver and John McDougall he helped establish the Board of Trade, predecessor of the Chamber of Commerce.

He was elected as a Member of the Legislative Assembly for Vermillion in Alberta's first provincial election in 1905. He left Edmonton in 1912 for Penticton, B.C., where he lived and grew apples for 13 years, before heading up to the Peace River area for his last stand at conquering wilderness. ■

Close-up of cougar guarding McDougall School entry.

NORWOOD SCHOOL • 1909

Renaissance Lends Style

9520-111 Avenue

NORWOOD SCHOOL, Edmonton's fourth oldest school, was built to serve the newly-created Norwood subdivision. Built in 1909, it was also Edmonton's largest school.

The three-storey Renaissance Style school opened to 400 students packed into its 10 classrooms. Generations have trooped through its doors since then, although in recent years, enrolment was about half what it was originally.

The school's exterior looks the same as it did back in 1909—red brick trimmed with Roman stone—except for the addition of a gymnasium during the 1960s. The top floor (originally built for assemblies as was typical at that time) is now converted into a library. In the basement, former playrooms have been changed into art and math labs.

The school was designed by architect Roland Lines, who was also responsible for Alex Taylor School, Firehall No. 2—now demolished—Old Scona High School and the old Royal Alexandra Hospital.

In 1906, two temporary buildings, one of one-room and another with two rooms, were installed north of the present school. But within a short time, the "Little Schools"—as they were known—were bursting at the seams with 51 students per room. As a result, conditions left a little to be desired. While students at the newly-built Alex Taylor School to the south enjoyed running water and indoor plumbing, their colleagues at Norwood made do with water pails and dippers and outdoor privies.

A nearby piggery, a nuisance ground and two brothels also brought complaints from parents. The piggery and nuisance ground were closed, while the brothels were relocated.

The basement for the present school was dug in the spring of 1907, by men using picks and shovels. Horse-drawn wagons

Norwood School retains its fine lines today.

hauled the earth away.

The cornerstone was laid in May of 1908, with samples of Alberta grain, current postage stamps, an Edmonton school board report for 1907 and five newspapers placed beneath it in a sealed box.

When the school opened on February 26, 1909, Margaret McCauley, daughter of founding school trustee Matt McCauley, was one of its nine teachers. One of the students that day was Eleanor Palmer, who later became Mrs. J.L. Cleary.

Mrs. Cleary, who served as nurse at

Norwood for 15 years, reflected about opening day in a speech given at a school reunion in the 1970s.

"We all gazed in wonder as we marched into the new school," she recalled. "Everything smelled so new. Instead of plasterboard painted black for blackboards, we had beautiful green boards. The drinking water fountains were a great attraction, to say nothing of indoor toilets.

"When Norwood School was completed, it was said to be the finest, most up-to-date school in Alberta." ■

LAMBTON BLOCK • 1914

Tales of Boom and Bust

11035-97 Street

LAWYERS and economic boom and bust figure heavily in the story of this plain brick structure built about 1914 for Edmonton lawyer John Robert Boyle.

Boyle, who was elected as a Liberal MLA to Alberta's first legislature, constructed the Lambton Block before the First World War. He named it after the Ontario county where he was born.

During another economic boom 66 years later, the block became the property of Martin Hattersley, another prominent Edmonton lawyer, in partnership with Leonard Hendrickson. The partners sold the apartment in 1980. But its new owners were foreclosed upon in 1985. The building is now owned by city mathematics teacher Dave Kolskog, who purchased it for $258,000 in 1986.

Original plans for the Lambton Block were prepared by Roland Lines, who designed numerous architectural masterpieces in this city before marching off to his death in the First World War. His plans show the odd-shaped building—it has six sides acknowledging its irregular lot—to have four stores on the main floor, all with separate basement access. The original suites were located on the second and third floors.

At some point in its history, the four stores were converted into apartments, as can be distinguished by the main floor's darker brick on the outside and its spartan hallways. The upper floors have been maintained in pristine fashion over the years, revealing the workmanship and style of a traditional era.

Boyle sold the building to the Dominion Life Assurance Company in 1925 for $25,500. As he had taken out a $30,000 mortgage with the company 11 years before, it is a strong likelihood that Boyle's building was barely holding its own.

Politics and judicial appointment was still in his future when Boyle came to Edmonton in 1894. He became a lawyer in 1899 in practice with Judge Hedley Taylor. He was elected an alderman to Edmonton's first city council in 1904 and served until 1905 when he was elected to the legislature for the Sturgeon riding. He went on to become minister of education, attorney general and a chief justice of the Alberta Supreme Court.

He ran for election with Nellie McClung in 1921, and became leader of the opposition when Herbert Greenfield's United Farmers of Alberta defeated Clifford Sifton's Liberal government. Boyle won the distinction of being the first in a long string of provincial Liberal leaders who would labor fruitlessly in their quest for power in wild rose country.

But a distinguished pioneer Albertan he has remained. Boyle died in 1936. The village of Boyle, 75 kilometres north-east of Edmonton, was named after him. ■

Right and opposite page:
Al Rashid Mosque, Canada's first, a tribute to Canadian tolerance.

AL RASHID MOSQUE • 1938

Canada's First Mosque

10107-111 Avenue

THE YEAR WAS 1938—Adolf Hitler was sowing the seeds of racial hate and the British Empire was still reeling from an unprecedented abdication. And in Edmonton, the fledgling Islamic congregation was gathered in Al Rashid Mosque—Canada's first mosque.

The humble one-storey brick building is distinguished by its corner minarets topped with Islamic crescents. When the mosque opened, it was situated at the corner of 101st

Street and 108th Avenue. Now it stands abandoned and out-flanked by the contemporary buildings of the Royal Alexandra Hospital.

While the property occupied by the mosque is now owned by the City of Edmonton and planned for future hospital use, the building remains the property of the Arabian Muslim Association. Save for the pigeons, the old mosque hasn't been used since 1980 when the Islamic congregation built a $2 million mosque in north-west Edmonton to accommodate its growing numbers. In 1986 Edmonton's Muslim population was estimated to number 16,000.

Unlike many Christian places of worship, there are no elaborate pews, organ, furniture, or art. The windows were clear and the faithful knelt or sat on the floor. A dome with a star was located on the central part of the roof, but was removed in the 1940s.

The building's future is uncertain. The Muslim Association was to preserve the building as an historic site, but has been unable to find funds or a new location. Moving costs alone were estimated at $120,000 in 1983. So the building estimated · to be worth $200,000, languished, unprotected even by so much as an insurance policy. That despite Alberta Culture's notation that "it is surprising to find the first Canadian mosque to be built only as late as 1937 and even more surprising to find it in Alberta rather than Toronto or Montreal."

The old mosque was constructed largely by Edmonton Muslims of Lebanese extraction. A 25th anniversary booklet notes "the prospect of building a mosque at that time looked hopeless, and the thought of a mosque inconceivable. The city Muslims were very limited in number and their resources meagre."

Work was halted two times due to lack of funding, but appeals to the Muslim and Arab communities in Alberta and Saskatchewan enabled construction to proceed. Total cost was $6,000.

The first religious function was the funeral of Ali Terrabain, an Edmonton pioneer businessman, in November 1938. Mayor John Fry officiated at the opening the following month. Abdullah Ussuf-Ali, a Muslim scholar from Bengal, India, dedicated and named the building after an Islamic prophet.

Fry told the Muslims that they should be proud of being Canadian citizens as "this could not happen in some lands which you are well aware of." He went on to say it was significant that people of many faiths were "sitting friendly together."

Saleem Ganam, an imam of the mosque, recalled in a 1986 interview that "the old-timers feared that it (the construction) would lead to more discrimination, that people would attack it and it would be destroyed. But Mayor Fry encouraged them to build and told them he would protect the building." ∎

GLENROSE HOSPITAL • 1911
Edmonton's Oldest Hospital
10230-111 Avenue

THE GLENROSE Rehabilitation Hospital is Edmonton's oldest standing medical facility. There are no more crutches or transplants planned for the landmark hospital, the "old red box" is scheduled for radical surgery—complete demolition.

Originally, the hospital was known as the Royal Alexandra Hospital from its construction in 1911 until the opening of the new Royal Alex in 1963. Little is left of the original classic English-inspired design. A $500,000 interior renovation in 1964 saw traditional touches, such as transoms, obscured. Only the original terrazzo floors, railings and bannisters offer a glimpse of another time.

In the 1950s, the classic front facade, with three floors of verandahs and an arched pediment with a scroll disappeared and were replaced by the more modern lines of the current foyer. While a dream for fire code designers, the current foyer pales when compared stylistically with its predecessor. Said *The Edmonton Bulletin* in 1910: "The main entrance to the building is imposing and in keeping with the pretentious nature of the entire hospital."

In 1986 there were 223 adult beds in the old hospital building, with another 55 pediatric beds in an adjoining annex. The annex, built in 1966, houses a school and hospital for emotionally and physically handicapped children. It will remain as part of the Glenrose when the old building is demolished.

The city-owned Royal Alex had its beginnings in 1899 when Reverend H.A. Gray, an Anglican archdeacon, opened the Boyle Street Hospital in a two-storey frame house at 102A Avenue and 97th Street. The name was changed to Edmonton City Hospital in 1906, the same year that a school of nursing was established. The following year, the Ladies Hospital Aid Society petitioned Queen Alexandra, consort of King Edward VII, to have the institution renamed in her honor.

The building, designed by Edmonton architect Roland Lines, was built on an eight-acre site purchased from the Hudson's Bay Company for $16,000. Two of the hospital's three sections cost $15,000 to construct.

Upon its opening ''25 patients were tranferred in horse-drawn and motor ambulances, several other automobiles, and carriages of friends.'' *The Edmonton Journal* noted at the time.

A 100-bed isolation ward was added in 1922, while the west section was completed in 1923. This new wing, designed by architect William Blakey, cost $300,000. It also increased the hospital's bed capacity to 300.

An annex for chronically-ill patients was added in 1948, while a maternity pavilion was built south of 111th Avenue in 1953. A new nurses' residence, near the maternity hospital, was completed in 1960.

Considered obsolete and outdated, a major chapter in the hospital's life ended with the completion of the Royal Alex's new 650-bed active treatment pavilion on Kingsway.

The old hospital was sold to the province for $1 and, after renovations, emerged as the Glenrose Provincial General Hospital a year later. Its name was changed to Glenrose Rehabilitation Hospital in 1983. ■

Revamped entry and 1911 wing of Old Queen Alex Hospital, now the Glenrose.

Grand lines of entry, H.A. Gray School.

H. ALLEN GRAY SCHOOL • 1914

Named After Cowboy Parson

12140-103 Street

THE SCHOOL was named after the first Anglican Bishop of Edmonton, Henry Allen Gray, who was called the "Cowboy Parson" after he spent his first six years in Canada—1886 to 1892, as a rancher near Calgary.

The educative efforts conducted here are no longer supervised by the Edmonton Public School Board. In 1983, the EPSB closed the building and it was leased to the Northern Alberta Institute of Technology.

Built in 1914, the stately edifice sports a classy finish of red brick and Bedford stone in a Collegiate Gothic Style. In a community largely known for humble housing, its lofty ornamental spires, shaped parapets, battlements and ornamental finials are a surprising sight for sore eyes.

While the exterior features classic details, NAIT students find the most modern of interior finishes. Only the foyers with their traditional ceramic tile and terrazzo, and the stairwells bear any resemblance to an older building.

The school was designed by the board's staff architect George E. Turner and cost $158,187. The first classes opened in May 1914, but H.A. Gray's official opening wasn't until the following September, when it was blessed by Bishop Gray.

Gray served as the city's first Anglican Bishop from 1914 to 1931. He began his service in Edmonton in 1895 at Holy Trinity Church. From 1897 to 1914, he served as rector of All Saints Church. He was a three-term member of the public school board, started the first Boy Scout troop in the city, served as chaplain of the 19th Alberta Dragoons and was a judge of the juvenile court. Gray retired to his native England due to poor health in 1931, where he died in 1939.

Highlands

*T*he Groat Estate was not the only subdivision planned for exclusive living during the pre-war period. In 1910, William J. Magrath and his partner Bidwell Holgate undertook to subdivide river lots 32 and 34 east of 65th Street on the high ground overlooking the North Saskatchewan River. They brought the extension of the street railway and the water and sewer system to the area, and on Ada Boulevard built themselves two of the most elegant homes in Alberta. The Highlands, as the new subdivision was named, soon attracted several of the most wealthy people in Edmonton, such as Mayor Charles May and coal magnate Robert Ritchie.

Full development of the community was curtailed by the economic recession which occurred with World War I, and during the 1920s even the Magraths and Holgates had to relinquish their mansions. Today, the neighborhood still retains many elements of pre-World War I grandeur, such as the Magrath, Holgate, Ash, Morehouse residences and the Gibbard Block, which once served as the main shopping centre for the community.

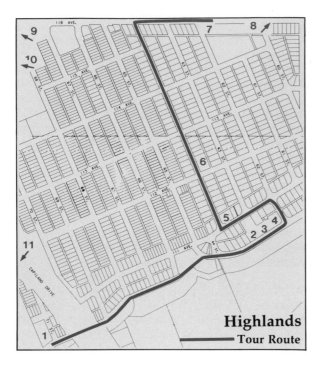

1. Schwermann Hall
2. Ash Residence
3. Magrath Mansion
4. Holgate Mansion
5. Morehouse House
6. Gibbard Block
7. Highlands Junior High School
8. Transit Hotel
9. Eastwood School
10. Parkdale Elementary School
11. Robertson House

SCHWERMANN HALL • 1926

Weathered College Needs Repair
7128 Ada Boulevard

THE WORN granite slab hallways attest to the thousands of students who have trudged through Concordia College.

Overlooking the panoramic North Saskatchewan River valley, the brick and stone three-storey edifice at the campus centre and the adjoining men's dormitory were erected in 1926 at a cost of $16,873. As well as the buildings, the cost included the real estate and a public address system considered to be a novelty at the time.

The college was named Concordia after the 15th century Lutheran writings called the *Book of Concord*. But in 1974 this central building was renamed Schwermann Hall, in honor of its first president Reverend Albert Schwermann, who helped to lay its cornerstone.

Over the years, Schwermann Hall has been surrounded by more recent buildings. And about 800 students can be found here now, compared to about 35 at the college's founding.

Owned and operated by the Lutheran Church Mission Synod since its founding, it is one of 17 throughout North America, offering senior high school classes as well as Bachelor of Arts and Science degrees in affiliation with the University of Alberta.

Schwermann Hall remains in use but its passage is beginning to show signs of wear. Little has been done, other than ongoing maintenance. A restoration program is planned.

The exterior is decorated with stone carvings and embellishments, including twin crests with the sign of the cross. Inside, vintage classrooms with transoms over doors are found. As well, there is a study hall, prayer chapel, art workshop and offices.

The hall and the dormitory were designed by the architectural firm of Magoon and MacDonald. The firm also designed four homes in 1930 for college instructors—known as faculty row—which were destroyed to make way for the Capilano Freeway.

Of its design, Alberta Culture notes that it presages many modern buildings in that its historical revival features have been greatly simplified and minimized. Although adorned with Gothic Revival details such as a pointed arch, finials and battlements at the main entry, the proportions and simplified squared silhouette are more modern than medieval.

The hall is joined with the men's dormitory to the east and to an administration building with science laboratories and more class-rooms to the west.

The college's original purpose, when started in 1921, was a preparatory training college for men in the preaching and teaching ministries of the Lutheran Church. It was first located in the Caledonian Temperance Hotel at 98th Street and 108th Avenue.

In 1924 the college's board of control purchased the John Fraser estate, then owned by the city. The purchase included John Fraser's original log cabin. Fraser, who died in 1919, was born in Jasper House in 1840, son of factor Colin Fraser.

His claim to River Lot 28 was staked in 1873 when he built the cabin. The cabin was removed in 1983 to make way for a new gymnasium. The cabin's whereabouts are now a mystery.

Before becoming the permanent western Canadian college in 1924, Concordia had begun in 1921 to provide education and religious instruction to the local Lutheran congregation, largely centred around Stony Plain.

Instrumental in its founding were the Reverend E. Eberhardt and its first principal (later president) Albert Schwermann. ■

ASH RESIDENCE • 1914

Residence Lavishly Enhanced
6256 Ada Boulevard

WILLIAM ASH, an early Edmonton jeweler, might not recognize his former Highlands home if he were alive to visit it today.

While the facade of the grand three-storey house, known as the Ash Residence, remains much as it was originally, the interior has been lavishly enhanced. The white wood frame house now bristles with numerous period embellishments, plus an impressive array of antiques added by its most recent owners.

Located two doors west of the famed Magrath Mansion, the home was a little more staid when built in 1914 for William and Jane Ash. They lived there until 1924, when they moved to a more humble home in Oliver.

The 2,600-square-foot house features a pillared south and west facing verandah on a concrete foundation cut to resemble stone. Maple flooring is found throughout the interior.

The most recent owners have spent $80,000 for restorations above the $275,000 they paid for the property in 1982. They virtually gutted the whole home, taking out 30 bins of lath and plaster. The subsequent improvements were many and varied.

Besides the wrap-around front porch, there is an enclosed rear porch destined to become a kitchen dinette. The second floor has front and back balconies.

From 1907 to 1928, Ash and his brother Sydney were proprietors of Ash Brothers Diamond Hall, a Jasper Avenue jewelry emporium. The business featured an elaborately detailed hall with ornate pillared display cases with elegant glass cabinets. It included a workshop ''for the manufacture of artistic jewellery,'' a 1911 article in *The Edmonton Bulletin* said. After it closed, Ash and his family moved to Toronto where he died in 1931. ∎

Renovated master bedroom of Ash residence.

MAGRATH MANSION • 1913

Home to Ukrainian Diocese

6240 Ada Boulevard

THIS SWANKY Georgian Style mansion, shrouded in trees and overlooking the North Saskatchewan River valley, is an exemplary monument to the economy of Alberta.

Designated a Provincial Historical Resource in 1975—the first such designation in Edmonton—the three-storey Magrath Mansion represents the climax of one of Edmonton's earliest and biggest real estate booms. The story is an archetypal tale of the rise and fall of Alberta capitalists, then and in years to come. These were men with big dreams and expensive tastes; they were also men who were out of step with the province's cyclical resource-based economy.

The red brick mansion, with full-width white verandah with sweeping porticos and carved Ionic wood columns, was built by real estate tycoon William J. Magrath in 1913. Magrath died seven years later. In 1933, his family was evicted by a city sheriff for nonpayment of taxes.

Magrath intended the house as a focal point and anchor to the community that he developed along the northeastern banks of the North Saskatchewan River. The community, which he named the Highlands, was one of the first to be marketed as a high-class residential area, complete with minimum building and development standards.

Since 1948, the mansion has been owned by the Ukrainian Catholic Episcopal Corporation of Western Canada. The diocese, which ministers to the needs of 44,000 Albertans, purchased the property from the city for $25,000. The church selected the mansion because it was large enough for all of the chancery's needs: a chapel, offices and accommodation for the bishop, priests and nuns.

Other than some fading of the silken wallpaper, few changes have occurred in the original decor and layout. While the formal dining room now serves as a chapel, the Czechoslovakian-made leaded glass mahogany china cabinet, mahogany wall panelling, light fixture, and grape-motif ceiling remain intact. Only a divider with a religious motif has been added.

In the basement, the Magrath's indoor pool is now the diocesan library and archives. The kitchen was moved into a former storage room in the basement. And the third floor— once containing a billiards room and ball room—was turned into accommodation for priests.

Magrath's wife Ada—after whom he named Ada Boulevard when he was developing the Highlands—imported the best of everything in her travels around the world. Hand-painted linen and silk wallpaper is found throughout. Viennese hand-painted cherubs dance on the hand-sculptured ceiling in the living room, now used as the chancery reception room.

The 14-room mansion was designed by architect Ernest W. Morehouse, who also designed a number of other Highlands homes and buildings. Accounts of the cost of the house vary—from $50,000 to $85,000. The mansion was built on an estate of 10 lots and the construction included a separate carriage house, which has since been sold for use as a private residence.

Magrath and his partner, Bidwell Holgate, paid prominent city capitalist John A. McDougall $35,000 for 23 lots — a year before the 1912 economic collapse.

Magrath and Holgate spent between $10,000 and $20,000 to bring streetcar service to the area, as well as other modern improvements rare in those days, including concrete sidewalks, street lighting, sewer and water mains.

The swanky Magrath Mansion.

Capital on Corinthian column, Magrath Mansion.

Like his partner, Magrath attempted to distance his private holdings from his business affairs by transferring title to his home for "one dollar and other valuable considerations" to his wife Ada. In October 1913, the Magraths valued their new home and estate at $60,000.

While this move may have staved off business creditors, the Magrath family's inability to pay city taxes saw them stripped of their Highlands properties in two stages. In 1927 the first properties were taken, and then in 1933, the mansion itself was sold to the city for the paltry sum of $1,050.

The mansion stands as a fitting tribute to Magrath, his dreams, and his accomplishments. ■

HOLGATE MANSION • 1912

Manor Retains Regal Character
6210 Ada Boulevard

THE TUDOR REVIVAL Holgate Mansion was built in 1912 by real estate entrepreneur Bidwell A. Holgate who came to Edmonton from Ontario in 1908.

The 5,500-square-foot, three-storey mansion is encircled by a verandah on three sides. It has a second floor balcony, as well as a number of sleeping porches. The house cost $35,000 to build and originally occupied a five-acre site.

Facing south, the rambling but regal mansion has a view of the North Saskatchewan River valley.

The garage and an outdoor swimming pool were installed by subsequent owners Michael and June Liknaitzky. Richard and Jeanie Vanderwell, who bought the house in 1983 for $265,000, said the house is in good structural condition, although the balconies and sleeping porches need repairs. Since buying the home, the Vanderwells have stripped carpeting from the main floor to expose the original oak flooring. They have also renovated the kitchen.

The front door opens to a vestibule with leaded glass windows. The foyer features oak parquet flooring and panelling, linen wallcoverings and a vintage brass light fixture. A mahogany-finished ladies' parlor, to the foyer's left, has hand-painted flower frescos on the ceiling, highlighted by ornate plaster molding or dentils.

The living room entrance on the other side of the foyer is flanked by oak pillars. Here oak panelling and ceiling beams are found. There is a hammered brass fireplace, as well as a leaded glass door to the verandah.

The dining room has a built-in oak china cabinet or breakfront with leaded glass doors. There are oak ceiling beams and linen wallcoverings. A smoking parlor or den has a tile fireplace and built-in shelving, plus an

original four-wall painting depicting the settlement of western Canada. A butler's pantry and the kitchen complete the main floor.

The second floor has five bedrooms, a sun porch and two bathrooms. Both bathrooms contain original tubs—one is seven feet long. Three more bedrooms and another bathroom are on the third floor.

Holgate and Magrath, who were partners in Magrath Holgate Company had made a fortune in Edmonton's real estate boom prior to the First World War. They developed the Highlands community as one of the city's first upper-crust neighborhoods. As part of that plan, the partners purchased a parcel of land, where the Holgate Mansion sits today, for $30,000 in 1912 from John A. McDougall.

The manor shuffled through numerous hands in the years to come. Eventually foreclosed upon in 1982, the mansion sat empty for about a year before being bought by the Vanderwells. ■

MOREHOUSE HOUSE • 1904

Georgian Revival Lovingly Maintained
11153 - 64 Street

THE MOREHOUSE HOUSE is remarkable both for the architect who built it, and for the high degree of originality maintained by owners to date.

The former residence of architect Ernest W. Morehouse bristles with traditional fixtures and finishings. While the gleam is the result of elbow-grease from its latest owners, Jerry and Linda Lack, they too were amazed at the resistance to modernize displayed by previous occupants.

Since purchasing the Georgian Revival two-storey in 1975, the Lacks have invested another $50,000 in repairs, renovations, and maintenance. Pride of ownership is reflected in the home's pristine condition. On the main floor the trim and fixtures were buffed with loving care. The living room has a bay window, coal-burning fireplace with original grating and oak mantle, and a decorative open-beam ceiling.

Sliding pocket doors still with original key, open to the formal dining room, a definite highlight of this home. The attention to detail displayed by artisans of that era is found in the orange tree pattern present in the crystal glass of the dining room's vintage brass and glass light fixture.

Georgian Revival architecture features broad eaves with brackets, a full-width verandah supported by twin boxed columns, a tall decorated chimney stack, symmetrical plan and a hipped roof with twin onamental dormers. Morehouse House, built in 1912 for $4,500, is a relatively modest example of this trend in Alberta's residential architecture.

Ernest Morehouse designed this home for himself, and a number of other Highlands residences for the area's developer, Magrath, Holgate and Company. More notable examples are the Magrath Mansion and the Holgate Mansion.

Other buildings designed by Morehouse include the neighboring Gibbard Block, built as one of the city's first luxury apartment blocks in 1913. The Highlands Methodist Church where he was an active member and a number of early commercial buildings also rank among his credits. *Alberta Past and Present*, written by John Blue, makes salutory mention of Morehouse:

''Edmonton is exceptionally fortunate in the number of men of high attainments who are to be found in its business and professional circles, and to this class belongs Ernest W. Morehouse, whose advancement along professional lines has been continuous, bringing him at length to an enviable position among the architects of Alberta.''

Morehouse married Miss Minnie L. Jaynes in 1892 and they had two children. After his arrival here, Morehouse established an architectural and contracting firm with Arthur Nesbitt. In 1914, Morehouse established his own company. He was an active member of the Alberta Association of Architects and served as its vice-president in 1921. ■

GIBBARD BLOCK • 1913

Old Building Fashionable Again
6427-112 Street

WILLIAM MAGRATH, Bidwell Holgate, and William Gibbard would probably be happy to see their charming apartment block turn up on the positive side of the balance sheet.

In the 1980s, the Gibbard Block—named for William T. Gibbard—emerged from a period of decay to become fashionable and profitable once again. The main floor of the Highlands building is home to the French restaurant La Bohème Café Galerie.

The success of restaurant owner Ernst Eder parallels the Gibbard Block's renaissance from aging disrepair to authentic delight.

Eder, an Austrian immigrant, came to Canada as a dancer in 1972 with $40 in his pocket. He opened La Bohème in 1979 with a second-hand stove and $60.

By 1985 he had secured half-ownership of the 11,000-square-foot building, which he said was worth $333,000. Eder has also invested $250,000 in plumbing, a new heating system, interior renovations and other improvements.

The building's architect was Ernest Morehouse. He designed numerous early Highlands homes, including those of early Edmonton capitalists William J. Magrath and Bidwell Holgate.

As Edmonton's population soared in the early 1900s, Magrath and Holgate developed the Highlands community, which included some of the city's earliest luxury homes. They also wanted a luxury apartment building in the area. But as the city's early real estate boom escalated, Magrath and Holgate leveraged their assets to acquire more and more prime real estate and other diversified industrial investments.

Consequently, another investor was required to build an apartment block. Enter William T. Gibbard, president of the Gibbard Furniture Company of Napanee, Ontario. For a one-third investment, Gibbard's name graced the block, and until 1914, 57th Street between 112th and 118th Avenues also carried his name.

The threesome purchased the site in October 1912 for ''one dollar and other valuable considerations'' from city clerk Manley Cryderman.

Some reports have indicated that the Gibbard Block was erected at a cost of $90,000. This is a distinct possibility, considering the inflationary boom times which existed in 1912, and the cost of importing the materials and craftsmen into an area that was little more than open farm land on the city's hinterland. And with stiff competition from the more central Arlington Apartments and LeMarchand Mansion, their business proposition needed all possible amenities if it was to succeed.

Unfortunately, Magrath, Holgate, and Gibbard's plans were washed up in the fall-out from that pre-war period of high hopes and high prices. Magrath died and his family lost his home. Holgate pulled out of his Ada Boulevard mansion with a quit claim and the shirt on his back. Gibbard died in 1920, and all of their interests in the Gibbard Block were foreclosed upon in a complicated legal action in 1926. ■

Magrath Mansion dining room, now used as a chapel.

Above: Refurbished living and dining rooms of Ash Residence.
Left: Vintage decorating, Morehouse House dining room.

185

HIGHLANDS SCHOOL • 1920
An Early Tale of Boom and Bust
11509-62 Street

BOOM AND BUST—it's a woeful tale with a familiar ring. This story isn't about real estate assembled at inflated prices in the early 1980s. Rather, it is about a school, similarly affected, but with beginnings pre-dating the First World War.

Highlands Junior High School was caught in that economic bust. Construction started in 1913, but when the war started the following year, funding was hard to come by.

So the school languished unoccupied until 1916, when the first floor of the two-storey brick and sandstone structure finally opened. However, it wasn't until 1920 that the building was completed at a total cost of $210,722.

The school also served as Edmonton's first normal school or teacher's college until 1923, with over 300 teachers graduating.

Highlands, with a crenellated roof line and an imposing central tower, was a duplicate of King Edward, a south side school which opened in 1913. Both schools were designed by George Turner, the Edmonton Public School Board's staff architect.

Prior to the opening of Highlands, classes in the area were held in three temporary wood frame buildings, one of which was preserved on the school grounds for several years as a janitor's residence. Parents chafed at the delays in construction, since a 1911 agreement which annexed Highlands to Edmonton specified the completion of a large permanent school. It wasn't until 1920 that sewer, water and electrical services were connected to Highlands.

In the 1980s, Highlands was still a hallowed hall of learning for students in Grades Seven to Nine. Its original 17 rooms were supplemented with an addition in 1958 that added five classrooms and new offices.

About $70,000 in renovations were carried out in 1970. The building was reported to be in good structural condition, but expensive to heat.

Inside, little remains of its original traditional grandeur. There is a wood-panelled foyer with terrazzo flooring, marble stairs and leaded glass windows. On the second, a leaded glass bay window is in the vice-principal's office, which has a trap-door access to the tower.

The halls have terrazzo flooring, but moldings are obscured with heavy coats of paint. Quaint overhead transoms have been covered because of fire regulations. The original coal-fired boilers, now converted to natural gas, labor dutifully in the basement.

Highlands was constructed at the end of one of the most prolific building periods the public school board has seen. There were 13 schools built from 1909 to 1914, the years in which Turner served as board architect.

Turner—along with Highlands—was a victim of the depression. Carried along with the euphoria of the economic boom, he submitted his resignation as an employee in the spring of 1914, and asked to be engaged as a consulting architect on a contractual basis. The school board agreed, but only hired him for three months. When the war started in August 1914, board cutbacks were immediate. Building operations were temporarily suspended and Turner's contract was one of the first to go. ■

TRANSIT HOTEL • 1908
Packingtown Watering Hole
12720 Fort Road

SANDWICHED BETWEEN high-rise apartments and old meat packing plants on the Fort Road, the Transit Hotel continues to ply refreshment upon thirsty clientele. But there have been changes.

When built, the boomtown structure went up in an area known informally as Packingtown, due to the proximity of the J.Y. Griffin and Burns meat packing plants.

The Transit's exterior no longer sports its original styling. The two-storey verandah and the finialed roof line are gone. The wood siding is covered with stucco. One storey additions have been built onto the north and east faces. Little remains of its original interior decor, save for doors and trim, decorative radiators and the old boiler.

When Patrick Dwyer bought the land it sits on in 1907 along with another 198 lots in the same area, he paid $3,000. The area is still known as the Dwyer subdivision. The hotel itself cost another $50,000.

In September 1908, under the headline, "New hotel in Packing-town," *The Edmonton Bulletin* reviewed the Transit's credentials.

"The Transit Hotel, the commodious new hostelry that will supply the hotel accommodations for Edmonton's thriving suburb commonly known as Packingtown opened to the public on Friday last."

The watering hole measured 32 by 80 feet, had 40 bedrooms and "the two upper flats were provided with lavatories and bathrooms." The first floor featured a "roomy rotunda," office, a dining room and a kitchen. The hotel was built with electricity and was supplied with hot and cold running water.

The Transit's location in Packingtown was no accident. It was strategically situated near the Grand Trunk Pacific Railway lines which came into Edmonton in 1909 and close to the

Transit Hotel, circa 1913, the hub of Packingtown.

J.Y. Griffin slaughterhouse which was built about the same time.

"At that time the only buildings in the vicinity were farms and were situated at fairly regular intervals of half a mile. The hotel which cost in the neighborhood of $50,000 looked at that time much like a 'Folly' but as things turned out it was just one further demonstration of western foresight," said *The North Edmonton Industrial Review* in 1913.

Boomtown architecture evolved from commercial subdivision practices. The lots were narrow and deep in order to maximize the number of commercial fronts that would be exposed to the street. Therefore architectural ornament was concentrated on the facade. ■

Left: Built-in oak cabinet in dining room, Holgate Mansion.
Opposite page: Tudor-Style exterior of Holgate Mansion.

EASTWOOD SCHOOL • 1924

Controversy Over Name

12038-81 Street

ONE OF ITS PRINCIPALS called it a shoe factory, Edmonton Public School Board trustees called it Frank Scott School and local residents insisted on calling it Eastwood School.

The school's austere lines prompted its principal in 1987, Jorn Brauer, to liken its design to that of an industrial structure in the business of manufacturing footwear.

Back in 1923, the EPSB named it Frank Scott School in honor of one of the sitting trustees. Unfortunately, they failed to consult the community, and after two petitions and a court case, reversed their decision in 1925.

By 1987, Eastwood Elementary and Junior High School was a centre of learning for 275 children from kindergarten to Grade Nine. A third are of Native background, mostly Cree.

The size of the school population and its ethnic composition are among the changes here since earlier times when overflowing classes forced double shifts and three-hour days in class for children in some grades. And from 1926 until the opening of Eastglen Composite High School in 1954, the district high school was located on the building's third floor.

Original building features included a glass block ceiling over the second floor, intended to allow natural light into the centre of the building from two skylights in the top floor above. But the skylights have been sealed in and the sunshine replaced with fluorescent lighting.

Extra wide halls were incorporated into the design to allow children indoor play space during inclement weather. On the second floor, the hall doubled as the school's original assembly area. The original stage and library were turned into offices after the hangar-like gymnasium annex was built onto the east face in 1936.

The building was constructed to replace the original Eastwood School, a wood frame two-storey at 120th Avenue and 80th Street built for $3,800 in 1913. Construction of the permanent brick and stone school was authorized by the EPSB in 1922. Designed by board architect Herbert Story, the building cost about $350,000.

Eastwood School was finished in tapestry brick of local manufacture with Pembina stone dressings from Entwistle. The third floor was not completed until 1926, when Eastwood High School opened under principal Ernest E. Hyde. The gymnasium was built 10 years later for $20,000.

The first principal of the permanent school was Charles B. Willis, who was noted for his pioneering efforts in the area of intelligence testing. Avid sportsman A.J. Skitch took over as principal in 1929, and remained at the helm for a remarkable 33 years.

During the period of school construction between 1920 and 1930, close attention was given to building costs which were reflected in the design. The result was a move towards economy of architectural ornament while maintaining contemporary western Canadian standards of classroom comfort and convenience. In keeping with this trend Eastwood school is modelled after a Collegiate Gothic Style. However, detailing has been greatly simplified.

The crenellated parapet, pointed arched entryway and broad three-storey pilastered strips are the telling hallmarks of the style incorporated into the design.

Although more modest than urban schools built before 1914, Eastwood represents the last of the Historic Revival Style schools constructed before World War II. ∎

PARKDALE SCHOOL • 1912

Alma Mater of Superstars

11648-85 Street

SEVEN MEMBERS of the famous Edmonton Commercial Grads basketball team first pounded the court on the third floor of Parkdale Elementary and Junior High School.

The Grads' starting line-up at one time was made up of Parkdale girls, and it was Miss Olive Thomson who gave them skills that the coach of the Edmonton Grads, J. Percy Page could use.

From 1914 until they were disbanded in 1940, the Grads won 502 of 522 games, held 108 local, provincial, national and international titles and were undisputed world champions for 17 years in a row. The inventor of basketball Dr. James Naismith called them the "finest basketball team that ever stepped out on a floor."

But future grads weren't the only ones to benefit from the Parkdale regimen. Edgar Millen, the RCMP constable who was killed in 1932 by Albert Johnson—the Mad Trapper of Rat Creek—studied here from 1913 to 1920. And so too did thousands of stalwart citizens and unsung heroes now scattered around the city, province and the globe. Their old alma mater still dominates the humble community and continues to serve the educational needs of its children.

Many renovations and paint jobs have been carried out over the years but some items endure. That includes the twin 1912 boilers built by J.A. Lockerbie Heating and Ventilation Limited of Edmonton laboring in the basement, a massive fan induction motor patented in 1905, the 12-inch high moldings with multitudinous layers of paint and one original slate blackboard. Of course the classrooms still have their separate cloakrooms and built-in corner cabinets and drawers.

Its traditional facade of brick with Bedford stone trim, while not the most ornate, still adds a gracious Gothic touch to one of the city's oldest neighborhoods. The three-storey building, similar to Ritchie and McCauley Schools, features a crenellated roof line, a crest inscribed with the year of construction, 1912, and the traditional separate boys and girls entrances.

Its Collegiate Gothic Style is considered a secular version of the Gothic Revival design used for churches and was common for educational buildings constructed across Canada from 1900 to 1925. Used to emulate the great institutions of learning like Oxford and Cambridge Universities, its distinguishing characteristics include buttressing, pointed Tudor arches and the crenellated roof.

It was designed by the Edmonton Public School Board building commissioner George Turner and was built in 1912 for $100,000 as part of the board's biggest ever building spree. Its official opening in April 1913 was delayed a month due to a $10,000 fire.

Built to relieve overcrowding at temporary schools in north Delton and Eastwood, another four classrooms were added to the third floor in 1919. Student enrolment in its early years was over 500 and rose to 651 in 1921.

In 1957 a gymnasium was built on the west side at a cost of $85,000. The former third floor drill hall of the Edmonton Grads was converted into classroom and library space. ■

SHERIFF ROBERTSON HOUSE • 1913
First Sheriff's Home
8120 Jasper Avenue

CROMDALE RESIDENTS remembered him as an elderly man, sitting in a rocking chair on the impressive 60-foot-wide porch with its sprawling view of the North Saskatchewan River valley.

He first came here in 1879 simply to sate his appetite for buffalo hunting. But for Walter Scott Robertson—who was to become the first sheriff of the Edmonton judicial district and a pioneer theatre and opera sponsor—the sight of the river valley took such a grip on him that he vowed to return with his wife and six children.

The enchanting house he built for his retirement was his to enjoy for only two years. Robertson died in 1915 at the age of 74.

Termed prairie-style architecture, the 2,000-square-foot house was designed by local architect Alfred Marigon Calderon, who also designed LeMarchand Mansion and McIntosh House.

Calderon was heavily influenced by renowed American architect Frank Lloyd Wright, who designed the first "prairie-style" house in Kamkakee, Illinois, in 1900. One trademark of the prairie style was the use of natural materials with little historical ornament.

Wright had incorporated a cruciform plan into many of his early designs and Calderon also did this in Robertson's house.

The most striking feature of the house is the octagonal rotunda with its two-storey ceiling featuring an octagonal skylight capped with a cupola. Interior lights provide night-time magic.

Calderon designed the rotunda with symmetry in mind. The oak door to the serving area adjoining the dining room and kitchen was built to compare favorably with an alcove seat that disguises a wood box.

The walls feature oak wainscotting with eight original Tiffany-style lamps in the corners.

In its cruciform design, the house is divided into four sections surrounding the central rotunda. At the front is the vestibule and the expansive porch with an overhang extending over a semi-circular carriage way.

On the west is the parlor with vintage sconce lighting fixtures. Double French doors open to a sun porch, while an opening leads to the dining room, which has the original three-quarter leatherette wainscotting on its walls.

On the east are two large bedrooms and a bathroom. The master bedroom has double French doors with transom to a sun porch. The other bedroom still has the original but fading pink and gold leaf design paper on the walls.

Robertson purchased the land for $800 and his building permit showed the house to have a value of $10,000. After his death, Robertson's widow continued to live in the house until 1919 when it was sold for $12,000 to lawyer Gordon Winkler.

In a 1908 interview with *The Edmonton Bulletin*, Robertson recalled:

"I felt that for dairying it would be the greatest country on the continent, and that with the railroads there would be great development. Besides that, there was and is, something in the climate or the country that makes men more daring than in the east. They are not afraid to take chances here."

During the Riel Rebellion in 1885, the Robertsons were one of three families brave enough to continue living outside the protective palisades of the fort. The other two were the Frank Oliver and John Cameron families.

Following page: Holy Trinity Ukrainian Catholic Church.

Edmonton Region

Most settlers who established the areas surrounding Fort Edmonton in the later 19th century were French. In St. Albert, Morinville, Bon Accord, Legal and other communities, Oblate Fathers of the Order of Mary Immaculate, such as Father Lacombe and Father Leduc, undertook to establish a genuine Francophone presence. Many vestiges of Franco-Albertan culture still remain, most of them religious. In St. Albert, Father Lacombe's Chapel remains the oldest building in Alberta. Nearby, the St. Albert Church and the Vital Grandin Centre reflect the continuing dedication of the Oblate bishops and priests, as do the Church of St. Jean Baptiste and Notre Dame

Convent in Morinville and the St. Vital Church in Beaumont.

By the 1890s, many other ethnic groups, particularly from eastern Europe, were making their presence felt in the Edmonton area. Architectural declarations of these cultures are also to be found in the communities surrounding Edmonton. The Holy Trinity Ukrainian Catholic Church on Highway 19, the Smeltzer House in Sherwood Park and the Multicultural Centre in Stony Plain all provide glimpses into the cultural diversity which came to predominate in northern Alberta.

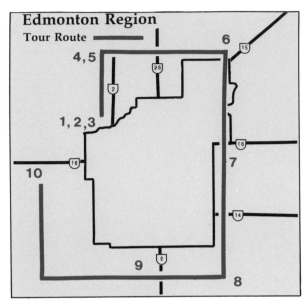

Edmonton Region

Tour Route ▬▬▬

1. *Vital Grandin Centre*
2. *Father Lacombe Chapel*
3. *St. Albert Roman Catholic Church*
4. *Notre Dame Convent*
5. *Church of St. Jean Baptiste*
6. *Alberta Hospital*
7. *Smeltzer House*
8. *St. Vital Church*
9. *Holy Trinity Ukrainian Church*
10. *Stony Plain Multicultural Centre*

VITAL GRANDIN CENTRE • 1887

A Tribute to a Saint
St. Albert

VITAL GRANDIN CENTRE, one of the first buildings erected in St. Albert, stands as a tribute to the early missionary efforts of the Roman Catholic order of the Oblates of Mary Immaculate (OMI).

Sitting atop Mission Hill and overlooking the Sturgeon River, the reconstructed building was originally the headquarters for Bishop Vital Grandin. By 1987 the three-storey building had become an historical house and administrative headquarters for OMI's Alberta and Saskatchewan district.

Since it was completed in 1887, many changes have occurred to the building at 5 St. Vital Avenue. The latest was a $1.2 million renovation in 1981 which returned the building to its early glory.

The centre—finished in cream-colored wood siding with white trim, a cedar shingle roof and log walls—is on a stone and brick foundation. After designation as a Provincial Historical Resource in 1978, Alberta Culture supervised and contributed $75,000 toward its restoration.

Inside, mementoes and historic artifacts illustrate the life of Grandin, as well as the arduous life and times of many Oblate missionaries.

Grandin, who became bishop of St. Albert in 1871, had been responsible for establishing the Catholic Church in western Canada. He has been declared "venerable" by the church—the first step toward sainthood.

Construction of the centre, also known as Grandin House and the Bishop's Palace, began in 1882. Due to lack of funds it wasn't completed until 1887.

The building was designed in the shape of the cross by Brother Patrick Bowes, with dormer windows and a majestic front staircase in a style typical of French Canadian convents of the 1800s. Logs were cut from the shores of Big Lake and floated down the Sturgeon River to St. Albert.

The centre was originally intended as a convent for the Grey Nuns, but they exchanged it with Grandin for his former quarters, since the bishop and missionaries were poorly housed at that time. It served as the bishop's residence until 1912, when the headquarters for the Episcopal See moved to Edmonton. Two bishops lived there—Grandin until his death in 1902, and Emile Legal who was to become Edmonton's first archbishop in 1912.

Grandin's three rooms on the main floor of the east wing are maintained today as an historical house for the public.

Grandin's study features an elaborate desk built by St. Albert Oblate Brothers. It was especially fashioned for Grandin to use standing up since he suffered from an arthritic back condition. A bust of Grandin, given to him by Father Albert Lacombe, sits on the desk.

In the reception area, cabinets contain his personal items, as well as those of Lacombe. These include a candle, one of three given to Grandin by Emperor Napoleon III of France.

A highlight of the main floor is the chapel. Opened in 1888, it includes original stained glass windows, Grandin's sanctuary lamp, a crozier, a ceremonial cross and an impressive hand-carved altar. The altar, fashioned by Brother Brochard in 1888 of local woods, features a three-dimensional scene of the Last Supper. ■

Opposite page, above: Bishop's Palace, now Vital Grandin Centre, St. Albert.
Right: Father Lacombe Chapel interior, 1928.

FATHER LACOMBE CHAPEL • 1861
Province's Oldest Standing Structure
St. Albert

THE BURSE—or container of cloths for Mass—of two Oblate missionaries who were massacred in the opening round of the 1885 Rebellion, and a candle-stand hand-made in Lac La Biche in 1857 rest in the modest white-washed church overlooking downtown St. Albert.

Today, thousands visit Father Lacombe Chapel where these historic artifacts are found. Built in 1861, the chapel is Alberta's oldest standing structure and was designated a Provincial Historical Resource by Alberta Culture in 1977.

Reverend Felix Fafard and Reverend Felix Marchand were among the first Oblates ordained in St. Albert. On Good Friday 1885, they were killed at Frog Lake by Cree Indians led by Chief Big Bear. Their burse rests on the chapel altar, with the candle-stand carved by Bishop Faraud to the right.

Originally made from three spruce trees cut on the south side of the Sturgeon River, the chapel was the beachhead for the missionary work of the Roman Catholic order of the Oblates of Mary Immaculate. The Oblates Episcopal See was immense—initially stretching from St. Boniface in Manitoba to the Rocky Mountains and from the 49th parallel to the Arctic Ocean.

The chapel on St. Vital Avenue was constructed by Father Albert Lacombe on a spot said to be chosen by Bishop Alexander Tache, with some prompting from Lacombe. It later became known as Mission Hill.

Lacombe first came to Alberta in 1852. He worked at the Lac St. Anne mission, but the poor soil, early frosts and bad location, convinced him to move closer to Fort Edmonton.

Tache approved the move and advised Lacombe to name the settlement St. Albert to commemorate Lacombe's patron saint. Some

accounts indicate that when completed, the chapel also served as Lacombe's residence, while others say he lived in a separate building.

The chapel was constructed by a work party of Metis under Lacombe's supervision on a spot now occupied by a statue of Father Lacombe. It was built in the post and sill method, originally without nails—a technique commonly used by the Hudson's Bay Company. Its dimensions were 20 by 40 feet. In 1864, unsuccessful goldminers from the banks of the North Saskatchewan River were enlisted to build an extension.

For six years the structure served as the Oblates' humble cathedral. Lacombe himself only stayed until 1870, reportedly saying that St. Albert, then with a burgeoning population of 1,000, had become too civilized.

With the building of a second and larger church that year, the original chapel was moved alongside it to serve as a sacristy. In 1900, the basement of the present brick church was built and services were conducted there until its completion in 1923.

The original chapel succumbed to use as a granary and storehouse before the Oblates moved to preserve it. In 1929, the building was moved to a location west of the present church. The flooring was replaced and the church enclosed in brick to protect it from the elements.

The building was used as a museum for church artifacts until its restoration and re-erection upon the present site between the current church and the Vital Grandin Centre in 1980-81. In 1982, the Oblates gave the building to the provincial government, and leased the land to the province for 99 years.

But the years and restoration have taken their toll. Without a basement or proper foundation, the chapel's flooring and timbers rotted. By 1986 only 40 per cent of the building was original. The roof, floor and parts of the wall have all had to be replaced. The pews and altar are also reconstructions.

Lacombe's contributions to the settlement of the Canadian prairies are numerous and legendary. They include translating the Bible into Cree, and building the first bridge in western Canada in St. Albert across the Sturgeon River.

He endangered his life on at least two occasions, once when he was grazed by a bullet when stopping warring factions of Cree and Blackfoot Indians, and when he aided the sick in the 1870 St. Albert smallpox epidemic.

The Natives called him Man with the Good Heart and Noble Soul. His role in pacifying Indians perturbed with the advent of the railway and the loss of their traditional way of life so impressed the president of the Canadian Pacific Railway Sir William Van Horne, that he granted temporary honorary president status to Lacombe.

Oblate curator Gerry Harnois reports that Lacombe immediately granted himself and a friend lifetime railway passes. "He was no dummy," Harnois observed.

Lacombe died in 1916 at the Lacombe Home for the destitute—which he founded—in Midnapore, south of Calgary. His heart is enshrined there and his body lies in the crypt at the St. Albert Church. ■

ST. ALBERT CHURCH • 1900

Grew From 1861 Mission
St. Albert

SITUATED atop a hill, behind a statue of Father Albert Lacombe, St. Albert Roman Catholic Church overlooks the city which grew from an historic early mission.

The church originally was intended as a cathedral after the mission—started in 1861 with Reverend Father Albert Lacombe and 20 Metis families—had grown to become the Episcopal See for Bishop Vital Grandin.

Plans called for a fancy cathedral for the new bishop and so the current church was started in 1900. The basement was built and pressed into service after the existing parish church—the second built at the mission—was destroyed by fire. The first church, Lacombe's chapel, remains as a museum.

Plans changed over the years and the church was completed 10 years later. The Bishop's See was transferred to Edmonton in 1912. And since the parish would be serving a town of only 500 people, a less ornate and slightly smaller church was built.

The Romanesque Revival Style structure is nestled in an enclave of church buildings, on what local residents affectionately call "the Holy Hill." The church stands out, with its red brick exterior, steep staircase, round Rose Window in the centre and bell tower to the east.

Corinthian columns and rounded arches mark the white-painted interior with dark oak pews. A simple, modern-style altar sits to the front of the sanctuary, which is flanked by two alcoves. The right alcove contains the altar with the brass tabernacle where the Sacrament of Holy Communion is kept. A round stained glass window of the Immaculate Heart of Mary is found at the back of this alcove. The baptismal font is located in the left alcove.

The only major structural change is the white-painted wall at the back of the sanctuary. Originally, there was a dark oak partition much further back. The partition gave way to the wall, which brings the priest and altar closer to the congregation.

Unfortunately, this renovation blocks off a stained glass window on the left of the sanctuary. The window depicts the Heart of Jesus and now is visible only to those going from behind the sanctuary to the basement.

Reminders of the church's rich past abound both inside and out. The bodies of Reverend Father Albert Lacombe, Bishop Grandin and Reverend Father Hippolyte Leduc, vicar-general at the time Grandin was bishop, lie in the basement crypt. A white-painted poplar altar carved by Oblate brothers in 1883, sits at the front of the crypt and is flanked by wooden angels. Display cases along the wall house artifacts from early church life.

Bishop Emil Legal is buried in a cemetery north of the nearby Star of the North Retreat House.

Brass candlesticks given to Grandin in 1874 by the government of France are still used. A statue of the Virgin Mary and the Christ Child sits just inside the entrance. The priceless statue survived a near disaster a few years ago, when a workman replacing the church carpet pulled on the hand of the Christ Child and it came apart. Fortunately, it was repaired with the assistance of the Provincial Museum. ■

Restored Notre Dame convent, Morinville.

NOTRE DAME CONVENT • 1909

Now Cultural Centre
Morinville

WHILE THE TIMES and interior decor may have changed, the purpose of the restored convent remains the enlightenment of the mind and spirit.

The Notre Dame Convent in Morinville, 30 kilometres north of Edmonton, was originally called the Convent Notre Dame de la Visitation. It was built in three stages for the Roman Catholic order of nuns, Les Filles de Jesus (Daughters of Jesus).

Although the three-storey brick building was vacated by the nuns in the 1960s, and later slated for demolition, it has been restored and most recently housed the Morinville Historical and Cultural Centre.

The central portion was constructed in 1909; the south wing in 1920; and the north wing in 1930. The building's architectural style is known as Second Empire, which was popular in the design of institutional buildings in Quebec and France in the 19th century. Its prominent features include a Mansard roof, dormer windows and a central tower.

The 36,000-square-foot building is now owned by the town. The centre's activities range from an annual heritage festival in August to ongoing pottery and art classes, community socials and weddings.

The building also houses the Morinville Museum, various period rooms, the town library, an historic research library, a chapel that is rented to various religious denominations, a conference room and an art gallery.

Historical centre president Norman Chalifoux recalled: "Our first meeting was standing up because there was no furniture, just $1,200 worth of broken windows, birds flying in and out, and some caved-in plaster ceilings."

Now, its period rooms reflect the history of Morinville and the convent. They include the St. Germain room, decorated in the style of a turn of the century law office, a convalescent room much as it was during the nuns' tenure, and the original chapel, with the history of the nuns' arrival in Morinville painted on the walls.

The central portion of the building has been restored similarly, but not exactly to its original self. The two wings have fairly modern facilities with some retention of the traditional decor, such as the transoms over the doors.

Part of the second floor and all of the third remains as the nuns left it, with such facilities as dormitories for boys and girls, and the nuns' quarters. Or as Chalifoux put it: "The girls to the south, the boys to the north, the nuns in the middle, and never the twain shall meet."

Les Filles de Jesus came to Canada from France in 1902 after a number of their schools had been closed. The first four nuns arrived in Morinville from St. Albert by sleigh on a winter day when the temperature reached minus 35 degrees. They had been invited to teach school in the fledgling French settlement by Reverend Joseph Arcand Ethier, the parish priest.

Soon after, the nuns would spend their summer soliciting donations from workers on the Grand Trunk Pacific Railway being built west of Edmonton. Sufficient monies were gathered to erect the central portion of the present building. It was loosely styled after the Mother House in Brittany, France.

From 1919 until the 1950s, the convent was also the provincial Mother House for the order in Alberta, Montana and California.

The Thibault School District purchased the building in 1968 and used it as an elementary school for the next nine years.

The convent was designated as a Provincial Historical Resource in 1978, as one of the few remaining old-style convents in Alberta. ∎

ST. JEAN BAPTISTE CHURCH • 1908

Church "Shakes in the Wind"
Morinville

DESPITE HEAVY WINDS that have kept it teetering since its construction, it has kept the faith and preserved the French fact in Morinville for years. Its spire still commands Morinville's skyline.

The Quebecois architectural influence on this triple-spired Roman Catholic brick edifice is no coincidence. The town, which numbered about 5,000 souls by 1986, and the surrounding area were originally settled by French Canadians just prior to the turn of the century. The town and the parish drew their names from one of the principal instigators of French Catholic settlement in Alberta—Reverend Jean Baptiste Morin.

It has almost always been a bilingual parish, with masses said in French and English. However, the primary focus has been on the French culture at the parish, which began in 1891. The present building is the third church.

While first glances show an elaborate interior, a closer examination reveals bending pillars and chipped paintwork. "The church is not in good condition structurally—it shakes in the wind," said Reverend Fernand Croteau, parish priest in 1986.

While $72,000 in renovations—including painting, lower stabilization, underpinning of the foundation and a new roof—were carried out in 1973, the superstructure still requires solidifying and the foundation needs reinforcement.

Shortly after its completion a moderate breeze shook the building, much to the chagrin of its pastor and parishioners. Despite follow-up repairs, the problem has remained to this day.

The church is one of the most elaborate and ornate Roman Catholic churches in Alberta, reminiscent of French-Canadian architecture, but with Gothic elements.

Detail of main spire, St. Jean Baptiste Church.

The pillars in the church support a barrel-vaulted ceiling, about 50 feet high, with tin-plated decorative moldings. In fact, all moldings and panelling in the church are made from painted tin.

But the most noteworthy items in the church are 18 massive oil paintings on canvas of Christ and St. John the Baptist. Some of the paintings are cracking and peeling.

The paintings were done in 1925 by Eustache Monty, who painted religious motifs in more than 200 churches in North America.

The first chapel was built in 1891, three kilometres west of the present townsite. The second hewn timber church was built in 1893. With donations and loans totalling $18,000, construction began on the present church in 1907. ∎

ALBERTA HOSPITAL • 1923

Largest Mental Institution
Oliver

THERE WAS many a departmental convolution just prior to the opening of the Institute for the Feeble Minded.

The predecessor of Alberta Hospital Edmonton—known by many as Oliver—officially opened its doors to those then referred to as "the chronically insane" on a warm Dominion Day in 1923.

The three-storey brick and stucco structure known as Building No. 1 was erected on bald prairie northeast of Edmonton. It was first planned by the department of education as a place of incarceration for mentally incapacitated children. Halfway through the planning stages it was turned over to the department of public health, which carried on planning it as "the Home and Training School for Mental Defectives."

Then in the spring of 1923, it was decided to change its nature to a mental hospital for insane adults. The first group of patients to arrive at Oliver included 47 veterans of the First World War.

Building No. 1 is the oldest part of the complex—other early buildings having since been torn down. It features a cruciform layout with crenellated roof line and front bay windows. An arched oak vestibule with terrazzo flooring greets the visitor. Inside, little remains of the original decor, save for interior windows and transoms.

Its design is an attempt at the English Jacobethan Revival Style, characterized by its multi-paned windows, shaped parapet, hip roof and bay windows.

By the late 1980s, the hospital was the largest psychiatric centre in the province, maintaining 650 active treatment beds for the mentally ill. ■

SMELTZER HOUSE • 1920

Sherwood Park Farm
Sherwood Park

A TWO-STOREY brick building, which once served as pioneer homesteader Maurice Smeltzer's farmhouse, was designated a Registered Historic Site in 1986 after a request from the County of Strathcona.

The tradionally-styled farmhouse, situated on a three-acre site near Broadmoor Golf Course, is out of character with encroaching suburbia. Owned by the county since 1977, the 1,800-square-foot building now serves as a community resource centre for visual and cultural programs. It was designated as one of the few surviving examples in the Sherwood Park area of Canadian Four-Square Architecture.

The Canadian Four-Square Style is a derivation of American Georgian Revival architecture. Characteristics include a squarish plan with a pyramidal or hipped roof, a single tall chimney or pair of them, a verandah and possibly one or more dormer windows. Occasionally, there was some classic detailing including dentils under the eaves and columns of pillars supporting the verandah.

The Smeltzer house was built of solid brick, all the way down to the seven-brick thick basement walls and footings. The walls have lath and plaster on top of two layers of brick with an air space between them.

The house features front and back porches, both topped with balconies. Hardwood flooring is found throughout—maple downstairs and fir upstairs. Moldings are the traditional 10-inch height.

The main floor has a parlor off the front entrance. It contains a vintage coal-burning fireplace accented with green ceramic tiles. Partial walls have been removed from the living and dining rooms, as well as two of the four upstairs bedrooms to create larger work areas for contemporary use.

Leaded glass and four-paned windows are in the living room, while the dining room has a combined built-in china cabinet and pass-through counter to a typical small kitchen work area. The kitchen retains its ancient sink and drain board.

The house was first heated by a coal furnace and cook stove. Rural telephone service had been available since 1912, while a gasoline generator and batteries provided electricity. Water was pumped electrically to provide pressure. It was finally connected to Edmonton Power in 1944.

Maurice Smeltzer was born in Huron County, Ontario, in 1867. He settled in Alberta in 1892. His arrival was part of what Alberta Culture calls "a minor land rush to the Edmonton area following completion of the Calgary and Edmonton Railway."

Maurice's wife, Eliza Pithie, came from Scotland and claimed to be a distant relative of poet Robbie Burns. The couple married in 1899 and their son Frank, was born in 1907.

Economic conditions forced Smeltzer to augment his agricultural income by working in Edmonton in the lumber and mining industries. After the turn of the century, he concentrated on his farm and won numerous agriculture medals and prizes.

Alberta Culture said Smeltzer's success is also reflected in the house he constructed in 1920. The farm once had 480 acres. He continued to farm until his death in 1938.

Strathcona County received $72,000 in grants from the Alberta government to facilitate the purchase of the farm. Since then, numerous repairs and renovations have been made. ■

ST. VITAL CHURCH • 1920

A Piece of Old Quebec
Beaumont

WITH ITS highly visible hilltop location and Beaumont unfolding about it, this landmark is a pièce de résistance of old Quebec in Alberta.

St. Vital Church and its community were intended as a bastion of Catholic faith and Francophone culture in a northwest frontier dangerously awash in Protestantism of the Anglophone variety.

While the town probably owes its existence to the church, by 1987 the church's pillars were being eroded. The cultural ones were moving over to make room for the English and the wooden ones in the basement had to be replaced periodically due to rotting from summer ground water.

It is still the largest church in town and French-speaking parishioners still make up about half of the faithful. But now there are two weekly English masses versus one in French.

When the economic boom of the 1970s and early 1980s drove city folk into Edmonton's hinterlands looking for affordable housing, Beaumont's population spiralled from just over 400 in 1973 to almost 4,000 by 1987.

The church underwent $80,000 worth of renovations and changes in the early 1980s, including the replacement of three large arched windows, new paint, carpeting and pews. In 1959, a sacristy was added to the east face.

The brick finished church features a cruciform design and a barrel-vaulted ceiling. There's a silver-finished central steeple flanked by statues on each corner. A block with the construction date is found to the left of the entrance.

A Casavant Frères organ of unspecified vintage is found in the rear choir loft. Access to the bell tower is via a ladder and trap door. Manual labor and a rope announce the celebration of the mass.

Alberta Culture described the church design as the result of a marriage of Quebec parish church designs and 18th century British classicism. Typical of the French Canadian style, the facade is characterized by a central engaged tower surmounted by a Baroque clocher. Two smaller towers placed on the corners of the face were also popular in these designs.

Beaumont's first church was a simple log structure, built around 1894. It was two kilometres south of the present church on a site chosen by Reverend Father Albert Lacombe.

In his book *Short Sketches of the History of the Catholic Churches and Missions in Central Alberta*, circa 1911, Archbishop Emile Legal wrote that the parish of Beaumont "has not the advantage of those special conditions which attract settlers, such as railroads, or coal mines, but is satisfied with the fertility of its soil, and owes its existence to the church built there a little after the arrival of the first settlers."

Parish pioneers first settled here about 1892, and a few years later Bishop Vital Grandin purchased 10 acres of land for the church upon the settlers' request. The parish was named St. Vital after the bishop's patron saint.

Reverend Father P. Perreault, of the religious order of the Oblates of Mary Immaculate, was the first to serve the fledgling Catholic community—once a month on a circuit basis.

A history of the parish by Annette (Lavigne) Gobiel noted that "his arrival was generally announced by a white flag hoisted on a long pole on the hill overlooking the colony." Before the church was built, mass was said in a settler's home. By 1898 there were 45 French-Canadian families and 30 English families in the parish.

But after struggling for many years to properly finish and furnish their humble church, parishioners were struck a blow when the building burned to the ground February 10th, 1918.

The Edmonton Evening Bulletin reported that all was lost, including the bell donated by Father Morin from the "old church at Vercheres. During the fire this bell, worn by long and faithful service, was melted into a long sheet of iron.

By November 1919, the basement of the new building was completed and the cornerstone was blessed. Gobeil's history notes that the church's dimensions were 50 by 100 feet and a 32-by-24-foot sanctuary. Five hundred loads of sand were brought in, three hundred loads of gravel, six hundred loads of rocks and 1,500 bags of cement. Everything except the cement was furnished and transported by the parishioners free of charge.

"Because of the exceptionally harsh winter, work did not resume until the end of May. On July 4th, 1920, the frame of the church was built and the 'St. Jean Baptiste' was celebrated. Father Normandeau sang his first mass exactly 25 years after the first mass by Father Morin in the first chapel in 1895." ■

Byzantine Pearl
Highway 19

HOLY TRINITY Ukrainian Catholic Church is an artistic and architectural pearl—a miniature Byzantine church with three almost perfect baroque spires pointing to the heavens above prairie flatlands. For its early parishioners, who were among the first Ukrainians to settle the province, it was a cultural and religious triumph when they built it in 1918 with their volunteer labor.

Sharing a 20-acre site with a graveyard and separate bell tower, this Eastern miniature is found about two kilometres south of Highway 19 just north of Edmonton International Airport.

Twentieth century conveniences come slowly to this impressive house of worship. Outhouses are still the commode of necessity, power lines were connected just a few years ago, and despite the propane-fired furnace, the church is still too cold to use year-round due to the total lack of insulation.

Finished in beige-painted wood siding with chocolate brown trim, the church is distinguished not only by its three chrome-colored octagonal cupolas—symbolic of the Holy Trinity, but also by its basilican plan and the fine detailing along its edges.

Holy Trinity was designed by architect and priest Reverend Father Philip Ruh, whose works stretch from Chicago to Edmonton, and around and in between. One of Ruh's more famous works, and a designated Historical Resource, is St. Josaphat's Cathedral in Edmonton.

Alberta Culture says Holy Trinity Chruch is considered one of the earliest, if not the first church to be designed by Ruh who arrived in Canada from Ukraine in 1911.

Ruh's studies in architecture were incomplete, and his ethnic background French, but an early posting to Ukraine brought about a life-long appreciation for the

Angels hover in dome of Holy Trinity Ukrainian Catholic Church.

language, culture, and people. As a result, his works were considered sometimes naive in expression and occasionally technically flawed. "Yet always there is that individual element which goes beyond mere stylistic nomenclature, as Ruh forged a body of work truly unique in Canada," says an Alberta Culture study of Ruh's works.

Ruh, who was born Phillippe Roux on August 6, 1883 in Bickenholtz, France, died in Winnipeg, Manitoba, October 24, 1962. The name of Ruh was a spelling he adopted after he joined the Byzantine rite.

The church is a wooden imitation of the ecclesiastical Baroque Style built of masonry during the late 17th to early 18th centuries in Ukraine. Classical features of this architectural style include the towers, the rose window which rests in the facade pediment, the fanlight over the entryway and round arched openings used throughout the building.

The impressive central dome completes the architect's interpretation of the Ukrainian Baroque Style and confirms his attempt to transport the traditional Ukrainian scene, as best as circumstances would allow, into newly settled lands.

Not only does Holy Trinity benefit from Ruh's design—it is also significantly blessed from floor to ceiling with the traditional religious painting of Peter Lipinski. His painstaking efforts are breathtaking in a structure of such humble size.

Lipinski, born in Ukraine in 1888, came to Canada in 1914. He lived in Edmonton until his death in 1975.

Highlights of Lipinski's work at Holy Trinity include painting the wainscotting and colonnades to resemble cut stone, motif borders, eight angels hovering in mandala formation inside the octagonal dome and oil paintings with integrating painted frames on canvas glued directly to the walls. Elaborate swirls, scrolls and border work abound.

Lipinski's work represents a faithful reconstitution of the Byzantine painting style as it existed in Ukraine at the turn of the century.

Lipinski painted 40 Alberta churches as elaborately as Holy Trinity—a marvelous accomplishment for which he was recognized with a scroll by Pope Pius XII.

Coming across such an unexpected oasis in a land often thought of as an architectural desert can be somewhat startling. But in the Ukrainian religious tradition, it was requisite of the rite that the house of worship be painted in such careful and loving fashion. Without it the church was considered unfinished. ■

MULTICULTURAL CENTRE • 1925

Unique Former School
Stony Plain

LOCATED in the Town of Stony Plain, this two-storey brick building was built in 1925 in the middle of an open farmer's field as the area's first regional high school. Now surrounded by the town, it is still owned by the County of Parkland school board number 31, but has been leased to the Stony Plain Multicultural Society since 1973 at $1 a year for 99 years.

The 300-member society subsequently renovated the structure and grounds to the tune of $135,000. While in sound structural condition, it required a massive overhaul and updating of the interior, electrical, mechanical and ventilation systems.

The building is now a centre of Alberta's cultural and historic fabric. Local art and handicrafts can be purchased in the centre's gift shop.

As a result of its architecture—unique to Alberta—its local history and enduring community use, the school was designated a Provincial Historical Resource in 1983.

Its architectural style—a Scottish design derived from the English arts and crafts movement—was popular in the late 19th century as a return to the indigenous buildings of Britain. Architect Stan Gotlieb, who prepared plans for a possible addition, described the school as "medieval in nature, with Gothic-Tudor influence."

The building's exterior features include a complex hip and gable roof—now covered in cedar shakes—multi-paned windows and a square bell-tower with pyramidal roof.

The structure was designed by the Edmonton architectural firm of Blakey, Blakey and Symonds, who also designed Christ Church in Edmonton.

Stony Plain Multicultural Heritage Centre, derived from English arts and crafts style.

Glossary

Compiled by Alberta Culture and Multiculturalism, Historic Sites Service

A

ARCADING: A line of arches raised on columns carved in relief as decoration on a solid wall.

ARCADING

ARTS and CRAFTS: English design movement of the 19th century based on traditional English forms stressing craftsmanship and organic forms in design.

B

BALCONET: A pseudo-balcony; a decorative railing placed on the sill outside a window.

BARREL VAULT: A vault of plain semi-circular cross-section.

BARREL VAULT

BAY WINDOW: A window formed in an angular projection of the wall beyond its general line.

BEAUX-ARTS CLASSICISM: A style taught at the Ecole des Beaux-Arts in Paris in the 19th century based on an eclectic mixture of historic classical elements.

BELLCAST ROOF: A roof, the eaves of which are flared out.

BELVEDERE: A roof top pavilion intended as a viewing platform.

BOOMTOWN FRONT ARCHITECTURE: A false front which hides the actual roof line, intended to increase the apparent size and dignity of frontier commercial architecture. Ornament is usually classical in origin. Overhanging cornices and round arched windows are common features.

BUTTRESS: An exterior attached pier intended to reinforce a wall.

C

CANADIAN FOUR-SQUARE STYLE: Derived from Georgian Colonial sources, the Four-Square residence is square in plan, usually 1 1/2 to 2 1/2 stories capped by a pyramidal or hipped roof. Ornament is classical in nature, but is used more sparingly than in Georgian Revival designs.

CHICAGO SCHOOL: A commercial style of architecture pioneered in Chicago in the late 19th century, used especially in tall buildings and characterized by steel or iron frame construction and triple-paned Chicago windows.

CLAPBOARD: The overlapping and wedge-shaped horizontal boards which cover a wood frame wall.

CLOCHER: French Canadian term for a bell tower located centrally on a church facade.

COLLEGIATE GOTHIC: A style derived from English medieval colleges adapted for use in 19th and 20th century North American education building designs.

COMMERCIAL STYLE: Refers to a type of late 19th century to early 20th century commercial building which is generally five to sixteen stories high. The character of their facades derives from the fenestration and ornamentation, which when present, is usually limited to the cornice and ground level.

COMMERCIAL STYLE

CORBELLING: A projection or series of steeped projections in masonry and especially in brick.

CORINTHIAN COLUMN: The most slender and ornate classical order. The Corinthian Order usually has a fluted shaft with leaf and scroll shapes in the capital.

CORINTHIAN COLUMN

CORNICE: Any projecting decorative moulding along the top of a building, wall, or arch.

CORNICE

CRENELLATED: A wall notched or indented at the top.

CUPOLA: A dome-shaped roof on a round base, often surmounting another dome.

D

DORIC COLUMN: A column of the classical Greek Doric order. The column may be smooth or fluted, the capital and base are of the simple cushion type.

DORMER: A window placed vertically in a sloping roof with a roof of its own.

DORMER

DOUBLE HUNG WINDOW: A two part window in which the counter-weighted panes slide up and down in the frame.

F

FACADE: The exterior face or wall of a building.

FINIAL: An ornament which is situated at the point of a spire or at the end of a gable.

FINIAL

FRENCH-CANADIAN CHURCH STYLE: The church type originating in Quebec generally characterized by a longitudinal medium pitch gable roof and a clocher located centrally on the facade.

G

GABLE: A vertically triangular portion of the end of a building having a double sloping roof; hence, gable roof.

GABLE

GEORGIAN REVIVAL: The 19th and 20th century revival of 18th century English architecture derived from classical, Renaissance and Baroque forms.

GOTHIC ARCH: Any arch with a point at its apex, characteristic of, but not confined to, Gothic architecture.

GOTHIC REVIVAL: The 19th century revival of medieval architecture characterized by pointed arches and complex ornamentation, including crockets, finials, gingerbread trim, and high pitched roofs.

GOTHIC REVIVAL

H

HALF-TIMBERING: Exposed timber foundations, supports, etc., the walls of which are filled in with plaster or other materials.

HIGH VICTORIAN GOTHIC REVIVAL: A middle phase of the

Gothic Revival, characterized by polychromatic ornament and an abundance of heavy, architectural detailing.

HIPPED ROOF: A roof sloped on all four sides; the sides meet at a centre ridge.

HIPPED ROOF

I

IONIC COLUMN: A column, of the classical Ionic order usually fluted, with large scroll shaped capitals.

IONIC COLUMN

J

JACOBETHAN REVIVAL: The 19th century revival of later 16th century Elizabethan and early 17th century Jacobean English architecture which combined Gothic and Renaissance elements.

JERKINHEAD ROOF: The end of a roof which is formed into a shape intermediate between a gable and a hip roof.

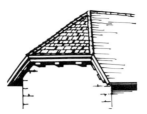

JERKINHEAD ROOF

K

KEYSTONE: In masonry, the central, often embellished, voussoir of an arch. Until the keystone is in place, no true arch action is incurred.

KEYSTONE

L

LANTERN: A windowed structure crowning a roof or dome.

LANTERN

LATE GOTHIC REVIVAL STYLE: The last of three phases of the Gothic Revival. It is distinguished from the High Victorian Gothic Revival in that the use of Gothic motifs is less emphatic.

M

MANSARD ROOF: A roof having a double slope on all four sides. The lower slope is longer and steeper than the upper.

MANSARD ROOF

MISSION STYLE: A type of structure usually built of wood and associated with early settlement periods. Characterized by a simple rectangular plan, gabled roof and absence of architectural ornament.

MODERNE STYLE: A style popularized in the 1920s to 1940s characterized by curved corners, strip windows, large unrelieved surfaces, and a generally streamlined appearance.

N

NICHE: A wall recess intended to hold a sculpture or other decorative element.

P

PALLADIAN MOTIF: A door or window in three parts, separated by posts, the two outer being flat-topped, and the central higher and arched.

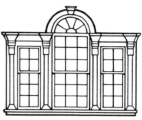

PALLADIAN MOTIF

PARAPET: A low wall, along the edge of a roof which may be crenellated or otherwise embellished.

PEDIMENT: The triangular gable end extending from the roof above the cornice which is often highly decorated. This element may also be found over a window or door.

PIER: A column or mass of masonry attached to a wall designed to support a concentrated load.

PILASTER: A shallow pier or pillar projecting only slightly from a wall.

PLAN: Line drawing made by projection of relative building parts on a horizontal plane.

PORTICO: A covered or roofed space at the entrance of a building. In a classical portico, the roof pediment is supported by columns.

POST and SILL CONSTRUCTION: A type of wood construction characterized by horizontal beams slotted into vertical posts.

PROVINCIAL HISTORIC RESOURCE: A building of considerable historic and/or architectural significance to the province. Because of its importance, alteration to the structure requires the approval of the Minister of Alberta Culture and Multiculturalism.

Q

QUEEN ANNE STYLE: A style of architecture employed in Canada between the 1870s and circa 1915 which was based on Elizabethan country home and cottage architecture.

QUEEN ANNE STYLE

QUOIN: Stones or brickwork located at the corners of a building usually employed as decorations or for reinforcing the external corner or edge of a wall.

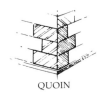

QUOIN

R

REGISTERED HISTORIC RESOURCE: A building which is deemed to be of importance in terms of historical and/or architectural evolution of

the province. The Minister of Alberta Culture and Multiculturalism must be notified 90 days in advance effecting any changes to the building.

RENAISSANCE REVIVAL STYLE: The 19th and early 20th century revival of 15th and 16th century architectural styles and motifs, most often as these occurred in Italy. This style is characterized by classical orders, round arches and symmetrical composition.

ROMANESQUE REVIVAL: The 19th and 20th century revival of 11th to 12th century motifs characterized by heavy round arches.

ROMANESQUE REVIVAL

ROSE WINDOW: A large round window containing tracery arranged in a radial manner.

S

SECOND EMPIRE STYLE: An eclectic style of architecture of French derivation characterized by classical ornament and mansard roofs.

SECOND EMPIRE STYLE

T

TAPESTRY BRICK: Brick which has at least one roughened face.

TERRACOTTA: Hard unglazed fired clay used for ornamental detail work and floor and roof tile.

TRANSOM: A horizontal bar separating a door from the window above it. A transom light is a window above a transom bar.

TRANSOM

TUDOR REVIVAL: The 19th and 20th century revival of English architecture of the early 16th century characterized by low pointed arches called Tudor arches.

TUDOR REVIVAL

TURRET: A small tower, often cantilevered.

U

UKRAINIAN-CANADIAN CHURCH STYLE: A church style imported from Ukraine which evolved from 10-11th

century Byzantine and 17th century Baroque architectural traditions.

UKRAINIAN-CANADIAN CHURCH STYLE

V

VENEER: A decorative facing with no structural function. Brick and terracotta are typical veneers.

W

WIDOW'S WALK: A walkway or platform on the apex of a roof.

Index